MATTERING PRESS

Mattering Press is an academic-led Open Access publisher that operates on a not-for-profit basis as a UK registered charity. It is committed to developing new publishing models that can widen the constituency of academic knowledge and provide authors with significant levels of support and feedback. All books are available to download for free or to purchase as hard copies. More at matteringpress.org.

The Press' work has been supported by: Centre for Invention and Social Process (Goldsmiths, University of London), European Association for the Study of Science and Technology, Hybrid Publishing Lab, infostreams, Institute for Social Futures (Lancaster University), OpenAIRE, Open Humanities Press, and Tetragon Publishing.

MAKING THIS BOOK

Mattering Press is keen to render more visible the unseen processes that go into the production of books. We would like to thank Natalie Gill and Joe Deville, who acted as the Press' coordinating editors for this book, Chris Kelty who acted as the book's overall reviewer alongside cross-reviews of each other's chapters by the authors, Steven Lovatt, for the copy editing, Tetragon for the typesetting, and Will Roscoe, Ed Akerboom and infostreams for formatting the html versions of this book.

INVENTING THE SOCIAL

EDITED BY

NOORTJE MARRES,
MICHAEL GUGGENHEIM
AND ALEX WILKIE

MATTERING PRESS

First edition published by Mattering Press, Manchester.

Freely available online at matteringpress.org/books/inventing-the-social

ISBN: 978-0-9955277-5-1 (pbk)
ISBN: 978-0-9955277-6-8 (ebk)

Mattering Press has made every effort to contact copyright holders and will be glad to rectify, in future editions, any errors or omissions brought to our notice.

CONTENTS

LIST OF FIGURES

CONTRIBUTORS

NEREA CALVILLO is an architect, researcher and curator, Assistant Professor at the Centre for Interdisciplinary Methodologies (University of Warwick) and unit master at the Architectural Association. The work produced at her office, C+ arquitectos, and her environmental visualization projects like *In the Air* have been presented, exhibited and published at international venues. Her research investigates the material, technological, political and social dimensions of environmental pollution. This has led her to analyse notions of toxicity, digital infrastructures of environmental monitoring, DIY and collaborative forms of production, smart cities and feminist approaches to sensing the environment.

NIGEL CLARK is Professor of social sustainability and human geography at the Lancaster Environment Centre, Lancaster University, UK. He is the author of *Inhuman Nature: Sociable Life on a Dynamic Planet* (2011) and co-editor (with Kathryn Yusoff) of a recent Theory, Culture & Society special issue on Geosocial Formations and the Anthropocene (2017). Current work includes the paleopolitics of the Mid Holocene, speculative volcanology, and the intersection of social and geological rifting.

CAROLIN GERLITZ is Professor of Digital Media and Methods at the University of Siegen and co-director of the Locating Media graduate school. She is member of the Digital Methods Initiative, University of Amsterdam, where she formerly worked as Assistant Professor of New Media and Digital Culture. She completed her PhD in Sociology at Goldsmiths, University of London. Among her research interests are digital media, methods, platform and app studies, quantification, calculation and sensor media.

MICHAEL GUGGENHEIM is Reader at the Department of Sociology, Goldsmiths, University of London, and a Co-Director of the Centre for Invention and Social Process (CISP). His research focuses on expertise and lay people in the fields of disaster management, buildings and cooking. He teaches inventive and visual methods and dreams of a different sociology.

ANDRÉS JAQUE is the founder of Office for Political Innovation (New York/ Madrid), and Director of the Advanced Architectural Design Program at Columbia University GSAPP. The work of the office includes awarded projects including 'IKEA Disobedients' (MoMA NY, 2011), 'Superpowers of Ten' (Lisbon, 2013) and COSMO PS1 (New York, 2015). His research work has been published in *Log, Threshold, Perspecta* or *Volume*; and his books include *Transmaterial Politics, PHANTOM. Mies as Rendered Society, Calculability* and *Different Kinds of Water Pouring Into a Swimming Pool.*

CHRISTOPHER KELTY is Professor at the University of California, Los Angeles. He is the author of *Two Bits: The Cultural Significance of Free Software* (Duke University Press, 2008), and *The Participant* (forthcoming, 2018).

LUCY KIMBELL is Director of the Innovation Insights Hub and Professor of Contemporary Design Practices at University of the Arts London and Associate Fellow at Said Business School, University of Oxford. She writes on and practices versions of design thinking and service design and works occasionally as an artist. She spent a year as AHRC design research fellow in Policy Lab, a team in the Cabinet Office, a department of the UK government. With Guy Julier, Lucy has undertaken two projects investigating social design commissioned by the AHRC.

BERND KRÄFTNER is an artist and researcher. He has realized numerous transdisciplinary research projects on and at the interfaces of science, society and the arts. He is a founder of the research group 'Shared Inc.' (Research Centre for Shared Incompetence) and teaches at the University of Applied Arts in Vienna at the Departments of Art & Science and Digital Art.

JUDITH KRÖLL is a sociologist. She is part of the transdisciplinary research group 'Shared Inc.' and Lecturer at the Department of Science and Technology Studies at the University of Vienna. She also works as a trainer with the Tomatis method.

NOORTJE MARRES is Associate Professor in the Centre for Interdisciplinary Methodologies (CIM) at the University of Warwick (UK). She studied science, technology and society (STS) at the University of Amsterdam and the Ecole des Mines (Paris). She was formerly the Director of the Centre for the Study of Invention and Social Process, Goldsmiths, University of London. Her book *Material Participation* (Palgrave) came out in paperback in 2015, and she published *Digital Sociology* (Polity) in 2017.

MIKE MICHAEL is a sociologist of science and technology, and a Professor in the Department of Sociology, Philosophy and Anthropology at the University of Exeter. His research interests have touched on the relation of everyday life to technoscience, the role of culture in biomedicine, and the interplay of design and social scientific perspectives. Recent major publications include *Actor-Network Theory: Trials, Trails and Translations* (Sage, 2017). He is currently writing books on Science and Technology Studies and Design (with Alex Wilkie) and on Speculative Research Methodology.

FABIAN MUNIESA, a researcher at Mines ParisTech (the Ecole des Mines de Paris) and a member of the Centre de Sociologie de l'Innovation, studies business life from a cultural perspective. He is the author of *The Provoked Economy: Economic Reality and the Performative Turn* (2014, Routledge), and the co-author of *Capitalization: A Cultural Guide* (2017, Presses des Mines). This latter book (not about fonts) is a study on the meaning of considering things in terms of assets, and society in terms of a society of investors.

CHRISTIAN NOLD is an artist, designer and researcher who builds participatory technologies for collective representation. He is a Research Associate in the Department of Geography at UCL. In the last decade he created large-scale public art projects such as the widely acclaimed 'Bio Mapping', 'Emotion

Mapping' and 'Bijlmer Euro' projects, which were staged with thousands of participants across the world. He wrote and edited *Emotional Cartography: Technologies of the Self*, (2009) *The Internet of People for a Post-Oil World* (2011) and *Autopsy of an Island Currency* (2014). His PhD was on the ontological politics of participatory sensing and the potential of design interventions.

MARSHA ROSENGARTEN is Professor in Sociology and a Director of the Centre for Invention and Social Process, Department of Sociology, Goldsmiths, University of London. She is co-author with Alex Wilkie and Martin Savransky of an edited collection *Speculative Research: The Lure of Possible Futures* (Routledge, 2017), co-author Mike Michael *Innovation and Biomedicine: Ethics, Evidence and Expectation in HIV* (Palgrave, 2013) and author of *HIV Interventions: Biomedicine and the Traffic in Information and Flesh* (University of Washington Press, 2009).

MARTIN SAVRANSKY is Lecturer and Director of the Unit of Play at the Department of Sociology, Goldsmiths, University of London. His works develops a philosophy of practices, weaving together a speculative pragmatism with an ecologically pluralistic politics. He is the author of *The Adventure of Relevance* (Palgrave, 2016), co-editor of *Speculative Research: The Lure of Possible Futures* (Routledge 2017), and guest-editor of a special issue titled 'Isabelle Stengers and The Dramatization of Philosophy' (forthcoming in SubStance). He is currently working on a second monograph under the title of *Around the Day in Eighty Worlds: Politics of the Pluriverse*.

ALEX WILKIE is a sociologist of science, technology and design and a designer. He is a Senior Lecturer in the Department of Design, at Goldsmiths, University of London where he is also a Director of the Centre for Invention and Social Process (CISP, Department of Sociology). Alex has recently been working on questions of aesthetics and speculation in relation to knowledge and inventive practices and has co-edited the volume *Studio Studies* (Routledge, 2015) with Ignacio Farías and *Speculative Research* (Routledge, 2017) with Martin Savransky and Marsha Rosengarten. He is currently writing a book on Science and Technology Studies and Design (with Mike Michael).

ACKNOWLEDGEMENTS

This book grew out of conversations that began at the Symposium *Inventing the Social*, which took place at Goldsmiths, University of London, on May 29–30, 2014. The symposium celebrated the ten-year anniversary of the interdisciplinary Centre for Invention and Social Process (CISP), based in the Department of Sociology at Goldsmiths. We would like to thank all the speakers and participants, who included not only most of the contributors to this volume, but also Andrew Barry, Lisa Blackman, Rebecca Coleman, William Davies, Maarten Derksen, Ignacio Farías, Michael Halewood, Javier Lezaun, Daniel Lopez, Anders Koed Madsen, Linsey McGoey, Liz Moor, Dan Neyland, David Oswell and Manuel Tironi. Thank you to Lucy Kimbell for her enthusiasm in joining the project, for proposing to have a conversation, and hosting it at Central Saint Martins. A final thanks to Natalie Gill, Joe Deville, Endre Dányi, Michaela Spencer, Uli Beisel and Julien McHardy of Mattering Press for giving time and making space to publish this project as a book, and for their excellent advice along the way.

I

INTRODUCTION: FROM PERFORMANCE TO INVENTING THE SOCIAL

Noortje Marres, Michael Guggenheim, Alex Wilkie

ACROSS MANY DIFFERENT DOMAINS, EFFORTS ARE UNDERWAY TO REINVENT ways of researching social life. Both in established fields of social inquiry, such as sociology and anthropology, and in disciplines such as art, design and architecture, there is an appetite for adventure, for moving beyond the customary distinctions between knowledge and art, and for combining the 'doing' 'researching' and 'making' of social life in potentially new ways. Designers, architects and artists are now re-framing their practices as novel forms of social research (Rosner, forthcoming; Mazé 2013), while social and cultural researchers are taking up artistic instruments and techniques to research society by other than textual means, such as drawing and installation art (Wakeford and Lury 2012; Wilkie 2017). However, while the projects of conjoining sociology and design, and more generally of rethinking epistemic and aesthetic engagement with social life, are increasingly widespread, they have raised many unanswered questions, such as: What are the specific qualities of such endeavours and the entities they produce? Can the aims of artistic intervention and social inquiry really be aligned in research practices? Is it possible to contribute to both knowledge and art at once, and should we even wish to?

To address such questions, we would do well to consider more carefully specific examples of the above forms of social research. Thus, the overall aim of this book is to introduce inventive approaches to social inquiry through the presentation of concrete projects and reflections on the contexts in which these projects are undertaken. At the outset, however, we want to offer a wider discussion of the intellectual background, methodological orientation and sensibilities that inform the projects and reflections presented here, and the commitment we think they have in common. Why use the term 'invention' in relation to social research? In what follows, we will describe the logics at work in the phrase 'inventing the social' and clarify what differentiates invention from innovation, and from performance, in relation to social life. We will argue that invention, unlike the other two terms, involves *an active search for alternative ways of combining representation of, and intervention in, social life.*

We will start by giving a brief introduction to what we take to be three key ingredients of established understandings of how social life is subject to design and artistic intervention. These approaches build on an old idea, namely that social life is not simply given – in the way that nature was previously assumed to be – but is performed, materially conditioned or constrained, and/or reflexive, i.e. it is transformable through knowledge, intervention and creativity. This will bring us to a discussion of the role of objects, technologies and environments in the accomplishment of social life, and of the difference between dominant ideals of the designability of social life and more inventive approaches to it. One of the main points we wish to make is that bringing together social research with arts and design practices makes possible new types of experimental intervention, that differ from narrow scientific experimentalism – moving away from from the idea that social science is able to *engineer* social phenomena like communities, collective behaviour and publics. Here, what might be understood as experimental procedures take on a very different appearance from their normative significance in modern science. Inventive social research finds its starting point in the inherent creativity of social life, and advances a particular form of experimental inquiry: it attempts to purposefully deploy creative aspects of social life – including performance, materiality, reflexivity – with the aim of rendering social phenomena interpretable and knowable. In the last part of this chapter we discuss what we view as markers of 'good' or pertinent inventions of sociality, namely experimentation as imagination (section four) and material intervention (section five).

SOCIAL LIFE AS TOGETHERNESS:
PERFORMATIVE, REFLEXIVE, AND MATERIAL

So, what does this rather awkward and counter-intuitive phrase 'inventing the social' mean? We want to start by considering some background assumptions shared by the contributions to this volume. Most important is the well-established view in the social sciences that social life is not something that simply exists out there, but is *made*: the very existence of social life depends on specific practices of display, representation, accounting and enactment. Society is not like nature was long presumed to be, something that exists independently of human intervention and needs only to be represented in order to be known. Society is not given but done; indeed, it is often difficult to separate the doing and the knowing of social life. Take, for example, a wedding celebration. It is both a way of practising togetherness and of making visible, and representable, the various relations and actors involved. It is also a way of making new relations. Importantly, this insight into the role of social practices is nothing new: it has long been championed by social theorists, and can be variously traced back to the works of Max Weber, Gabriel Tarde, Alfred North Whitehead, John Dewey, John Austin, Ludwig Wittgenstein, Alfred Schütz, and Harold Garfinkel (for a discussion see Halewood 2014). According to these – in many respects very different – authors and the intellectual traditions they represent, social life is accomplished through rituals, representations, accounts, and dramatisations of togetherness: it is a consequence of our deliberate orientation towards others. In this view, then, there is no such thing as a society that exists independently of performative acts.[1] Perhaps the most pertinent version of such a perspective is Garfinkel's (1967) generous idea of the 'methodical character' of social life, and his claim that social life is accomplished through everyday practices of 'accounting for social life as part of social life' (Thielmann 2012).

Different intellectual labels have been offered to identify this insight, from interpretative sociology to performance studies, but if we accept a looseness of terminology, we can say that they invoke the same basic idea: the active or deliberate curation, instantiation, representation and dramatisation of social bonds is critical to the very existence of the entity called society and the phenomenon of sociability. Thus, it has been argued that social life has a dramaturgy (Goffman 1959), is reflexive (Woolgar 1988), and is marked by looping effects between how people are labelled – say, as foreigners – and how they understand themselves (Hacking 1995). This is to say that the basic idea of what we might call the artificiality of social life has become fairly well established over the course of the twentieth century. However, it has been argued that current proposals to 'engineer' social life, as in 'smart' urban laboratories, are raising new challenges for the understanding of social life as performed (e.g. Calvillo and Halpern 2016). Contemporary phenomena like the rise of social media platforms, and the digital city, have granted fresh relevance to the idea that social life is artificial, as we will discuss in more detail below.

It is important to recognise that not only social research, but also arts and design disciplines have, for some time, drawn attention to the special role of technology and material entities – such as buildings – in the conduct and performance of social life. The idea of the materiality of social life is of crucial importance in understanding how invention may be a characteristic of social research. Sociologists and anthropologists have long argued that it is not just practices, rituals and ideas that inform the ongoing performance of social life, but also the settings (such as buildings), infrastructures (such as electricity and radio) and environments (mountains, cities, the air) in which it unfolds. In social research, this attention to materiality is today mostly associated with Actor-Network Theory (ANT) (Michael 2016) and with anthropological approaches like material culture studies (Miller 1987; Hicks 2010). In social theory, ANT is known for introducing the concept of the non-human as an actor (Callon 1986; Latour 1992). Here, the idea that society is performed or made becomes directly associated with material and technological practices of engineering and design, such as attempts to design an electric vehicle (Callon 1986) the installation of 'sleeping policemen' in the street (Latour 1992), and the famous ANT slogan 'society is technology made durable'.[2] However, as Calvillo reminds us in her contribution to this book, the idea that material practices contribute to the invention of social life is much older. The long history of architectural utopias and attempts to create new forms of society through buildings is testament to this idea (see also Guggenheim 2014). This realisation is also critical for understanding why exchanges between social research and arts and design are becoming pertinent today. Or, to put it another way, architects and designers will not be surprised to hear it said that buildings and artefacts *do things*. 'Of course they do things' comes the reply – 'it's our job to *make* them do things!'. For designers and architects, the question is *how* things do things. Still, it is not self-evident how what architects and designers do 'to' society, relates to how sociologists understand it.

It is also increasingly recognised that social research itself, not just social life, is constituted by material practices (Lezaun 2007; Wyatt 2008). Drawing on John Austin's philosophy of language, sociologists have argued that material devices initially developed by social scientists to represent society – such as focus groups or surveys – may actually influence the conduct of social life or even generate forms of sociality (Muniesa et al. 2007; Law, Ruppert and Savage 2013). Such studies of the performativity of research methods strive to reveal the myriad of practical and material interventions that lurk below the surface of the official endeavour to represent society. Some of this work has explicitly challenged the representational understanding of social research, arguing that knowledge objects, such as focus groups and opinion polls, do not just refer to external states of affairs, but may actively constitute the very phenomena they purport to represent, such as opinions and preferences (Osborne and Rose 1999). Performative perspectives on social research reveal a troubling circumstance: devices that ostensibly serve to report on social life in actual fact influence it. A stock market index or opinion poll does not simply re-present the state of the economy or the public, but actively enrols audiences in arrangements for knowing and acting on the economy and the public. Moreover, the reverse is also true: phenomena that ostensibly serve as occasions for the enactment of social and public life – say a public debate organised by government or policy actors – at the same time enable the production of data, analysis and knowledge about it (Lezaun and Soneryd 2007). In short, devices that have been designed to represent a phenomenon – society, publics – actively work to shape or even create it.

Recent work that combines social research with arts and design practices builds on these insights into the performance of social life, but also moves beyond them. The implicit claim of performative analysis of social research devices is that 'social research is always already an intervention' but that this is not sufficiently appreciated in representational social science, and public discourse more widely (Law 2004). In this view, one needs to adopt a performative perspective – and its favoured research methodology, ethnography – to appreciate that observational social methods, such as survey research, do not simply represent social life, but act on and in it. By contrast, the project of inventing the social does *not* begin with a critique of the blind spots of representational [social] science, which must learn to acknowledge performativity. Instead, it begins with the idea that social life and social research are performed, and seeks to put this insight to use in a generative way, in collaboration with disciplines such as architecture, arts, computing and design. Here the starting point is not the forgetting of intervention, which performative approaches can subsequently claim to recover, but engagement with the creative competencies of other disciplines, and the question of how social research may share in these creative competencies. In our view, the difference between representational and performative approaches in social research methodology does *not* hinge on the question of whether research constitutes a form of intervention or not, but on the types of connection between representation and intervention that are made, enabled, and explored in social research. To acknowledge the performativity of social research is but a first step. To rethink social research based on this understanding means to invent the social.

FROM ANALYSING PERFORMATIVITY TO INVENTING THE SOCIAL

Inventive approaches to social research explore different ways of combining doing, making and knowing social life, of connecting representation and intervention. In mixing social research and arts and design practices to this end, inventive research takes up a diverse range of techniques and methods, from the design of material displays for survey findings, as in the case of Lucy Kimbell's 'Pindices' (2005), to the use of design prototypes to facilitate discussions of a public issue, as in Nold's chapter (this volume) on the use of participatory design to elicit views of local residents on noise pollution around Heathrow. Each of these projects is idiosyncratic, but they share an important feature highlighted in Lury and Wakeford's (2012) introduction to the book *Inventive Methods*, which states that to inquire into a given phenomenon is to participate in it. For Lury and Wakeford, inventive methods are the means by which 'the social world is not only investigated, but may also be engaged. [...] To describe [methods] as inventive is to seek to realise the potential of this engagement, whether this is as intervention, interference or refraction' (Lury and Wakeford 2012: 6). From this insight a number of critical questions arise: can social research serve as an occasion for inventive engagement with social life? If participation is in some sense inevitable, could social research actively contribute to generating sociality? Crucially, however, for Lury and Wakeford the purpose of inventive methods is not to design new forms of living together from scratch but 'to enable the happening of the social world – its ongoingness, relationality, contingency and sensuousness – to be investigated' (Lury and Wakeford 2012: 2). In formulating this proposal, Lury and Wakeford make an important move beyond the critique of representational social science, to pose the question of how the creative capacities of social research might be purposefully or methodologically deployed.

Importantly, this invitation to combine social research and arts and design practices addresses an important contemporary ethical and political challenge that faces social research and design disciplines alike. As inventive research combines representing and intervening in social life, it offers a different vision of what it means to experiment on – or rather with – social life, one that may provide an alternative to more limited ideals of scientific experimentalism that have recently gained ascendency in voguish fields such as computational social science, behavioural governance, and smart city design. Indeed, this is a further reason why we must now move beyond the critique of representationalism. It seems to us that the performative proposition – the view that social methods do not merely describe social reality but actively inform and participate in its enactment – has now become a truism, as social research is today expected to be interventionist. In the wake of social media and other technologies, the idea that social life is somehow artificial, and can be curated, designed or even engineered, has become increasingly prominent. Take for example the recent large-scale Facebook experiments, in which the social media platform deliberately modified particular platform settings by introducing an 'I voted button' on election day, to see if voter turnout could thereby be increased, and more generally to demonstrate the degree to which 'social behaviour is amenable to online intervention' (Bond et al. 2012). Such experiments may not, strictly speaking, be new – indeed they invoke early twentieth-century experiments in deploying social network analysis for reform purposes (Mayer 2012; Guggenheim 2012). They do signal, however, that the ideal of a purely representational social science is today less prominent in public discourses themselves and, in turn, that accounts – idealised or not – of experimental intervention in social life are becoming more so.

In this context, it becomes apparent why the critique of narrow scientific representationalism – of the view that social science merely represents phenomena that exist independently out there in external reality – is at the very least *incomplete*. In light of the idealisation of the instrumental deployment of social science research (as discussed in Muniesa's chapter on behaviouralism, this volume), what is required in addition is a critique of narrow scientific experimentalism – of the idea that social science is able to *engineer* social phenomena like communities, networks and publics. This, we want to argue, is *not* a form of social research that participates, nor one that invents, insofar as it ignores the creativity of social life itself, treating it instead as a passive object of knowledge, control and optimisation. Retrospectively, one could say that the performative critique of representation – its insistence that social science actively shapes the phenomena that it purports to describe – only works insofar as the idea of interventionist social science, of social engineering and the malleability of society remains discredited. Only in that context could performative understandings of social research claim it as their special insight that social science does not merely represent but also intervenes in the social world. To be sure, performative studies of social research did reflect on the demise of the modern ideal of the malleability of society (Law 2004; see also Woolgar et al. 2009), but these reflections translated into a cultivated scepticism vis-a-vis purposeful and planned societal intervention as such.

How do inventive approaches to social research address this situation? One way is by challenging methodological indifference, the way in which scientific methodology risks remaining unresponsive to the phenomenon under study (Stengers 2017). In this respect, there is another important difference between performative and inventive approaches in social research. Social studies of performativity tend to frame social methods as an object of inquiry – they wish to demonstrate how social research, say a census, does not simply represent but enacts social reality (Law and Urry 2004). By contrast, inventive approaches tend to regard the enactment of social phenomena not as a topic to be exposed or described, but as a research task or challenge: can we do it? Can we contribute to the creative articulation of social phenomena (Guggenheim et al., this volume)? As we have noted, inventive approaches take to task not just representationalism but also interventionism: instrumentalist ideals of experimental intervention in society, such as the behavioural nudge policy pursued by the UK government, are founded on the passivity of social phenomena. It is presumed that social phenomena are out there to be known and acted upon. Inventive approaches deem this presumption not just ethically but also methodologically unsound: conducting research on society always means actively engaging with social settings and actors – with techniques to which the researched are not indifferent. The contributions to this book take as their starting point the experimentality of social life. That is to say, following Matthias Gross, the authors treat society as an experiment: a 'sociological perspective [that] has got nothing to do with the idea of sociologists as experimenters in white coats. It is rather to be understood as called forth by the observation that in modern societies, social practices increasingly present themselves as experiments via a willingness to remain open to new forms of experience' (Gross and Krohn 2005: 80; see also Marres 2012). Inventive research takes this experimentality of social life as the occasion to reconfigure social research.

This is also to say that in shifting our attention away from the critique of social scientific representationalism as such, we do *not* move from representation to intervention as the primary concern. Instead we ask, what kinds of passages between representation and intervention are opened up by adopting an inventive approach to social life? An alternative experimentalism in social research is still to be invented insofar as to engage in this type of social inquiry is to recognise that there are many possible inter-articulations between knowledge and intervention. In making this point, we follow Lury and Wakeford's insistence in *Inventive Methods* that research constitutes a form of participation. But we also differ from their approach. In choosing 'inventing the social' as the title for this book, we foreground a specific interest in not only the methods, but also the objects and objectives of creative forms of social inquiry.[3] Many of the contributions to this book translate sociological ideas and sensibilities into arts and design research practices. Thus, Andre Jaque's chapter deploys the sociological distinction between the backstage and the frontstage of social and public life, while Christian Nold draws on insights from social studies of science and technology in examining the 'provocational capacities' of technological devices to elicit public debate and issue articulation in a specific setting, namely a neighbourhood in the proximity of Heathrow airport affected by sound pollution. For others, the primary interest is in the possibility of exchange – of collaboration – between arts and design and social research. Our intended audience for this book is all those engaged in social and cultural research, design, computing, art and architecture who are interested in the exchange of capacities, knowledges and sensibilities between these fields, to make possible new ways of combining knowing, doing and intervening in social life.

In creatively combining representing and intervening, inventive approaches to social inquiry actively seek to transform the ongoing practices that constitute social life as occasions for social inquiry (Marres 2014). Inventive social research assumes the performativity of its methods in the curation of its objects of study (Wilkie 2014; Guggenheim 2015), and in doing so it can be seen to follow the Marx-inspired dictum that, although social studies have long described the performative effects of social science concepts, methods and measures, the point is to deploy them (Marres and Moats 2015; Kimbell, this volume). In other words, the difference between performativity and invention is not only a theoretical, but also a methodological question to be addressed in specific practices of research. Once we consider the possibility that social research may curate, provoke, or even generate social formations, we may become curious about the creative potential of our own knowledge practices. What are the possible roles that researchers can adopt in the curation of social situations, and how do and might they interact with various co-inventors, be they human – in the case of research subjects for example – or non-human, in the form of instruments, devices and so on? What role can tools and technologies play, from drawing pens to audio equipment (e.g. Michael 2004), prototypes and Twitter Bots (e.g. Wilkie et al. 2015), and hyperlinks, social media buttons, hashtags and Web scrapers (Rogers 2013) in the curation of social formations? And finally, what are the criteria of success of inventive social research?

GOOD INVENTIONS: EXPERIMENT AS IMAGINATION

It should now be obvious that, in our view, inventive approaches to social research are experimental. Above we have specified this notion in terms of the commitment to combine representation and intervention in social research. Practically, this means applying the term in two ways. First, the willingness to try out new methods, practices and techniques that are different from those presumed to define or belong to a home discipline, whether, for example, surveys or fieldwork in social research or modelling and prototyping practices in design and architecture. Second, taking an interest in forms of expression and knowledge that do not merely seek to represent social reality but seek to 'make visible phenomena in a form in which they could never possibly be lived, never otherwise made manifest' (Brown 2012: 69).[4] Experimental social research seeks to articulate social phenomena not simply through describing them but by deliberately modifying settings and by inducing or provoking actors to behave and express themselves in ways they would probably not of their own accord. However, it is important to emphasise that the development of experimental approaches to social research is not just about adopting experimental methods from the natural sciences. As noted, invention entails a departure from methodological indifference to the object of inquiry – an affirmation that social research involves active participation in social life. If to inquire is to participate, and it is impossible to avoid intervention, then we may as well try to become good at it, i.e. to learn the artful diligence and response-ableness of experimentation.

Furthermore, if the imperative of clinical intervention is to improve a medical disorder – a definition that, arguably, informs how intervention is commonly understood – then what new kinds of intervention does creative experimentation make possible: does it ameliorate, add, enhance, provoke, reverse, challenge, accommodate?

Among those who have developed an experimental methodology specifically for social research, the aforementioned and pioneering ethnomethodologist Harold Garfinkel stands out. He famously noted that in order to understand society, we need to conduct experiments as 'aids to our sluggish imagination' (Garfinkel 1967: 38): to render visible what is going on in social situations it is not enough to carefully describe what happens, we must also provoke accounts. If we want to really grasp social processes we must somehow *invite*, *persuade*, or (to put it more strongly) *provoke* actors and situations to generate accounts, and to produce expressions and articulations of social reality. However, and as the sociologist Alvin Gouldner (1970) has pointed out, there are remarkable similarities between, on the one hand, Garfinkel's interventionist approach and, on the other hand, interventions in social and public life undertaken under the rubric of performance art and activism. Gouldner gives the example of the provocative methods used by the Amsterdam-based Provo movement to render visible the true nature of society. Provo mobilised a visible and material police force by releasing a small number of chickens on the Prinsengracht in Amsterdam one Saturday morning, thereby demonstrating the fear and anxiety of the Amsterdam authorities (Gouldner 1970; see also Marres 2012).

But what is arguably more apparent today than it was in the 1970s is the experimentality of social life itself: not just artists and activists, but also everyday actors themselves continuously engage in experimentation on (with) our forms of living, behaviours and habitats – as in living experiments, in mundane forms of digital self-presentation (social media), and in a wider turn to what Francisca Gromme (2015) refers to as 'governance by pilot'. In this context, the question for social researchers and knowledge practitioners more generally becomes: what can we add to experiments already underway (Guggenheim et al., this volume; Marres 2012)? Awareness of the experimentality of social life changes what it means to undertake experiments in social research. In this context, it makes sense to adopt a minimal definition of experimental social inquiry, one that foregrounds the tactical modification of social settings, architectures and situations in order to render explicit latent social phenomena. As such, to experiment, first and foremost, means to intervene in social life, not necessarily with an instrumental goal in mind but to highlight social formations (Kimbell, this volume). Neither is the aim necessarily to scale the experiment up to a population, but rather to make visible, audible and tangible collective processes and problems that would otherwise be invisible, remain latent or exist as virtual phenomena, or *in potentia* (Savranksy, this volume; Lezaun et al. 2017).

While this definition is in need of further development, this way of framing the methodology of inventive social inquiry can help to clarify the relation between knowledge and creativity in these practices. Crucially, inventive social research does *not* proceed by adding creativity to more traditional, evidence-based forms of social research. The very idea that social research suffers from a creative deficit that needs to be addressed in order to make social research more engaging is, in our view, misguided. There are plenty of fictions, visions, and fantasies already at work in social research. The notion of a creativity deficit wrongly suggests a strict opposition between forms of knowledge and intervention grounded in facts and those that are grounded in the imagination. As philosophers of science such as Karl Popper, Alfred North Whitehead and Isabelle Stengers have long reminded us, imagination is not the opposite of truth; fiction is not the opposite of fact. Inquiry (knowledge) *requires* imagination. As Stengers (2002) pointed out in her retelling of Galilei Galileo's classic physics experiments, science always starts with an idea, a fiction, a 'what if?' What if weight made no difference to the velocity with which things fall?

The deployment of the imagination, and the generation of phenomena that are not given in the world, is not something that an inventive approach adds to empirical research – it is an approach and material reality that the arts, sciences and humanities have long shared. As the design researcher Daniela Rosner (forthcoming) points out, design, too, 'is always asking "what if?"' of the social worlds it inhabits: it imagines scenarios, tries out different shapes and ways of doing things. However, Rosner also insists that asking 'what if' – introducing new scenarios and prototypes into social life – does not mean losing one's interest in what is already given in the world: it does not entail a shift from loyalty to 'what is' to 'what might be'; and it does not mean exchanging empiricism for speculation (Savransky et al. 2017). Instead, as Marsha Rosengarten shows in her contribution to this volume, practising inquiry by way of creative intervention is about engaging with what is already ongoing, already happening in the world with an explicit view to what *might be* in the world *in a different mode*. And this project does not belong to any one discipline, but is best understood as a shared undertaking across fields. Inventive inquiry may be pursued with the aid of social research methods such as participant observation, as well as through art and design practice. Its aim is to develop new ways of deploying the imagination as a method for knowing and intervening in social life, and to this end a variety of methodological traditions can be mobilised.

GOOD INVENTIONS:
MATERIALITIES AND TECHNICITIES

The role of the imagination covers one aspect of the kinds of experiments that distinguish inventive approaches to understanding social life from descriptive, performative approaches. Another important feature is that material, aesthetic and technical milieus enable distinctive kinds of interactions with users, audiences and institutions of social research. An imaginary that is materialised in artefacts, architectures and everyday devices has different qualities than imaginations that are materialised in texts or laboratory set-ups. The 'what if?' of a tract on socialist utopia or a physics experiment is relatively difficult to engage with unless you do not need to wait for your revolution, or are trained in the field, but the 'what if?' of an app or a sweater can be tested very quickly. To create imaginative experiments, we need the right – meaning well-designed – devices. Social research now takes account of the materiality of the social in many different ways. However, we need to go further than this: the pressing question today, in our view, is whether social research can reflexively deploy things, environments and non-humans to make an ostensible difference to our forms of life, and to how we live together.

It is now commonplace to point out that non-humans actively participate in social life. For example, we typically interact with bots on our phones, we find their messages in our inboxes and we are lured into bot-enhanced advertising, marketing and lobbying in our everyday interactions on social media, and many of us reflect on these novel yet mundane circumstances. Remarkably, however, even if non-humans are acknowledged as a significant presence in social life, this does not mean that society is now widely recognised as being hybrid – involving a co-mingling of humans and machines. On the contrary, human forms of sociability are, on the whole, firmly upheld and prioritised in the world of designed sociability. Examples of this, such as social media platforms, tend to materialise distinctively human forms of social organisation (Marres & Gerlitz, this volume): the friend network, the community, social behaviour. Contemporary forms of designed sociality tend to invoke classic social forms. This is another reason why we want to affirm experimentality, and why we need to exercise our skills in other than descriptive/observational forms of inquiry. It is not enough to empiricise the question of the social (Boltanski 2011), and to describe the social theories invoked by the actors themselves to account for social life. Now that we have established the generative capacities of devices, objects and settings in social life, the question arises: how does their participation in social life *make a difference* to our forms of life; can they inspire alternative forms of knowing and doing? This experimentalisation of social life is inherently *in question* (this is part of what makes an experiment): we do not already know how to conduct, understand and change contemporary social life, and no one knows what forms of inquiry and intervention are the most adequate for this purpose (not even the actors themselves).

To adopt an inventive approach to social inquiry, then, is not to jump on the technological determinist bandwagon and to believe that it is new technologies that have the power to produce new societies. Rather, the aim is to create experiments that can serve to articulate, explicate and elaborate ways of (not) living together that are already ongoing. As many of the contributions to this book show, the experimental explication of social forms often depends on tactical (as well as literal) operations upon materialities: moving materials from the cellar to the exhibition space (Jaque, this volume), or exchanging bricks with helium (Calvillo, this volume), or, for that matter, the re-programming of bots (Wilkie & Michael, this volume), or introducing soft toys to a medical measuring tool (Guggenheim, Kroell and Kraftner, this volume).

Jaque's paper offers a fascinating account of the type of experimental renegotiation of social forms that we have in mind. His Barcelona Pavilion experiment produced a form of assembly that went against the organisational forms and logics of the social composed and given concrete form by self-appointed executors of the ideas of the architect Mies van der Rohe (the 'Mies Society'): their obsession with stabilisation and purification was exposed as limited in scope and un-lively. Jaque's pavilion intervention demonstrates the cost of stabilisation, exposing how this commitment rendered particular kinds of assembly invisible and impracticable. However, his attempt to address this by staging some of these invisible assemblies in the pavilion also comes at a cost, as it threatens to render un-doable particular modes of assembly like the Mies Society. This is an excellent example of the 'coming out of things' (Marres, 2012): the outing of hybrid collectives and the explication of experimental forms of togetherness by way of material intervention. It also demonstrates a political truth: that the work of re-assembling the social is likely to generate tensions and conflicts; one society's assembly, to put it somewhat inelegantly, is another's dis-assembly.

Many of the material inventions described in this volume are modest and low-key: the experimental practices of social research we are presenting here do not aspire to the heroic design of large-scale knowledge infrastructures. Rather, ad-hocism, bricolage, hacking, glitching and prototyping are the interventions of choice (Jencks and Silver 1973; Corsín, Jimenez and Estalella 2010). Certainly, this is partly due to the financial restrictions researchers are under. The nimbleness and playfulness enabled by small-scale interventions also have a deeper connection to experimental practices: preferring to be materially and resource light, such endeavours do not wish to impose their inventions on the world, but rather to operate in the mode of making material suggestions, offerings, and attempts at indicating that a different society is possible.

CONCLUSION

In sum, then, inventive approaches to social research must be distinguished both from performative social studies and from attempts to reinstate social engineering as a viable paradigm. On the one hand, inventive approaches do not seek to describe the performance of social reality, but rather treat performativity as an effect that may be purposefully deployed in social research. However, to move from performance to invention does not require the endorsement of the simplistic ideal of the designability of social life. Inventive social inquiry precisely seeks to carve out an alternative to the ideal of the designable society. The two approaches, or experimental regimes, if you will – designability versus invention – are markedly different, in two ways: first, from the standpoint of the designable society, experimental capacities are an attribute of technical apparatuses or architectures. It is the online platform, or the smart city architecture that is presumed to enable experimental intervention into an external object (society) – as for example in recent policy preoccupations where creativity as an economic object can be stimulated by urban planning (Farías and Wilkie 2015: 2). Inventive approaches, by contrast, find their starting point in the experimentality of social life and social situations themselves.

From the standpoint of the designability of society, the latter are presumed to be largely passive, they are to be acted upon by technology and innovation, and technology is assumed to align itself with this purposeful invention. Here the assumption is that the social world will comply with the goals of social design ('and if it won't we'll try something else'). By contrast, inventive approaches to social inquiry are para-instrumental: they *expect* social situations to push back against our social theories, and they deliberately look for recalcitrance in materials and situations: the aim is to press societies' 'buttons' and in doing so to activate latent social realities. Here, resistance is not noise, and neither is it simply anarchic: it has methodological value. The aims and goals of experimental social inquiry are here assumed to require situational adjustment. This, indeed, is what social research is all about: the adjustment of the practices and aims of inquiry during the process of research signals that we have learnt something.

NOTES

1 A word of caution is necessary here regarding the performance of social life. For Austin (1962), performativity in language – statements that bring into being states of affairs, such as marriage or war – require particular 'felicity conditions', meaning that certain circumstances need to obtain in order for them to work. For example, they may need to be pronounced by an appropriate actor (priest, head of state) or in a particular place (a church or press conference). If these conditions of felicity are not in place, then such statements will not 'act' appropriately, i.e. they will not work.

2 Things quickly become complicated, however, when, for instance, actor-network theorists such as Bruno Latour disavow the concept of the social. Latour mischievously adopted Margaret Thatcher's phrase that there is no such thing as society (Latour 2005). As Marres and Gerlitz suggest in their contribution, 'inventing the social' can also be framed as a project to recover the specificity of social forms in the face of ANT's (and Thatcherite) indifference.

3 Lury and Wakeford are interested in invention as a property of method. In their account, method is what constitutes the interface between social research and art. In presenting invention in this light, their approach has the advantage of foregrounding the question of *how* research operates in the world, but it also has the effect of suspending, or downplaying, the question of what forms of collaboration and types of exchange are possible between social research and creative disciplines in the practice of social research. Reinstating the more abstract notion of 'method' inevitably distracts from – and at times, brackets – the issue of collaboration, the exchanges of competencies that are possible between the domains, fields, sites, technologies and genealogies of social research, design, art, and architecture.

4 In this regard, inventive social inquiry returns us to a classic maxim of structuralist sociology: to gain knowledge of society requires the explication of dynamics that are not readily observable.

REFERENCES

Austin, J. L., *How to Do Things with Words*, 2nd edn (Oxford: University Press, 1975 [1962]).

Barry, A., and N. Thrift., 'Gabriel Tarde: Imitation, Invention and Economy', *Economy and Society*, 36.4 (2007), 509–25.

Boltanski, L., *On Critique: A Sociology of Emancipation* (Cambridge; Malden, MA: Polity, 2011).

Bond, R. M., et al., 'A 61-Million-Person Experiment in Social Influence and Political Mobilisation', *Nature*, 489. 7415 (2012), 295–98.

Callon, M., 'Some Elements of a Sociology of Translation: Domestication of the Scallops and the Fishermen of St. Brieuc Bay', in J. Law, ed., *Power, Action and Belief: A New*

Sociology of Knowledge? (Abingdon, Oxon; New York, NY: Routledge, 1986), pp. 196–223.

Callon, M., 'The Sociology of an Actor-Network: The Case of the Electric Vehicle' in M. Callon et al., eds, *Mapping the Dynamics of Science and Technology* (London: Macmillan, 1986), pp. 19–34.

Callon, M., and J. Law., 'Agency and the Hybrid Collectif'. *The South Atlantic Quarterly*, 94 (1995), 481–507.

Calvillo, N., et al., eds, 'Testbed as urban epistemology', in S., Marvin, A., Luque-Ayala, and C. McFarlane, *Smart Urbanism: Utopian Vision or False dawn?* (Abingdon, Oxon; New York, NY: Routledge, 2016), pp. 145–167.

Farías, I., and A. Wilkie, 'Studio studies: Notes for a research programme' in I. Farías and A. Wilkie, eds, *Studio studies: Operations, topologies and displacements.* (Abingdon, Oxon; New York, NY: Routledge, 2015), pp. 1–21.

Ford, L. S., 'Creativity in a Future Key', in R. C. Neville, ed., *New Essays in Metaphysics* (Albany, New York: State University of New York Press, 1986), pp. 179–197.

Garfinkel, H., *Studies in Ethnomethodology* (Cambridge: Polity Press, 1967).

Goffman, E., *The Presentation of Self in Everyday Life* (New York: Anchor, 1959).

Gouldner, A. W., 'Ethnomethodology: Sociology as Happening', in *The Coming Crises of Western Sociology* (London and New York: Basic Books, 1970), pp. 390–5.

Grommé, F., 'Governance by pilot projects: Experimenting with surveillance in Dutch crime control' (PhD thesis, Institute for Social Science Research, University of Amsterdam, 2015).

Gross, M., and W. Krohn, 'Society as Experiment: Sociological Foundations for a Self-Experimental Society', *History of the Human Sciences*, 18.2 (2015), 63–86.

Guggenheim, M., 'Mutable Immobiles. Change of Use of Buildings as a Problem of Quasi-Technologies', in Ignacio Farias and Thomas Bender, eds, *Urban Assemblages. How Actor Network Theory Transforms Urban Studies.* (London and New York: Routledge, 2012), pp.161–78.

—— 'Laboratizing and De-laboratizing the World: Changing Sociological Concepts for Places of Knowledge Production', *History of the Human Sciences*, 25.1(2012), 99–118.

—— 'From Prototyping to Allotyping: The Invention of Change of Use and the Crisis of Building Types, *Journal of Cultural Economy*, 7.1 (2014), pp. 411–33.

—— 'The Media of Sociology: Tight or Loose Translations', *British Journal of Sociology*, 66.2 (2015), 345–72.

Hacking, I., *Representing and Intervening* (Cambridge, England: Cambridge University Press, 1983).

Halewood, M., *Rethinking the Social through Durkheim, Marx, Weber and Whitehead.* (London: Anthem Press, 2014).

Hicks, D., and M. C., Beaudry, eds, *The Oxford Handbook of Material Culture Studies* (Oxford: Oxford University Press, 2010).

Jiménez, A. C., A., Estalella, and Z. Collective, 'The Interior Design of [Free] Knowledge', *Journal of Cultural Economy*, 7.4 (2014), pp. 493–515.

Latour, B., 'Where are the Missing Masses, Sociology of a Few Mundane Artefacts' in W., Bijker and J., Law, eds, *Shaping Technology-Building Society. Studies in Sociotechnical Change* (Cambridge: MIT Press, 1992), pp. 225–59.

—— 'Do Scientific Objects Have a History? Pastuer and Whitehead in a Bath of Lactic Acid', *Common Knowledge* 5.1 (1996), 76–91.

—— *Reassembling the social: An Introduction to Actor-NetworkTheory.* (Clarendon Lectures. Oxford: Oxford University Press, 2005).

Law, J., *After Method: Mess in Social Science Research* (London and New York: Routledge, 2004).

Law, J., and J. Urry, 'Enacting the Social', *Economy and Society*, 33.3 (2004), 390–410.

Lezaun, J., 'A Market of Opinions: the Political Epistemology of Focus Groups'. *The Sociological Review*, 55.52 (2007), 130–51.

Lezaun, J., and L. Soneryd., 'Consulting Citizens: Technologies of Elicitation and the Mobility of Publics', *Public Understanding of Science*, 16.3 (2007), 279–97.

Lezaun, J., N. Marres and M. Tironi, 'Experiments in Participation', in C. Miller et al., eds, *Handbook of Science and Technology Studies*, vol 4 (Cambridge: MIT Press, forthcoming).

Lury, C., and N. Wakeford, 'Introduction' in C. Lury and N. Wakeford, eds, *Inventive Methods: The Happening of the Social* (London and New York: Routledge, 2012), pp. 1–24.

—— eds., *Inventive Methods: The Happening of the Social.* (London; New York, NY: Routledge, 2012).

Marres, N., *Material Participation: Technology, the Environment and Every Publics.* (Basingstoke: Palgrave, 2012).

—— 'Who is Afraid of the Green Cloud? On the Environmental Rendering of Controversy, CSISP Working Paper Nr. 2. (2013) <http://www.gold.ac.uk/media/Marres_NuageVert_Controversy_analysis%20copy.pdf> [accessed 30 April 2018].

—— *Digital Sociology: the Re-invention of Social Research* (Cambridge: Polity, 2017).

Mayer, K., 'Objectifying Social Structures: Network Visualisation as Means of Social Optimisation', *Theory and Psychology*, 22.162 (2012).

Mazé, R., ed, *SWITCH! Design and Everyday Energy Ecologies* (Stockholm: Interactive Institute Swedish ICT, 2013).

Michael, M., *Actor Network Theory: Trials, Trails and Translations* (New York and London: Sage, 2016).

—— 'On Making Data Social: Heterogeneity in Sociological Practice', *Qualitative Research*. 4.1 (2004), 5–23.

—— *Actor Network Theory: Trials, Trails and Translations* (Los Angeles, CA; London; New Delhi; Singapore; Washignton, CD; Melbourne: Sage, 2016).

Muniesa, F., Y. Millo and M. Callon., 'An Introduction to Market Devices', *The Sociological Review*, 55. s2 (2007), 1–12.

Osborne, T., and N. Rose, 'Do the Social Sciences Create Phenomena?: The Example of Public Opinion Research', *The British Journal of Sociology*, 50.3 (1999), 367–96.

Rogers, R., *Digital Methods* (Cambridge: MIT Press, 2013).

Rosner, D., *Integrative Inquiry: A Reflexive Approach to Design Research* (Cambridge: MIT Press, forthcoming).

Savransky, M., A. Wilkie and M. Rosengarten, 'The Lure of Possible Futures: On Speculative Research', in Wilkie, A., et al., eds, *Speculative Research: The Lure of Possible Futures* (Abingdon, Oxon; New York, NY: Routledge, 2017), pp.1–18.

Shaviro, S., *Without Criteria: Kant, Whitehead, Deleuze, and Aesthetics* (Cambridge, MA: MIT Press, 2009).

——*Discognition* (Watkins Media Limited, 2016).

Stengers, I., 'The Thousand and One Sexes of Science', in *Power and invention: situating science* (Minnesota: The University of Minnesota Press, 1997), pp.133–52.

——A Constructivist Reading of Process and Reality' *Theory, Culture & Society*, 25.4 (2008), 91–110.

——*Cosmopolitics* (Minnesota: University of Minnesota Press, 2010).

Thielmann, T., 'Taking into Account. Harold Garfinkels Beitrag für eine Theorie sozialer Medien', in: *Zeitschrift für Medienwissenschaft*, 6 (2012), 85–102.

Wakeford, N., 'Don't Go All the Way: Revisiting 'Misplaced Concretism' in G.Bowker and S. Timmermans, eds, *Boundary Objects and Beyond: Working with Leigh Star* (Cambridge: MIT Press, 2012).

Whitehead, A. N., *Science and the Modern World* (New York, NY: The Free Press, 1997 [1926]).

Wilkie, A., 'User Assemblages in Design: an Ethnographic Study' (PhD Thesis, Goldsmiths, University of London, 2010).

——'Prototyping as Event: Designing the Future of Obesity', *Journal of Cultural Economy*, 7.4 (2014), 476–492.

Wilkie, A., et al., *Speculative Techniques. Speculative research: The Lure of Possible Futures* (Abingdon, Oxon; New York, NY, Routledge: 2017), 111–13.

Wilkie, A. (2018) 'Studios, Publics, Problems', in A., Boucher, et al., *Energy Babble*. (Manchester: Mattering Press, forthcoming).

Wilkie, A., M. Michael and M. Plummer-Fernandez., 'Speculative Method and Twitter: Bots, Energy and Three Conceptual Characters', *The Sociological Review*, 63 (2015), 79–101.

Woolgar, S., ed., *Knowledge and Reflexivity: New Frontiers in the Sociology of Knowledge*. (Thousand Oaks: Sage Publications, 2008).

Woolgar, S., C. Coopmans and D. Neyland, 'Does STS Mean Business?' *Organisation*, 16.1 (2009), 5–30.

PROJECTS

2

INVITING ATMOSPHERES TO THE ARCHITECTURE TABLE

Nerea Calvillo

BUILDING THE SOCIAL

IN STS (SCIENCE, TECHNOLOGY AND SOCIETY) AND FEMINIST STUDIES OF technoscience there has been much discussion about the ways in which the social can be redefined by expanding it to more-than-humans, from an inclusive invitation to a parliament of things (Latour 1993), to messier and more entangled modes of co-habitation (Haraway 2003: 1991). In this context, this chapter asks if and how other disciplines can contribute to this debate, specifically by discussing the attempt in the field of architecture to build the social from air. Architecture is a discipline that manifests expertise in managing inert more-than-humans, while at the same time being deeply intertwined with the social, as it builds spaces with materials to be inhabited by humans. The question I want to explore here in response to the topic of this issue concerns the ways in which architecture articulates this relationship. Can, for example, architecture construct, facilitate or design the social, or is it 'just' its container, with no agency of its own? More particularly, can architecture, as a practice, *design* the socialities needed *for a good life* (e.g. Braidotti 2012)?

Architects have long thought about how to invent the social through buildings[1]. There are, however, some problems with this approach. In order to unfold them let us take as a reference utopian projects that intended to create socialist and communist societies, such as residential communities in the nineteenth century or communal housing at the beginning of the twentieth. These projects assumed a direct causal relationship between spatial organisation and the social, whereby a certain material configuration could enhance a specific human behaviour, and even construct complex social organisations such as socialism, for instance (e.g. Buchli 1998). Crucially, however, both architecture and the social were conceived as static materials: architecture as that which concerned buildings as finished and stable entities, and the social as a unified and immutable set of social relations.

Studies of architecture have demonstrated that this causal and static way of inventing the social through buildings did not succeed, in part because it did not take into consideration the fluidity of the social (e.g. Guggenheim 2014; Vanderburgh and Russell Ellis 2001) and in part because it had a narrow understanding of what architecture is, limiting it to the built environment. One way to move away from this framework is to reduce the expectations of architecture and shift from *constructing the social* to *facilitating socialities*. Another path is to gain a more processual and experimental understanding of inventing socialities with/through buildings where architectural practice can learn from STS and feminist research.

French sociologist of science and philosopher Bruno Latour (2005) developed the notion of 'sociotechnical assemblages' to highlight that things are not only a material assemblage, but are also composed of the social entities that use, produce, or represent them, as well as institutions, contracts, humans, more-than-humans, and so on, distributed in space and time. Thinking about the built environment as a sociotechnical assemblage expands the number of actors involved in making those buildings what they are to include the social entities to which they are already connected, and also the necessarily implied associated temporalities. Recent work in STS, inspired by ANT (Actor-Network Theory), provides accounts of material participation (Marres 2012; Marres and Lezaun 2011) that acknowledge the agency of the built environment i.e. what it can 'do' in relation to the engagement of actors in communities, problems and publics. In this view, things (and therefore buildings) acquire their agency and political capacities depending on how they are deployed, which implies that the socialities facilitated by buildings cannot be completely predetermined, by architecture design for instance, and are necessarily experimental.

In order to assess this shift to the processual, as well as the ability of architectural practice to design socialities, in this chapter I propose to think and work with a dynamic and seemingly intangible material: air. Although air has been largely ignored throughout architectural history (Banham 1969), during the 1960s and 1970s there was a proliferation of inflatable structures that used air to explore the lightness, ephemerality, transparency and transportability of new plastics. This took place in the context of an attempt to propose new ways of living that were closer to everyday, popular culture and that might thereby facilitate political resistance (Dessauce 1999; Topham 2002). The project I discuss here, although sharing certain aesthetic qualities with these earlier ventures, was conceived differently. Firstly, the Polivagina was not conceived as addressing air through its structural capacity, but drew on its invisibility and dynamism to destabilise architectural practice, requiring a transformation of methods, techniques, materials and forms of organisation. Secondly, it acknowledges that the social is not simply the result of the inhabitation of inflatable structures: the air is already social. German philosopher and cultural theorist Peter Sloterdijk, in his work on social foams (2005), proposes that sociality is not only about human exchanges of information (Wakeford 2011), but is a foam that includes humans, structures, and the air and climate that brings them together. If this is so, then taking air into account in architecture shifts attention beyond boundaries, such as walls and roofs, to what is in between them, working with humidity, pressure, smell, toxicity and breath.

However, when Sloterdijk discusses architecture he makes a direct translation of foam to physical enclosures, where architecture becomes a set of containers at different scales, from the cell to the urban. In this direct translation three potentials of his specific proposal for how humans and more-than-humans can be brought together are lost. Firstly, the atmospheres created by these architectures are hardly described, and so their involvement in the construction of socialities cannot be traced. Secondly, Sloterdijk focuses on architectural objects as finished and stable entities, and has little appreciation of the production of architecture itself as a space where socialities are generated. And lastly, the social effects of buildings are described in generic and representational terms. For example, Sloterdijk describes the apartment as a symbol of society's individualism, but he does not specify the relationships between material assemblages and particular practices that make him draw this conclusion. In order to test the potentials of Sloterdijk's conceptual proposal this chapter addresses these absences by making three moves. Firstly, instead of using Sloterdijk's metaphorical reading of architecture as an enclosure, it uses his notion of 'air design' (2005: 140) to think about architecture not simply as creating envelopes for climate control, but as involving the actual design of atmospheres where the air is not only a conditioner of well-being but also a material for the construction of certain modes of sociality. Secondly, it takes the process of architectural design and construction as its main site of inquiry into the design of socialities. Finally, the chapter proposes a conceptual framework to describe (or sense) the after-effects of construction: the socialities that emerge during the inhabitation of an atmospheric space, which are spontaneous, fragile and in constant transformation.

Two advantages are gained by reconceiving architecture as dealing with atmospheres (or atmospheric assemblages), rather than with objects. Firstly, such a reappraisal destabilises conventional ways of practising architecture, which, just as when an accident happens and infrastructures break, makes visible their capacities and controversies (Star 1999). Including air as a construction material and as an object of design transforms design from an attempt to control the capacities of a future building and regulate its inhabitants, to an experimental set-up that embraces uncertainty. Design, here, is no longer about deciding how to create a shape and assemble components, but is rather conceived as a practice concerned with how to design the construction process as an experiment. The second advantage of this reappraisal is that it opens up a space for experimenting with the design of socialities, which do not necessarily take place only after the project is finished, but are in permanent development and transformation. As such, 'doing architecture' is no longer a process that ends with the construction of a building, but a constant reassembly of materials, humans, ideas, and so on (Guggenheim 2009; Yaneva 2009). In other words, architecture is viewed as a continual three-dimensional material invention of the social. This approach, drawing on STS and Sloterdijk, can begin to describe how the social can be (in part) designed with matter and atmospheres.

CONSTRUCTING WITH HELIUM AND AIR

This speculative proposal is part of an ongoing practice-based research project that will be illustrated in narrative and visual means through the installation 'The Polivagina of Fan Riots' (Polivagina).[2] The project was designed by C+arquitectos – the office directed by the author of this article – for the art event Fan Riots curated by Ivan Lopez Munuera for the SOS4.8 music festival, in Murcia[3]. The Polivagina became an exploration of how to take seriously the application of (atmospheric) more-than-humans to architecture, taking in this case air and helium as the main materials for construction. This decision was made as an intellectual challenge, but also because it helped to respond to many of the demands of the curator, the existing building, the building regulations and the climate. Examples include the need to completely transform a seven-hundred m² space that could not be touched[4]; to host art installations, performances and round-tables; to 'attract' party-goers whose main interest in a festival may not be art; to deal with a limited budget; and to work within the time constraints of two days to set up the project and five hours to dismantle it. These conditions, seeming almost contradictory, could only be brought together by means of a light structure or some sort of inflatable, but this would have driven the project over budget. We therefore asked ourselves the following questions: Does air design necessarily imply the creation of a controlled envelope (such as those referred to by Sloterdijk)? What are the limits of atmospheres? Do they need continuous physical boundaries?

Due to all these constraints we invited helium, a common atmospheric element renowned for its lightness, as our main guest, and contained it in an ordinary object: a polyamide balloon. This invitation was not a peaceful one, as the helium was brought in gas bottles and forced with pressure into the balloons. This was necessary, however, as it was only when thus enclosed

FIG. 2.1 Helium bottles used to inflate the balloons (photo: Nerea Calvillo)

that it could perform its structural function. Even when enclosed, compared with bricks, stone or concrete, gases – in this case helium – have very different properties: they have fluidity and can move, change and react. Gases are, by nature, volatile, and for that reason difficult to control. Architects, typically trained in mechanics rather than in thermodynamics, are in most cases not prepared or equipped to deal with their properties. This, of course, does not mean that there are no previous references or existing centres of expertise: as the abovementioned inflatable projects in architecture, arts and industry show, architects have developed techniques to keep large membranes inflated. Polivagina, however, was a permeable membrane composed of micro inflated units, rather than a capsule filled with structural conditioned air. The balloons-as-containers used in Polivagina therefore added an extra dimension of complexity and technical difficulty. As balloons are not used in architectural construction, manufacturers do not provide the required technical specifications stating how they perform (how much they lift, for example), there are no building codes or regulations covering their usage, and there is little or no expertise in how to assemble balloons in such circumstances.

Pushed by these uncertainties we framed the project as a *'cosmopolitical experiment'* (Hinchliffe et al. 2003), in order to explore other ways of knowing that may enable a different composition of the world. For this purpose, we wondered how we could bring those invisible agents to the project, in the same way as Hinchliffe et al. had to decide how to encourage water voles – the elusive animals they were trying to detect – to inhabit their urban site. We did so by taking helium's agency into account in material terms, learning about its material performance by engaging with the small differences between the gas' properties and attributes, because 'this openness to difference, which is borne out of a looser kind of sense, a knowing around rather than a knowledge of, is a vital means to allow for nonhuman knowledgeabilities' (Hinchliffe et al. 2003: 653). Given this, we collected stories, experiences, and expertise about helium from domains outside architectural construction, making use of experts in corporate conference design and decoration, or drawing on our own experiences of childhood birthday parties or wedding catalogues. Having collated this knowledge, we then tested a number of small prototypes at home, counting weights, lifting times, trying out ways of sticking, attaching, gluing or tying them together; while beginning to understand how to attune three interrelated and processual aspects of aerostatic things: envelopment, inflation and buoyancy (McCormack 2009). Attunement was gradually achieved as the architects became more sensitive to very small changes in the quantity of helium injected when feeling the tension of the stretching polyamide, or to the unexpected choreography that the balloons initiated in response to subtle currents of breeze through, for example, an open door.

Instead of trying to limit the balloons' capacities, we aimed to explore and exploit them: to create more entanglements and more means of addressing this gas by multiplying the agents involved to include not only humans – such as the many festival volunteers who joined the construction – but also other gases. Once on site we had to invite naturally occurring air to fill the balloons. Because air is heavier than helium, it could counteract the unpredictably strong lifting capacity of helium, in a dialogue where we, humans, became only mediators. The question now is whether these encounters with non-humans gave rise to new relations and modes of becoming between humans and more-than-humans. By observing what occurred in the design and construction process it could be argued that various changes occurred in how architecture is practised. Furthermore, the design process also gave rise to outcomes, or desired socialities, that were imagined and anticipated by the architects, whilst other socialites emerged unexpectedly.

EFFECTS IN THE MAKING OF ARCHITECTURE

The first effect of taking atmospheric more-than-human agency into account is that it requires a conceptual and practical change in what architectural design means. Instead of being a process that defines how things are assembled prior to construction (or even during construction), taking air into account forces the whole process to become experimental. The object of design is the experiment itself and no longer a formal configuration. Instead of having to define every construction detail (which is the tendency towards which architectural practice keeps moving), what has to be defined are the conditions of experimentation, moving from drawings to protocols, a similar shift to that made in music in the 1970s by John Cage and his contemporaries. In the Polivagina the design of the experimental setting implied the definition of fixed elements (a number of balloon arches) that meant random filling, distribution of time, labour and learning processes for the students with whom we built the installation, and the acceptance of failure, even though stressful and painful, as part of the process. This move towards the design of an experimental setting demands a redefinition of what control means in design, and pushes to deal with uncertainty, making design a performative and emergent practice that blurs the boundaries between design and construction by substituting embodied movements in space for drawings and models.

New socialities between humans emerged during the construction process. While we were designing the experimental setting, helium's unexpectedly strong lifting capacity destroyed our dome-like assemblages every night. Due to time

FIG. 2.2 Celebration of the construction of the first arch of the structure (photo: Nerea Calvillo)

constraints and our inability to govern the balloons, the social organisation of the team had to be adjusted and a redistribution of power and decision-making took place. Architects were no longer the ones explaining what and how to build, and they did not even coordinate tasks. The group dissolved into small, self-organised and ever changing experimentation groups that would make decisions and share their findings on their own.

And yet, although it may resonate with practices of collaborative design, participatory design or co-design, this architectural engagement was a different process: there was neither a shared understanding among the various stakeholders of what was taking place (e.g. Kvan 2000), nor an awareness of the organisational contexts in which this form of cooperative design (e.g. Suchman et al. 2003) was enacted. Furthermore, unlike in co-design or participatory design (e.g. Sanders and Stappers 2008; Wilkie 2011), we were not designing with future users in mind. In this cosmopolitical experiment decisions were not

FIG. 2.3   Assembling the different domes (photo: Nerea Calvillo)

negotiated or agreed upon. Instead it became a distributed, untraceable decision making process, with no time for agreements or discussions, and which
included aggressive moments, tears and a lot of stress. The division of labour
hierarchies between designers and producers dissolved, since there were no
experts; those involved acquired the appropriate knowledge, skills and experience through the process. Arguably, and if we think of this project in terms
of involvement-in-design and human/more-than-human participation, we in
fact co-designed *with* helium and air, by letting them speak as 'we' collectively
adapted to one another.

   The fact that the team became a group of 'makers' as well as mediators with
the air affected not only the social structure of construction but also the construction technique itself. Instead of hitting, breaking and assembling materials with
tools, the (human) body became the main instrument to build with through
embodied practices of touching, holding, catching, lifting, hugging and so on,
with the help of domestic implements such as scissors, tape and string. If 'the

FIG. 2.4   Balloon assembling process (photo: Nerea Calvillo)

materiality of things becoming lighter than air is generative of distinctive modes of experiencing' – or sensing – aerostatic space (McCormack 2009: 27), and relates to movement and a privileged point of view (Adey 2010; McCormack 2009), the sensing experience of being *with* air was a more intimate, non-representational and an embodied one. Echoing the specific movements that early twentieth century skyscraper construction workers developed in order to construct when hanging in the air (McCormack 2015a), we developed our own movements, not for being *in* the air, but for being *with* the air: holding it with our arms, pushing it with our knees, displacing it with our chest. Practices of material assemblage were replaced by practices of soft material care.

In this context, human bodies, as Hinchliffe et al. (2003) propose in their cosmopolitical experiment, have to learn to be affected (Latour 2004) by gases in order to become experimental instruments trained to measure, for instance, how much a 45 cm balloon lifts depending on its shape, in a similar fashion as the bodies of nineteenth-century chemists became epistemic instruments that

FIG. 2.5 Practices of embodied material care (photo: Nerea Calvillo)

provided specific types of knowledge (Roberts 1995). Indeed, since the strength or agility normally needed in other types of construction were not required, other types of bodies could participate in the assemblage of the installation, thus redefining who can participate in a construction process.

The cosmopolitical experiment also had other effects, such as expanding the number of agents involved and redistributing agencies and power relations, creating new socialities through this expansion. Again, the elevating force of helium, its resistance to being confined and its overall recalcitrance (Tironi and Calvillo 2016), caused the biggest conflicts and controversies. Very slowly, the 90 cm balloons pulled the whole structure up, until the highest parts of the domes reached a point where they triggered a laser detector in the ceiling, activating the fire alarm. This incident, three hours before opening, initiated a whole institutional conflict, bringing together the building security guards, institutional representatives of the cultural complex, the 90 cm balloons, the festival promoters and ourselves. The city council technicians proposed technical solutions to lower the structure, but the balloons had achieved equilibrium and we had lost control over them, so there was no way of bringing them down without dismantling the overall structure. Another option, bursting the bigger balloons, although acceptable from our side, was rejected by the promoters of the festival, who prioritised the aesthetics and decided to push for an administrative solution. So after two hours of phone calls and meetings the issue was handed over to the municipal and regional authorities, confronting security, aesthetics, budget and time.

The solution adopted was to replace the laser smoke detector with a whole crew of fire-fighters, who became the main supervisors of the building, the event and the installation. Interestingly enough, this not only redistributed power relations – as now the fire-fighters could decide what would or would not take place – but also transformed the newly-invested representatives of control and power into the public themselves, since the fire-fighters now took selfies, listened to the round-tables and watched the video art pieces themselves. So conflict can

FIG. 2.6 Firefighters who replaced the smoke detectors, and who, in the process, took on the role of supervising the exhibition as well as taking selfies (photo: Nerea Calvillo)

cause other forms of temporary sociality to emerge, expanding the number of agents involved by making people from different contexts come together and discuss issues such as public events regulations, institutional security protocols, fire-fighter budgets and so on. Throughout this process redistributions may take place and temporary publics be constituted.

THE AFTER-EFFECTS: ATMOSPHERIC ATTUNEMENTS

In the above, we have discussed how the mediation between humans and more-than-humans through atmospheric elements in architecture turns the design and construction process into a cosmopolitical experiment, which affects how design is practised, and facilitates the design or emergence of certain socialities between humans and more-than-humans. Nevertheless, the design of socialities does not end in the production process, as the 'inhabitation' of the project also included the production of sociality. We now turn to an assessment of how the installation, once built and installed, was capable of stimulating and facilitating these socialities. To do this we will look at the installation as an experimental device in itself, 'because experimental devices are not instruments for normative intervention, they have important moral and political capacities in and of themselves' (Marres 2012: 3).

To detect these capacities, and following anthropologist Kathleen Stewart (2011), we can consider the socialities produced by Polivagina as 'atmospheric attunements'. Kathleen Stewart's concept is useful because it accounts for temporary, sometimes conscious and sometimes unconscious adaptations and transmissions of effects, not only between humans, but also with non-humans: 'an intimate compositional process of dwelling in spaces that bears gestures, gestates, worlds. Here, things matter not because how they are represented, but because they have qualities, rhythms, forces, relations and movements' (idem: 445). Stewart's concept is also interesting because not only does it account for the production of effects, but it is also a kind of mattering or world-making that involves the air, the space, humans and others, and could be interpreted as producing socialities in a spatial foam.

FIG. 2.7 Atmospheric attunements inside the Polivagina during a performance (photo: Nerea Calvillo)

Within the Polivagina, due to the unstable equilibrium between air and helium, the skin moved, crashed and became unstitched; it was alive, producing strangeness and fragility, constructing an atmosphere of attention and a collective sensation of participating in something ephemeral or not fully finished, a space in transition, holding the tension of a structure just about to self-disassemble in front of the eyes of the spectators. Yet this collective and indeterminate attunement (Anderson 2009) with gases is precisely why 'proliferating little worlds of all kinds that form up around conditions, practices, manias, pacings, scenes of absorption, styles of living, forms of attachment (or detachment), identities, and imaginaries' (ibid: 446) could be sensed.

My attention to the liveliness and world-making capacity of the air has, until now, left another materiality unattended: the balloon as a 'device for making atmospheric things' (McCormack 2015b), and more specifically, its polyamide. Here I want to argue that an attunement to this light film, with its mechanical strength, barrier properties and reflective silver finish, facilitated the constitution of publics around specific issues. Evoking Kathleen Stewart's account of the different ways in which the colour red played a role in the material, affective and symbolic New England (Stewart 2015), the reflectivity of the silver-coloured material multiplied like a kaleidoscope throughout the space. It diffused its limits, reflected light, hid furtive hugs and distorted smiling faces; it multiplied Michael Jackson's fans to infinity, reminded someone of Warhol's Factory and made us desire Warhol's Silver Clouds – such were the unexpected effects of this silver-coloured material. People who attend music festivals mostly go to listen to concerts, and yet this colour itself seemed to attract the music fans. The installation was identified as a 'cool' selfie location for self-representation and collectiveness, spreading by word of mouth and bringing people in. Visitors took pictures of themselves in different locations, identifying preferred spots depending on the intensity and colour of the light, the openness of the mesh or the ease with which they could photograph each other. This effect was designed and planned, as a sort of practical aesthetics, 'engaged in thinking about and devising modes of sensory and affective apprehensions of the world' (McCormack 2015b: 105), and as demarking 'possible sites for experimenting with experience' (ibid: 106). The intention was that, once inside, visitors would engage with the art pieces and join round-tables and performances, and this is indeed what happened. Visitors who had never been exposed to such contexts not only listened, but also engaged in the debates. The strangeness of the space and the fact that they inhabited it in their own ways empowered them, as one of the visitors mentioned, to ask, question and speak their minds. So the visitors, including festival-goers as well as cleaners, firemen, technicians and guards, thanks to some extent to the polyamide, engaged with various issues including, but not limited to fan emancipation and queer politics, producing 'new collaborative spacetimes of experimental togetherness, new forms of association' (ibid: 105). However, and importantly, this did not result in the constitution of a new parliament. This attunement took place at specific moments and through temporary and fragile engagements, beyond any possible control.

FIG. 2.8 Visitors attuning to the balloons and art installations (photo: Nerea Calvillo)

And yet other than human publics participated in Fan Riots. It can be argued that part of the success of this emergence of publics was due to the opening up of architecture to the ordinary and the banal. This was primarily effected by the presence of the balloons (see Topham 2002), but playfulness also entered with people's transitions through the space, transforming the way in which art is usually engaged with: dancing in front of art pieces or kissing while watching videos about transgender experiences. Playful practices became recontextualised, hybridising institutionalised formats of cultural exchange. These hybridisation practices also took place the other way around: the displacement of the installation to the main scenarios produced the emergence of creative practices. While the installation was being dismantled, the balloons recovered their usual condition and were taken outside tied to a string and given out to the passionate fans dancing at the main stage. Unexpected (for an architectural installation) atmospheric attunements emerged here: people feeling the joy of a surprise gift, sharing the balloons as a collective treat among their friends, and creatively transforming them into hats, t-shirts or masks. Some people even took them home, expanding the physical network of the festival to domestic spaces.

FIG. 2.9 Music fan posing with balloons repurposed as a dress (photo: Nerea Calvillo)

CONCLUSIONS

Working with air is an exercise in empirical speculation where STS is put to work in architectural practice and which involves developing a more processual way of understanding how socialities can be designed *with* buildings. By focusing on the material, technical and symbolic properties of gases, the design and construction process of the Polivagina and the socialities that emerged during its use, we have been able to identify how architecture is not only about buildings, but about all the various processes that constitute sociotechnical assemblages in permanent transformation, as well as what the installation could do in relation to the social. The movement, instability and flow of the air distributed hierarchical roles and created a collective affect of attention. The lightness of air enabled other bodies and practices to participate in the construction. The lack of history or technical specifications of balloons transformed the design process into a laboratory. It also enabled other publics to participate through a collective affect of celebration, introducing banality and the everyday into artistic and academic contexts.[5] Last, but not least, helium's resistance to being confined or domesticated brought about a controversy that increased the number of actors involved in the process, and transformed the process itself from a design and production context to an institutional and political one.

These socialities were not facilitated by a specific shape or spatial organisation, as other architectural projects have attempted, but by working with atmospheric materials. Even though in accounts of material participation it has been demonstrated that more-than-humans do not have inherent political and social agency, and that they can only acquire it in specific settings (Marres 2012), the case of the Polivagina shows that the agency of these gases became very active precisely because they were a dynamic, rare and unexpected guest.

As mentioned in the Introduction, the advantage of shifting from architecture as an object to dynamic atmospheres is twofold. The first is that it destabilises architectural practices, transforming them into cosmopolitical experiments. For some time, scholars interested in ANT have taken an experimental approach to buildings (Guggenheim 2009; Marres 2012). This chapter, however, demonstrates that atmospheric approaches to experimentation should take buildings-in-the-making into consideration and acknowledge the lack of order in which ideas, materials and actors are assembled. In the case of Polivagina the agency of air demands not only different recombinations of matter, humans and ideas, but different practices to do so. Thus, it is not about changing the order of materials (as in other accounts of architecture), or the order in which humans participate (as in practices of co-design, where users also participate in the initial design phases), but about finding new practices of construction and inhabitation, such as horizontal and self-organised construction teams or playful spectatorship. And yet this experimentation does not acquire its political capacities through variation, as Marres proposes for demonstrational devices (2012), but by embracing uncertainty, which has strong effects in architectural practice where the project cannot be predicted or previously defined, but is performative and non-representational.

The second advantage of shifting to dynamic atmospheres is that it opens up spaces for designing socialities (e.g. in the design and construction phases), and other types of affects with material entities (such as atmospheric attunements). But most importantly, it offers the possibility of designing desirable socialities with political and/or transformative capacities. Building with air calls for feminist or queer construction practices to which anybody can contribute and in which practices of assembly are replaced by practices of care. To better understand this relationship between more-than-humans and socialities I would like to propose one last speculation: that the cosmopolitical experiment may be better read as a process of conviviality, as a temporary co-habitation with more-than-humans. What if through Haraway's Companion Species manifesto (2003), we imagine that helium and air became our companion species?

Gases are not dogs or any other conventional companion species, but thinking about them using Haraway's framework may help us engage with two propositions. The first one is to think of our relationship with the air – a composition of gases and particles (and any other material, for that matter) – not as something out there to be managed, but as material with which we have intimate bodily and affective attunements (Choy 2010; Shapiro 2015). The second proposition is to see how in architecture there can be ways of engaging with more-than-humans other than by control and domestication, but instead through processes of mutual training and learning to be affected, where the value of the interaction does not depend on an economy of affection. Because as Haraway claims in her dog-human co-habitation, 'dog's value and life does not depend on the human's perception that the dogs love them. Rather, the dog has to do his or her job' (2003: 38), which is precisely what the helium balloons did. Even though we established some sort of physical and chemical affect, some sort of 'animacy' (Chen 2012) with helium balloons, they did not respond to our care, but carried on rising, destroying the installation. And yet temporary, fragile and instant moments of equilibrium can be achieved by constantly looking at what emerges from the relationship, which can challenge modes of sociality precisely because we are not used to them. Everyone needs to learn how to engage, and in this process new relationships can emerge. The question, paraphrasing Haraway, is 'how might an ethics and politics committed to the flourishing of significant otherness be learned from taking *air-human* relationship seriously?'[6] (Haraway 2003: 3).

So, inviting atmospheric more-than-humans to architecture's table may be a means to propose a different view of how socialities can be facilitated with atmospheres. It can also contribute to STS by showing how working with air can invent the social in ways not possible without intervening with specific materials, and how socialities can be designed not through discourse or human-only interactions, but through human and more-than-human atmospheres. The level of design and control of this process is still uncertain, and requires more experimentation.

ACKNOWLEDGEMENTS

An early version of this paper was presented at the Third Ordinary Sociology Meeting in Madrid 2015. I am grateful for the comments made by the audience. I would also like to thank Marina Fernández, my courageous colleague throughout the cosmopolitical experiment; Iván López Munuera, for commissioning it and his support and trust in the project; and Miguel Mesa del Castillo and the team of architecture students of Alicante for engaging in the experiment with enthusiasm and patience. My gratitude also to the editors of this book and to the two anonymous reviewers for their helpful comments.

NOTES

1 Architects' conceptions of how to invent the social have shifted throughout history. For instance, in the Baroque period, architecture was a tool to represent power. With the advent of the new state and changes in society of the late nineteenth century and beginning of the twentieth, architecture had to accompany and represent societal changes such as modernisation and industrialisation, as Le Corbusier extensively discussed. In the 1970s a more modest wave in Europe focused on small scale architecture, exploring through

design how small design decisions affect how people inhabit spaces (such as the work of Herzberger in the Netherlands or the Smithsons in the United Kingdom).

2 The name Polivagina was chosen as an allusion to Pussy Riot, but also in reference to the reformulation of the idea of the vagina as a contested space developed by feminists in the 1970s (see Munuera, 2014).

3 It was designed at C+arquitectos by Nerea Calvillo with Marina Fernandez, and built with a group of students from Alicante University architecture school at a workshop directed by Miguel Mesa del Castillo.

4 This is how 'flexible' buildings were conceived and built in the 1990s.

5 Which will demand, in fact, other ethical and aesthetic modes of evaluating architecture.

6 'Dog-human' in the original.

REFERENCES

Adey, P., *Aerial Life: Spaces, Mobilities, Affects* (London: Wiley-Blackwell, 2010).

Anderson, B., 'Affective atmospheres', *Emotion, Space and Society*, 2 (2009), 77–81.

Banham, R., *The Architecture of the Well-Tempered Environment* (London: The Architecture Press, 1969).

Braidotti, R., *Nomadic Theory: The Portable Rosi Braidotti* (New York: Columbia University Press, 2012).

Buchli, V., 'Moisei Ginzburg's Narkomfin Communal House in Moscow: Contesting the Social and Material World', *Journal of the Society of Architectural Historians*, 57 (1998), 160–81.

Chen, M. Y., *Animacies. Biopolitics, Racial Mattering and Queer Affect* (Durham and London: Duke University Press, 2012).

Choy, T., 'Air's Substantiations', in K. S. Rajan, ed., *Lively Capital: Biotechnologies, Ethics and Governance in Global Markets* (Durham: Duke University Press, 2010), pp. 121–54.

Dessauce, M., *The Inflatable Moment. Pneumatics and Protest in '68* (New York: Princeton Architectural Press, 1999).

Farías, I., 'Planes Maestros como Cosmogramas: La Articulación de Fuerzas Oceánicas y Formas Urbanas Tras el Tsunami de 2010 en Chile', *Revista Pléyade* (2014),119–42.

Foucault, M., *Vigilar y castigar: Nacimiento de la prisión* (Madrid: Siglo XXI, 2010).

Guggenheim, M., 'Building memory: Architecture, Networks and Users', *Memory Studies*, 2 (2009), 39–53.

——'From Prototyping to Allotyping', *Journal of Cultural Economy*, 7.4 (2014), 411–33.

Haraway, D., *Simians, Cyborgs and Women: The Reinvention of Nature* (New York: Champman and Hall, 1990).

——*The Companion Species Manifesto. Dogs, People and Significant Otherness* (Chicago: Prickly Paradigm Press, 2003).

Hinchliffe, S., et al., 'Urban Wild things: A Cosmopolitical Experiment', *Environment and Urban Planning D: Society and Space,* 23 (2003), 643–58.

Kvan, T., 'Collaborative Design: What is it?', *Automation in Construction,* 9 (2000), 409–15.

Latour, B., *We Have Never Been Modern* (Cambridge: Harvard University Press, 1993).

——'How to Talk About the Body? The Normative Dimension of Science Studies', *Body & Society,* 10 (2004), 205–29.

——*Reassembling the Social. An Introduction to Actor-Network-Theory* (Oxford: Oxford University Press, 2005).

Lopez M., I., 'Fan Riots', *Arquitectura: Revista del Colegio Oficial de Arquitectos de Madrid* (2014), 20–5.

Marres, N., *Material Participation: Technology, the Environment and Everyday Publics* (London: Palgrave Macmillan, 2012).

Marres, N., and J. Lezaun, 'Materials and Devices of the Public: an Introduction', *Economy and Society*, 40 (2011), 489–509.

McCormack, D. P., 'Atmospheric Choreographies and Air-Conditioned Bodies', in V. Hunter, ed., *Moving Sites. Investigating Site-Specific Dance Performance* (London, New York: Routledge, 2015a), pp. 79–94.

——'Devices for Doing Atmospheric Things', in P. Vanni, ed., *Non-Representational Methodologies* (London, New York: Routledge, 2015b), pp. 89–111.

——'Aerostatic Spacing: on Things Becoming Lighter than Air', *Transactions of the Institute of British Geographers,* 34 (2009), 25–41.

Roberts, L., 'The Death of the Sensuous Chemist: The "New Chemistry" and the Transformation of Sensuous Technology', *Studies in History and Philosophy of Science*, Part A 26 (1995), 503–29.

Sanders, E. B. N., and P. J. Stappers, 'Co-creation and the New Landscapes of Design', *CoDesign*, 4.5 (2008), 5–18.

Shapiro, N., 'Attuning to the Chemosphere: Domestic Formaldehyde, Bodily Reasoning, and the Chemical Sublime', *Cultural Anthropology*, 30 (2015), 368–93.

Sloterdijk, P., *Esferas III* (Barcelona: Siruela, 2005).

Star, S. L., 'The Ethnography of Infrastructure', *American Behavioral Scientist*, 43 (1999), 377–91.

Stewart, K., 'Atmospheric Attunements', *Environment and Urban Planning D: Society and Space*, 29 (2011), 445–53.

Suchman, L., J. Blomberg, and R. Trigg, 'Back to work: Renewing Old Agendas for Cooperative Design', in M. Kyng et al., eds, *Computers and Design in Context* (Cambridge: MIT Press, 2003), pp. 267–87.

Tironi, M., and N. Calvillo, 'Water and Air: Territories, Tactics and the Elemental Textility of Urban Cosmopolitics', in I. Farías and A. Blok, eds, *Urban Cosmopolitics* (London, New York: Routledge, 2016), pp. 207–24.

Topham, S., *Blow Up. Inflatable Art, Architecture and Design* (London: Prestel, 2002).

Vanderburgh, J., D. Russell and W. Ellis, 'A Dialectics of Determination: Social Truth-Claims in Architectural Writing, 1970–1995', in A. Piotrowski and J. W. Robinson, eds, *The Discipline of Architecture* (Minneapolis: University of Minnesota Press, 2001), pp.103–126.

Wakeford, N., 'Beyond the Individual. Replacing the Network Society with Social Foam: a Revolution for Corporate Ethnography?', *Ethnographic Praxis in Industry Conference Proceedings* (2011), 240–55.

Wilkie, A., 'Regimes of Design, Logics of Users', *Athenea Digital*, 11 (2011), 317–34.

Yaneva, A., *Made by the Office for Metropolitan Architecture: An Ethnography of Design* (Rotterdam: 010 Publishers, 2009).

3

INCUBATIONS: INVENTING PREVENTIVE ASSEMBLAGES

Michael Guggenheim, Bernd Kräftner, Judith Kröll

In remembrance of Stefan Beck

INCUBATIONS: A METHODS PRIMER

THIS CHAPTER INTRODUCES, IN A PROGRAMMATIC FORM, OUR OWN TAKE on inventing the social. Incubations take off from current attempts in the social sciences to create 'inventive methods' (Lury and Wakeford 2011), speculative methods (Wilkie et al. 2016) and design experiments (Binder et al. 2015), or to expand the methods and devices of social science beyond texts (Becker 2007). But incubations are not so much a specific method as an attempt to reorient the basic assumptions of social science towards a strong notion of inventing the social. What follows is programmatic account followed up by one example. But this account is also skewed, as it rationalises a messy process. Rather than create a blueprint, a recipe or a toolbox, we began with a variety of projects (Guggenheim et al. 2006; Kräftner and Xperiment! 2005; Kräftner et al. 2010; Guggenheim et al. 2016; Guggenheim 2011) that finally prompted us to think about what holds these projects together. Incubations, as should become obvious, are not rule-bound practices, but attempts to invent the social under specific circumstances. The following account merely suggests, based on experience, what to pay attention to when embarking on your own incubation.

To begin with, here is a definition: An incubation is a socio-technical device that uses situational, social and time-based pressure to invent the social and represent it with a wide variety of media. This idea draws conceptually on three historical meanings of incubation that appear to be unrelated to the problems of social research, yet which contribute in important ways to our definition of incubation as an approach to inventing the social. First, in Classical antiquity, an incubation is a healing process that is attempted when usual forms of healing do not work (Meier 1949). A patient is brought to a temple and sleeps there, where she experiences dreams. If she has the 'right' dream, she is healed. From this first meaning, we can learn two things: incubations are *experimental* forms that replace other, more standard forms of practice. More specifically, they experimentalise lay-expert co-operation: Rather than an expert applying external knowledge and medication to the lay person, in an incubation the expert helps the lay person to have new kinds of experiences.

Second, an incubator is a pressure cooker, a device invented in the laboratory of Robert Boyle by his assistant Denis Papin (Papin 1681). The pressure cooker uses pressure to fuse ingredients in novel ways. It speeds up chemical processes and softens ingredients. From this second meaning we can learn that incubations bring actors and actants together, applying to them a kind of pressure that reconnects them in novel ways. Incubations re-order social situations by intervening in them.

Third, the term 'incubator' became applied, around 1880, to a new device that creates a safe environment for premature babies. These early incubators, however, being made from non-transparent materials, created a barrier between mother and child that in some cases led mothers to stop caring about their babies. Pierre Constant Budin thus invented a version made from glass, which preserved the delicate atmosphere needed for the care of the infant without creating an opaque barrier between mother and child (Baker 2000: 323). The incubator thus became a device that shielded a precious being from the world, while at the same time allowing primary care. Later, incubators became complex and expensive technical devices with ventilation and heating. To finance them, they were exhibited, which in time led to ubiquitous incubator shows at trade fairs, zoos, fairgrounds such as Coney Island, and other unlikely places (Silverman 1979). For our purposes then, an incubator is also, based on this third definition, a device for carefully creating unusual and unlikely consumption contexts for delicate objects of social scientific knowledge.[1]

From this description it also follows what an incubation is not. Firstly, an incubation cannot, and should not, be defined in terms of the media it uses (such as 'documentary photography', 'art installation' or 'ethnography'). An incubation can be any of these, but incubations do not start with such media in mind. Secondly, an incubation is not an 'intervention', as opposed to a scientific research project or an art project. An incubation is all of these, and can result in any of them, but at its heart it cannot be reduced to any of them exclusively. Third, an incubation is not a project in which artists and social scientists collaborate in an inter- or trans-disciplinary way in the sense that social scientists do science and artists do art and then these two things are combined. An incubation includes strategies, elements, material and epistemic practices from both of these fields, but it does not neatly separate them into art and social science. To start with separate media, technologies, professions, spheres and skills, and to ponder how these can be brought together, is the opposite of the logic of an incubation. It is an artefact of organisational specialisation, but to begin with an incubation this specialisation has to be resolved first, rather than becoming the problem of the project itself. An incubation needs to draw on whatever technologies, logics and skills seem necessary, rather than being defined by them from the outset.

We begin the article by explaining how incubations are a particular form of inventing the social. We then discuss a particular project, 'Straight from the Heart: Prevention Indices and Divinations of Researchers' with regard to the three main characteristics of incubations given above: the creation of an experimental situation, the application of pressure and the design of a careful presentation context.

INCUBATIONS AS INVENTING THE SOCIAL

Before we present our example, it will be helpful to clarify how incubations are a form of inventing the social. The phrase 'inventing the social' can be understood in multiple ways. First, by inventing the social we can understand what Hans Joas has termed 'the creativity of action' (Joas 1996). Such a notion of inventing the social refers to a sociological conception of agency, specified in different ways in the writings of classical social theorists influenced by pragmatism, such as G. H. Mead, Alfred Schütz, Herbert Blumer, Berger and Luckmann, and Harold Garfinkel, which foregrounds the creativity, contingency, inventiveness and production of novel forms of sociality in all forms of action. This first view of inventing the social opposes structuralist and rationalist accounts of action by stressing that even in the most humble interactions, novel forms of the social constantly emerge, and that the role of the social scientist is to observe how this emergence takes place.

We can adopt this view for the practice of social science. If any kind of interaction invents the social, then any practice of a social scientist invents the social too. This is the second version of inventing the social. As Law and Urry put it, 'theories and methods are protocols for modes of questioning or interacting which also *produce* realities' (Law & Urry 2004: 395). Thus every text on a social practice not only describes it, but also adds a new version of it to the world. Methods are inherently inventive (Lury & Wakeford 2011).

A third version of inventing the social adds what Ian Hacking has called 'looping effects' to the picture (Hacking 1995). Re-descriptions of the social offer actors new ways of understanding themselves, and produce new forms of action by adapting or resisting these descriptions. Take as an example the way that the term 'performativity' has been used in social studies of finance (MacKenzie & Millo 2003). Economists, when they describe the world as being run by efficient markets, do not merely describe this world, but equip the actors with concepts and devices that then perform the very things the economists purport to describe. This kind of argument is primarily directed against a traditional sociological critique of economics which claims that economists do not adequately describe social realities. In a different theoretical register, Pierre Bourdieu has observed very similar things in the case of opinion surveys. Bourdieu demonstrates that questionnaires make people express 'opinions' on topics they would not have opinions about were they not participating in a survey (Bourdieu 1984:.412 ff.; Law 2009). According to this view, efficient markets and opinion surveys *do* perform what they do, but this is at least in part because social scientists equip actors with the means of enacting these things. Inventing the social would then mean that social scientists equip the world with the means to create new worlds.

These three versions are descriptive and do not presume that the actors they refer to actively *seek* to invent the social. The invention of the social is here a by-product of ordinary or social scientific actions. In particular, in the case of performativity, it is an important part of the analysis that it claims to *reveal* the performative elements of what economists or survey researchers conceive of as *description*. All these three versions, then, describe features of (particular kinds) of actions, not differences *between* kinds of actions. They ignore the possibility of actions or forms of social science that do *not* invent the social.[2] All three notions are part of a theoretical debate about the concept of action or what it means to do social science, rather than a debate about different kinds of actions or social science.

A fourth form of inventing the social can be seen in lay practices that experimentalise the social in formats that are similar to social science, in 'experiments in living' (Marres 2012). This fourth form, it could be argued, is a systematic transport of the breaching experiment (Garfinkel 1967) into practices of the self. It is a form of creating the social by lay people through the means of effecting systematic breaches and changes in their own conditions of living (also see Whatmore 2009). It is here that incubation as 'inventing the social' comes into its own, where it specifies a *particular* practice rather than a re-description of generic practices.

But such experimentalisations of the social have rarely been taken up by social scientists, because to do so would be to break with a number of assumptions about how to conduct social science. To understand this break, it will help to look at some typical descriptions of such experimentalisations. For example, Law and Urry, in the article cited above, argue for a move from re-describing social research to re-designing it: 'If social investigation makes worlds, then it can, in some measure, think about the worlds it wants to help to make' (Law & Urry 2004: 391). For Law and Urry, what follows are different assumptions about what we could call the form of the world. For them, social worlds should be invented as 'multiple' and 'complex' (Law & Urry 2004: 397–404).

Yet multiplicity (Mol 2003) and complexity (Law & Mol 2002) have been used in this research tradition primarily as descriptions. If we are to understand them as inventionist terms, we can perhaps best conceptualise them as differing from the tradition of action research (Fals Borda 2001). In most action research, the world is imagined not as multiple and complex, but as shot through with power relations, and the goal of the researcher is not so much to allow other forms of complexity and multiplicities, but to change the world in ways that are conceived of as more just by the social scientists. To understand multiplicity and complexity as elements of a form of inventing the social implies that any attempt to invent the social aims at *complicating* things and *opening up* possible actions for any participant, rather than closing them down.

For Law and Urry, the problem of complexity and multiplicity is interwoven with the different *forms* that social science takes. When they write that they want to 'imagine ... fluid and decentred modes for knowing the world allegorically, indirectly, perhaps pictorially, sensuously, poetically, a social science of partial connections' (Law & Urry 2004: 400), these suggestions echo the criteria for what Luciana Parisi calls 'speculative methods' (Parisi 2012). For Parisi, a speculative method 'demands of thought to become felt, fact to become poten- tial, imagination to supersede observation, object to affect method, method to become transformative of the object' (Parisi 2012: 241). Such a method 'may contribute to push social research towards the *designing of unknown objects* by exposing their particular perspectives about the importance of an event' (Parisi 2012: 242).

In their different ways, these accounts of social science converge in a move from purely textual accounts of the social, to different pictorial, sensual and objectual accounts of inventing the social. This expansion of the media of social science is surely welcome (see Guggenheim 2015). The traditional scepticism within social science against other than textual media is unfounded, and given the practice of the natural sciences, rather hinders than enables better translations of the world. Elsewhere we have explained that social scientists often assume a media determinism for visual media. As expressed in the statements above, they believe that visual representations are in themselves more or less objective, or more or less capable of inventing the social (Guggenheim 2015).

But we suggest reading this shift to the visual, objectual and so on as indicative of an underlying problem: If 'theories and methods are protocols for modes of questioning or interacting which also *produce* realities', as Law and Urry claim in the quote above, then the focus of research shifts from an end result to the practice of doing it. Instead of focusing on the research articles as accounts of what has been done during a research project, incubations as a particular kind of inventing the social imply a focus on the 'modes of questioning or interacting which produces realities'.

This is where the three characteristics of incubations mentioned in the introduction become relevant. To question and interact in order to produce realities suggests first of all suitable setups; second, it suggests some form of pressure to soften established situations; and third, it suggests carefully designed products in adequate consumption contexts.

In our view, such a shift implies moving away from taking methods as pre-existing tools that can be used for all kinds of realities. It certainly asks us to refrain from *identifying* a researcher with particular theories and methods. To say, 'I am an ethnomethodologist' or 'I do ANT' would imply a strange way of inventing the social. Rather than questioning and interacting, to identify with a theory or method in such a way would assume a machinic idea of theories and methods. Moreover, such an idea would make theories and methods part of the identities of researchers. It would assume a world with which a researcher always interacts in the same way. This is highly unlikely to invent relevant forms of the social, if we imagine the social world to be complex and multiple.

Instead, an incubation asks us to understand research problems as requiring *adequate* ways to question and interact with them. Rather than beginning with a particular method, or particular media, an incubation begins with a problem, and the call to question and interact with it in ways such that the social is invented in novel and adequate ways.

The reason why incubations often move away from purely textual forms of research can be found in the three dimensions of incubations given above.

In many cases, the search for adequate experimental situations and adequate forms of pressure and consumption contexts *does* lead away from purely textual modes of doing research, but not for the sake of non-textual approaches as such, but because purely textual approaches are often inadequate to incubate a given problem. As can be seen from the example that follows, one main problem here is that incubation often requires working together and interacting with a multiplicity of actors. For many of these actors, what is a normal mode of data production and presentation for a social scientist is a highly unusual way to interact with the world. Such a radically asymmetric protocol for inventing the social is, however, rather unlikely to work. The reason why scholars such as Law and Urry ask for the visual and the poetic lies probably here: it aims for a format in which the asymmetry between the production of social science and other actors is flattened.

This, however, should not be read – as it far too often is in defences of visual sociology (see for example Leavy 2008: 344) – as an attempt at popularising social science with other media. The logic behind such ideas of popularisation suggests that images are easier to understand than texts. Social scientists do their difficult job, and once they have finished, they use images to make it easier for lay audiences to understand it. This, however, leaves the asymmetries between different media and between social scientists and their audiences intact, and merely serves to dumb down social science.

In contrast, incubations aim to invent the social by challenging the practices of social science as much as those of the other actors involved in a particular incubation. An incubation is not based on the fiction that the power differentials between researcher and researched can easily be flattened. Rather, it takes the power differentials seriously by creating challenges for the researcher and the researched. By denying the idea that the researcher can simply enter a situation with theories and methods that she masters, symmetry is achieved by loosening the researcher's grip on what she thinks she knows what to do, and how to do it. This is why the organisation founded by two of the present authors (BK and JK) is called 'Research Centre for Shared Incompetence'. How is it possible, then, to invent the social?

CREATE AN EXPERIMENTAL SETUP

Incubation in antiquity was an experimental setup that was only used once other methods had failed. It was a form of hope in experimental methods: 'Therapeutic optimism is unlimited and never punished' remarks Meier in his standard book on incubations in antiquity (Meier 1949: 59). The patient sleeps on the steps of the temple and dreams. What matters is the *right* dream, and the right dream cannot be planned for. Whether it was the right dream is only known after the fact, when the patient wakes up. Incubations cannot be repeated, planned or standardised. In incubations the expert does not so much apply her superior knowledge, but rather accompanies a lay person on an experimental path. The same is true for incubations in social science.

This means that great care is needed in deciding where and how incubations in social science should be housed. Social science departments may not be the most suitable places to do so. The organisational background that we have found to be the most enabling for our project work is a mixture of direct funding for specific projects, combined with either specialised departments devoted to non-disciplinary research, or a (loose) attachment to STS, sociology or anthropology departments. Since funding explicitly for incubations does not exist, we depend on funding possibilities that at least encourage projects at the border of social science and the arts.

Incubations need materials, some of them costly, others simply unusual at social science departments. Working with materials requires machines and studios (Farias & Wilkie 2015). The offices and seminar rooms in social science departments are often not very convenient for the multiple affordances of an incubation. Work with humans necessitates spaces that are comfortable and that do not implicitly replicate the affect and organisational structure of offices. Universities are also not strictly suitable for incubations, because they tend to formalise acceptable forms of research, both by specifying discipline-specific standards and by increasingly restricting ethical review procedures, which are formulated according a very particular kind of research that depends, for example, on anonymisation (Clark 2012).

STRAIGHT FROM THE HEART: PREVENTION INDICES AND DIVINATIONS OF RESEARCHERS (2008)

The project on which we report had its beginnings in unusual circumstances. As a group, we already had extensive experience of conducting incubations. Our collaboration began three years previously when we were directors of the exhibitions 'die wahr/falsch inc.', a ten-module exhibition in Vienna (Guggenheim et al. 2006). Already for that collaboration we began working in a mode in which there was no clear-cut division of labour, and in which all the team members carried out the conceptual and practical work together. For that exhibition, BK and MG had already collaborated with the late Stefan Beck at the Institute for European Anthropology at Humboldt University Berlin for a module titled 'Who With Whom. Heredity in Action' on Thalassemia in Cyprus.

The beginning of 'Straight from the Heart' lay in another project of Stefan Beck and his research group, entitled 'Preventive Selves – Interdisciplinary Investigations into an Emergent Form of Life'. This was a collaboration with the department for general practitioners at the Charité (the university hospital). 'Preventive Selves' sought to understand why people, although they are aware of various truths about how to prevent cardiovascular diseases (such as the fact that unhealthy eating habits or smoking increases the risk) do not adhere to this knowledge. They researched the lived realities of particular groups at risk (migrants) (Niewöhner et al. 2011), but also the interaction between GPs and patients in consulting sessions (Heintze et al. 2010). The project members themselves identified its key shortcoming: observing and interviewing 'preventive selves' did not really give a full picture of these selves.

The project leaders asked us whether we could contribute to the project by exploring new methods of thinking about what they called 'preventive assemblages' (Niewöhner et al. 2011). From the very start, we decided not to focus again on patients and their role in the assemblage, as we felt that their role was already overdetermined by the research of the project itself, as well as by the many other research projects that either sought to improve prevention or were critical of the governmental logics of state-led prevention projects. Instead, we decided that we would turn the logic of experts and patients around and create preventive assemblages with the project members themselves. We would intervene in the making of preventive assemblages at the level of those who develop these concepts, which includes ourselves.

How would it be possible for us to collaborate with anthropologists and doctors to think about and invent professional preventive selves, rather than produce prevention as a solution to which the population should adhere? What could be a suitable setup for doing so? Our basic idea was to build a laboratory that would allow us to explore a number of methods to produce various versions of preventive selves.

First we needed to create an organisational setting that would allow us to operate such methods. We knew from the beginning that, for practical reasons, our laboratory would best be set up at the respective institutes. We needed to create a space not within the control of these institutes – a liminal space that would clearly indicate that this was not part of the ongoing practices of these departments. In the case of the Department of European Anthropology, we could use a corridor that connected two parts of the department. It had a balcony that was often used by smokers. It also had a sink. It was neither an office nor a classroom, and it contained some ragged furniture that we could make use of. On the same floor as the Department of Medicine was a former dental clinic, now abandoned. We set up our laboratory there, in a bright, empty, tiled space (Fig. 3.1).

A room does not determine an organisational environment. Research environments are not only spatially, but also organisationally and practically tightly controlled through disciplinary practices, organisational rules and ethical reviews, and these prescribe what kinds of the social can be invented. Our project took place in a complex organisational space: our research participants were also our research funders, and they owned the spaces in which our experiments took place. At the same time, the research project did not need to undergo ethical review, as, at least at that time, sociological and anthropological research in Germany did not need to undergo ethical review, and also the project took place below the radar of any overseeing body. But we were crucially aware of the fact that the project took part within an organisational environment in which ethical issues are seen as crucial, and further, in which ethical and methodological standards are very different for the two groups.

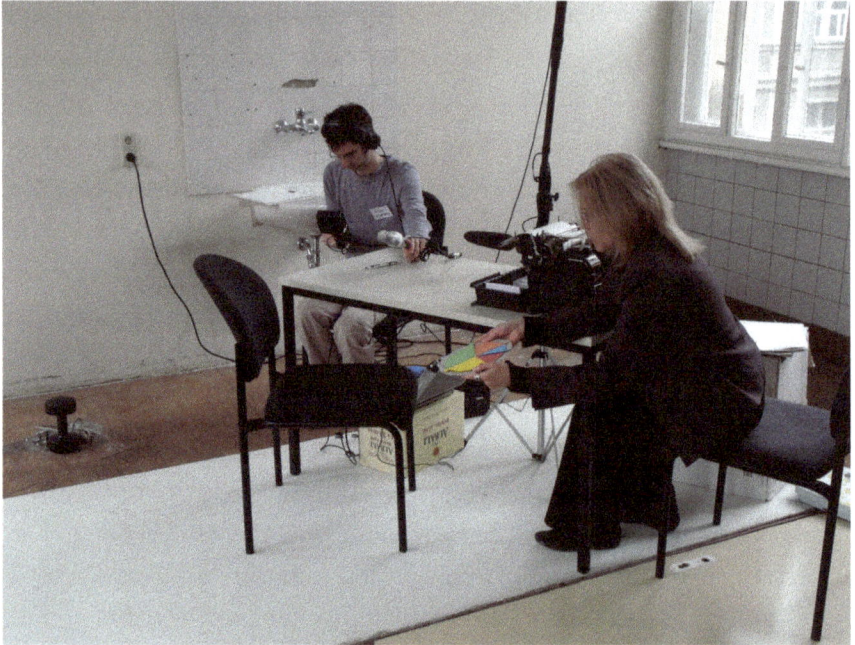

FIG. 3.1 The prevention laboratory at the Department of General Practice, Charité, Humboldt University (photo: Bernd Kräftner)

The logic of ethical review aims at *preventing* too much invention of the social. Ethical review is by its very nature conservative. It is geared towards preserving the social world as it is. It assumes that research participants have a right not to be bothered by researchers and that researchers need to guarantee demonstrable benefits to society if they want to bother other people. Particularly in the social sciences researchers are assigned the position of documenting the ethical review without being able to influence, control or even change social situations.

But incubations work against this logic by aiming to provoke, change, influence and ultimately invent new forms of the social. The methods used in 'Straight From the Heart' could potentially be challenging to the research participants, who were themselves researchers. We thought that we would need to establish a space that would set out its own rules, but at the same time make the research participants aware of this unusual situation and create the possibility of discussing it with them. To accomplish this, we developed an informed consent sheet that notified participants of their rights to object and disagree with the research altogether, to provide alternatives to it, to stop us from continuing, to intervene in the procedures, and to obtain the material produced.

This model for informed consent became a device for creating a research environment of our own definition, rather than simply copying an existing logic of negotiating the relationship between researcher and researched. The model functions by openly contesting existing definitions of informed consent, but it also invites the test persons to contest our notion of informed consent.

Our project also highlighted a crucial problem with the consent forms themselves: even when they are considered as a basis for discussion, rather than simply a form that is signed, they focus on abstract options of action to be taken in particular situations that are yet unknown to the participants. It is only in, and more often after exposure to particular situations that research participants can form an opinion, an emotion or a (dis)agreement. This is precisely what happened. No participant challenged our review form, and signed it without further ado, some of them slightly bemused at the wording that gave them more power than other forms. Yet during the sessions, the participants did not exercise this power to challenge what we did. They would be interested in our research, they would ask us about particular steps, but no one considered different courses of action. Some of them would be rather confused, and even felt misled afterwards.

The experimental space was not only set by discursive means, but at the very beginning of each session was enacted by two events. First, when entering the space, we presented the participants with a variety of things they could consume (Fig. 3.2).

We offered them ostensibly healthy food such as apples, but also ostensibly unhealthy foods such as cheap cakes and chocolate. We also offered them cigarettes, wine and schnapps. The gesture of offering such a variety of consumables was on the surface a gesture of hospitality. But it also gestured at the organisational space in which this was taking place. Smoking in the buildings of the university is forbidden, as is drinking alcohol at work. As our experiments took place immediately before, during, or after the participants' work, these were also offers to break written and unwritten codes of the organisation. When

FIG. 3.2 Consumption offers at the Department of European Anthropology, Humboldt University (photo: Bernd Kräftner)

asked, we explicitly claimed to take responsibility for breaking these rules, yet obviously, we could not guarantee what would happen. Our gesture of hospitality was at the same time an invitation to a performative negotiation of the nexus of the logics of prevention, a challenge to how these are built into the rules of workspaces and an exploration of the desire of groups and individuals to transgress these rules. Smokers happily accepted our offers to smoke, and some drank wine.

At the same time, our offers of food created a liminal space in the very organisations in which the experiments were conducted, and produced data on how to negotiate such a space. On a basic level it gave us data about how many people consumed which kinds of goods. On a more sophisticated level, it gave us recordings of conversations about how the research participants created and negotiated this space.

Second, after discussing informed consent, the next step was to ask the participants whether we could take a drop of blood from them (Fig. 3.3).

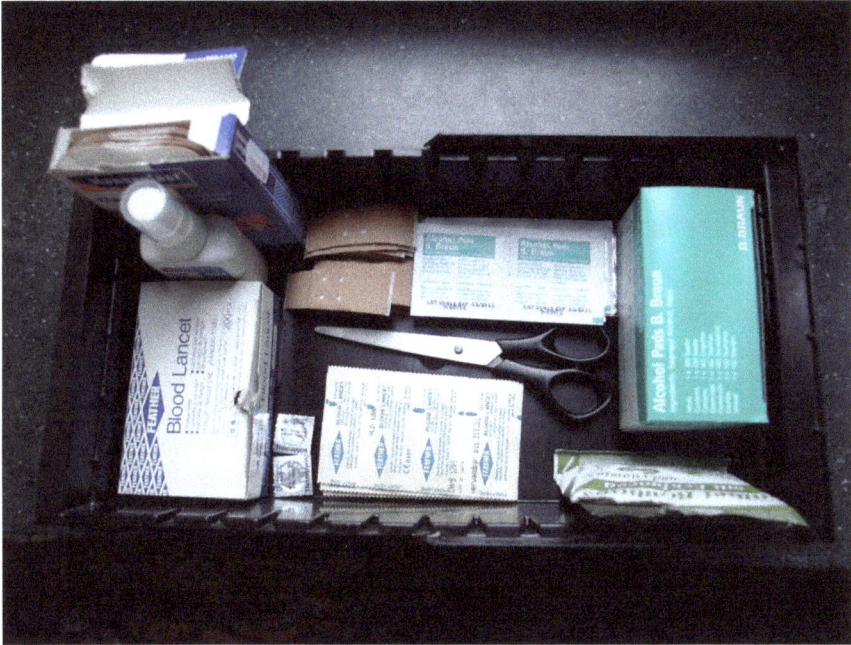

FIG. 3.3 Kit for blood taking (photo: Bernd Kräftner)

We made it clear that there was *no* medical justification for this procedure (we used the blood later as a central element of the posters for the exhibition: see the discussion in section 4 below). The blood-taking became a prompt to create a social situation in which the relationship between researcher and researched was put to test (and which would result in a visible product of this test: a drop of blood). This opened up the issue of why people allow their bodily integrity to be challenged, and for what reasons such a transgression can occur.

We offered that we would take the blood, or that they could do it themselves (many of the participants were doctors, and thus used to doing it). We would also point out that the person who would take the blood, Bernd Kräftner, was originally a trained doctor, and thus technically allowed to do so, yet that he had not practiced for more than twenty years. Rather than putting the blood away in a capillary tube, we would drop it onto a piece of paper. Thus the blood did not disappear, but remained visible for the participants.

Asking for a drop of blood had a similar effect to offering food. It questioned and created a space that is usually taken for granted in research. It pointed to the fact that breaking boundaries of the skin and taking bodily fluid is a procedure we are used to under specific conditions. Giving a non-medical justification opened a space to discuss the logics of violating bodily boundaries. At the same time, the offer that they do it themselves and the explanation of our own (lack of) qualifications to do it, questioned the expert-lay divide ingrained in research practices. The offer, after all, was not merely a choice, but also opened up the unspoken assumption that researchers are better qualified to do what they do than their research subjects. Our offer explicitly acknowledged that at least the doctors among the participants were probably better qualified to do it than we were.

APPLYING PRESSURE:
NEW FORMS OF PROVOCATIVE CONTAINMENT

The other two characteristics of an incubation both refer to the uses of controlled environments. The first, the pressure cooker, is historically a precedent of the second, the baby incubator. Both are spaces that control atmospheres (also see Calvillo, this volume). But while the baby incubator tries to care for particularly vulnerable beings, the pressure cooker transforms and softens objects.

As John Evelyn reported at the first demonstration of a pressure cooker by Denis Papin at the Royal Society in 1682, it is a procedure 'by which the hardest bones of beef itself, and mutton, were made as soft as cheese' (Evelyn 2009: 393). Such a softening of the materials is exactly what is intended in a research incubation. Hardened positions, worldviews and bodily practices stabilised by habitus are softened and opened up to collective transformation.

Incubations do not produce pressure on the participants because we oppose their views, even if they may be politically opposed to ours. For an incubation to work, it needs to apply pressure to *all* of those involved, including the incubators, to produce new situations and new solutions to commonly perceived problems.

A common version of pressure in incubations resembles what Lezaun, Muniesa and Vikkelso call 'provocative containment', a term they use to describe the experiments in social psychology of Lewin, Moreno and Milgram. Provocative containment is the idea that researchers can create a space in which they 'choreograph situations of induced spontaneity' (Lezaun et al. 2013: 279; also see Brown 2012). While Lezaun et al. situate 'provocative containment' as a research practice in a specific epoch, and see its remnants in artistic, therapeutic and managerial practices, incubations reinvent it as social research, but with a twist.

What distinguishes the pressure of incubations from those earlier experiments is that the latter aim to solve social problems, as defined in social psychology, while the former try to open up and change how we look at certain issues. While the social psychologists usually 'realised' something they knew and intended, but which did not exist in its pure form outside the laboratory (democracy, authority etc.) (Lezaun et al. 2013: 289), incubations instead aim to explore an issue and create new worlds. In the words of Vinciane Despret, it is a matter of 'genesis', 'of raising more interesting questions that enable more articulated answers, and therefore more articulated identities' (Despret 2004: 125).

What emerges in the incubation is not simply 'data' that we then use to test a hypothesis, but rather, the 'choreography' or performance is a central outcome itself, a pressure-induced invention of the social. For this reason, it is part and parcel of the incubation to be open for interruption and interrogation by the participants before, during and after. Also, the props and the control exercised over the participants have no hidden meaning or plot. There may be surprise, in the sense that the incubators know what is coming next while the participants do not, but nothing is hidden from their view.

The laboratory for testing ideas of prevention implied pressure of this kind from the beginning. The set-up was explicitly informed by the organisational logics of provocative containments. It was an artificial space, governed by an artificial logic that had no equivalence in the world outside our experiment. It was a laboratory space in the narrow sense of the word: it was a controlled space that aimed for 'placeless' and 'inconsequential' intervention (Guggenheim 2012).

The laboratory did not aim to produce a knowledge that is specific to a time or place, or that would change the world outside the laboratory. Rather, we sought to produce a knowledge that could only be produced by the specific laboratory. As a pressure-inducing mechanism the laboratory was specifically targeted to what we assumed to be a research problem: that doctors and anthropologists, precisely because they work on the topic of prevention, are very difficult research participants when it comes to their own ideas and behaviours of prevention. Their habitus – as is ours, as incubators – is geared towards turning questions regarding their own ideas and lives towards 'problems', that are considered to be off-topic, too personal, too complex and irrelevant to explore (see the 'unclassifiable professor' in Bourdieu 1984: 418).

Pressure induced in the laboratory has two sources. First, the strange organisational space, which explicitly suspends normal interaction protocols, as outlined in the previous section. Second, more specifically, pressure is induced by prompts for the research participants to do certain tasks, such as the offer of food, or the request for a drop of blood. In the latter example it is also obvious that the pressure induced does not only affect the research participants but also us: the task is a task that mediates the relationship between the researcher and researched. Other than in the cases of provocative containment, incubators do not control the situation behind the backs of the research participants. Instead, we create and open up a situation that has to be negotiated by us and them together. The researchers are not observers, and neither are they puppet-masters that create a spectacle, but they are implicated in the negotiation of the social.

Other such tasks consisted, for example, in an adapted version of SEIQoL, an established test for assessing the quality of life (Hickey et al. 1996). In SEIQoL, a participant freely names five elements central to her life (such as, for example, family, work, playing volleyball, going to the pub, attending the opera), and rates these relative to each other with the help of a five-segment colour wheel. The advantage of this method with regard to other quality of life measurements is that the results are quantifiable and comparable, yet are based on individual choices for those elements of life, rather than on predefined ones. For the participants, this was a well-known and unsurprising device.

FIG. 3.4 SEIQoL with soft toys (photo: Bernd Kräftner)

But then we added a surprise element. After they had completed the task, we asked them to pair a soft-toy animal to each of their elements and explain the selection (Fig. 3.4).

Further, the participants were asked to answer a number of questions regarding their ideas about prevention, and specifically about the implied futures of prevention, culminating in the question 'When you have grown older, will you have thought enough about whether you did enough to live longer?'[3] Such questions are not usual in surveys, because they do not assume that the respondents will have an opinion about what is asked. Even though the participants deal professionally with the subject-matter of the questions, it seems likely that the questions will actually instigate new thoughts because of their complexity. But these questions are also atypical of expert interviews, because they address, in the modus of prevention, the future of the experts' bodies themselves, and not their views about the world. They ask the respondent to transport herself into the future, to invent a situation in which she thinks back on her own life and

83

answer in the present about this future situation. They help the respondent to invent her own future.

Pressure in an incubation is theatrical, similar to the examples of Lezaun et al. (2013). It is a prompt to act in new ways. But it is also different, because it is not about staging unwitting participants, but about making them reflect on and explore their relation to the world.

CREATING CAREFUL CONSUMPTION
CONTEXTS FOR DELICATE OBJECTS

The third incubator, the baby incubator, was developed as a very unusual technical object. It was first and foremost an incredibly complex technical step to create an atmosphere for babies. But the design of the incubator also had to mediate between the needs of mothers and doctors. Incubators had to allow two groups to care for babies: mothers, and experts such as doctors and nurses. The invention of glass incubators allowed the needs of these two main groups to be calibrated: it allowed the experts to control the environment, while at the same time it allowed communication by mothers with their infants. Incubators, then, are devices that balance and mediate between closeness and distance, between impermeable boundaries and bodily closeness, between sight and touch, between professionals and lay users. In a later phase, this mediation included a third element, namely audiences that did not have an obvious connection to the babies. The reasons were historically specific: to finance the expensive technology, some doctors decided to show them to the general public at a cost. This was so successful that soon there were incubator shows in zoos, on Coney Island and in other such places.

Similarly, incubations in social science need to balance and mediate between the researchers, the research participants and wider audiences. The balance is similar to that of a baby incubator. What is the right distance between the researchers, the research participants and other audiences? What are adequate means to create such a balance? How can the delicate interactions during the research process be preserved and made public?

A particular problem of incubations is that the route of translations from the world to the research result is not fixed. The research article is but one among many options in which an incubation can be presented to the public. As incubations are very often local and situational inventions, specific for particular constituencies and audiences, they very often profit from installations, performances, and exhibitions and other place-specific presentation forms. These allow for different forms of translating the originating research materials into *materially inventive* forms. If incubations can be said to invent the social, then a central element of these new forms of the social is their adequate translation into materialisations.

When carrying out incubations, we never have a predefined idea of what the end result will be in terms of the media used. Terms such as 'exhibition' are merely convenient placeholders for locally specific forms of presentation. They are convenient precisely because 'exhibitions' are not media specific, but allow for a suitable combination of drawings, photographs, performances, texts and audio material. The guiding question then is always which presentation format translates the originating material in a way that is both true to the originating research problem and adds the right kind of surprise.

For the project on prevention, we initially intended to stage an exhibition. Given that the exhibition had to take place at the Department of European Anthropology, we were confined to a corridor with two opposing walls and no usable floor-space. To mitigate these space restrictions we decided to create a series of posters. The posters would refer back to scientific posters that often hang on these walls and those of the Department of General Medicine.

The first poster was deliberately designed to resemble one that doctors might present at a conference (Fig. 3.5).

It was planned according to the same rules that govern the design of such posters: it contained a layout that would give an overview of the research question, the methods, and the research participants.

The other sixteen posters were based on two materials gained during the experiment, namely the drops of blood we took at the beginning and the soft toys used in the quality of life tests. We used both of these as backgrounds to contain the other forms of data gathered (Fig. 3.6, Fig. 3.7).

FIG. 3.5 Introductory Poster (image: the authors)

FIG. 3.6 Example poster based on flying animals (image: Bernd Kräftner)

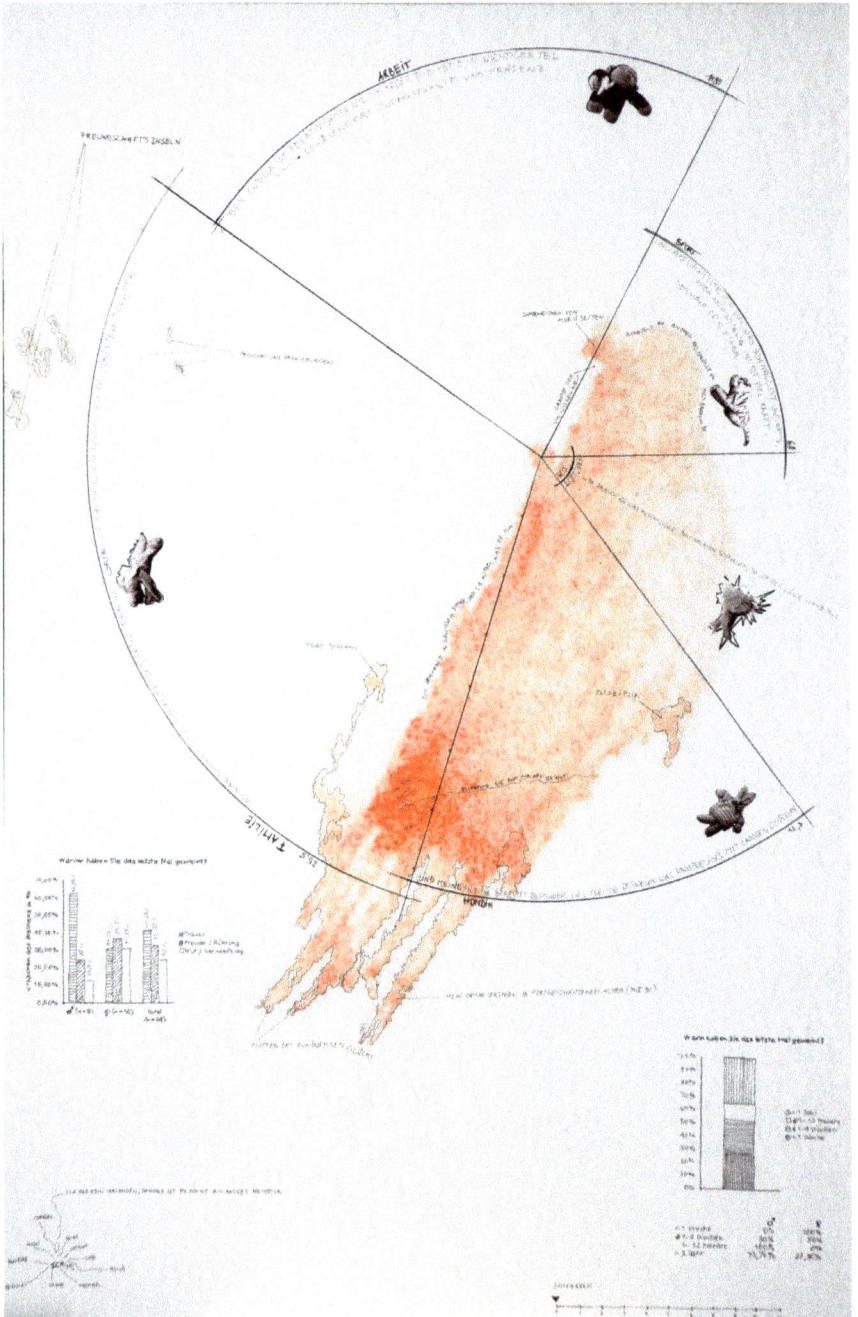

FIG. 3.7 Example poster based on blood (image: Bernd Kräftner)

Both posters refer back to ancient forms of prevention and of forecasting, namely those of haruspicy (divination by entrails) and augury (divination by the patterns made by birds in flight) (Cicero 1923). Forecasting the future of our bodies, exhorting ourselves to live longer and better, is now framed in a normative terminology of modern facts. We can analyse this terminology and critique it as a form of governmentality. As an incubation, we chose to transform it and bring it back, so highlighting parallels with earlier ways of dealing with the problem of forecasting bodily futures. We returned to the idea that the future of our bodies can be found in our blood. Yet in our version, this future is not found in a blood test, but in the appearance of blood itself.

Onto these two kinds of divination we plotted the various kinds of data gathered by our experiments, namely the qualitative answers given to various questionnaires, the outcomes of SEIQoL, and the drawings the participants were asked to do to explain the relationship between them and the medical system. The data then invent the social in yet another way: rather than following established routes of either aggregating data and losing the individual, or focusing on individuals at the expense of aggregation, new social bodies were presented, in which numbers and qualitative data emerged as collective divinations.

CONCLUSION: WHEN NOT TO DO INCUBATIONS

As with other powerful technologies, there are risks and side effects inherent in the use of incubations. There are also many conditions for which the use of an incubation is at best pointless and at worst dangerous. It may seem from the above that incubations can be used to invent the social anywhere and at any time. But incubations are fraught with problems, and these should not be omitted. Also, inventing the social is not a goal in itself. Invention is not better per se than non-invention. The idea of inventing the social runs the risk of following a modernist logic of celebrating invention for itself.

But apart from the organisational, reputational and practical difficulties, as related throughout this text, there are also a number of occasions when incubations are not very helpful. Incubations are needed when situations appear to be stuck in routines, and when 'more of the same' would not help to produce particular outcomes. Here, incubations are the perfect means of translating a situation and coming up with new forms of describing and representing such situations. However, if a phenomenon is new, unknown, or of such a large scale as to require an overview, then an incubation is of little help.

Incubations work best when applied to stable and continuous situations, involving persons who know what they want, and to organisations that function smoothly, but are in danger of becoming stuck in routines. Here, incubations can create new translations and transformations that allow for enlightenment and serendipity. If a situation, an organisation or the persons involved are highly unstable, an incubation is of little help. If we are confronted with a social dispute and one side needs help in the form of arguments (textual, visual or otherwise), an incubation operates as a detour and may merely exacerbate the situation. If a situation is very fraught with internal and unresolved difficulties, unless all participants agree to it, an incubation may similarly make matters worse. Also, an incubation is not a mediation or a form of therapy, and the people doing them are not mediators or arbiters for conflicts. The use of incubations happens at your own risk. But do not be scared of it.

NOTES

1 Today, business incubators are a conceptual legacy of baby incubators: instead of a machine, these are organisations to stabilise and nurture a fragile object.

2 For example, ethnographers of professions, such as doctors or economists, give professionals the tools to understand themselves *as* professionals, who then may use these descriptions for their own purposes.

3 The questions are influenced by the famous questionnaire of Max Frisch (Frisch 1974). It contains questions such as 'Would you prefer to have died, or live on as an animal? Which one?'

REFERENCES

Baker, J. P., 'The Incubator and the Medical Discovery of the Premature Infant', *Journal of Perinatology*, 5 (2000), 321–28.

Becker, H. S., *Telling About Society* (Chicago: University of Chicago Press, 2007).

Binder, T., E. Brandt, P. Ehn, and J. Halse, 'Democratic Design Experiments: Between Parliament and Laboratory', *CoDesign*, 11.3–4 (2015), 152–65.

Despret, V., 'The Body We Care for: Figures of Anthropo-Zoo-Genesis', *Body & Society*, 10.2–3 (2004), 111–34.

Bourdieu, P., *Distinction. A Social Critique of the Judgement of Taste* (London: Routledge, 1984).

Brown, S. D., 'Experiment: Abstract Experimentalism' in N. Wakeford & C. Lury, eds, *Inventive Methods: The Happening of the Social* (London: Routledge, 2012), pp. 61–75.

Cicero, M. T., *De Senectute; De Amicitia; De Divinatione* (Cambridge, MA.; London: Harvard University Press, 1923).

Clark, A., 'Visual Ethics in a Contemporary Landscape', in S. Pink, ed., *Advances in Visual Methodology* (London: SAGE, 2012), pp. 17–36.

Evelyn, J., '*Diary and Correspondence of John Evelyn*' (Whitefish, MT: Kessinger Publishing, 2009/1850).

Fals Borda, O., 'Participatory (Action) Research in Social Theory: Origins and Challenges', in P. Reason & H. Bradbury, eds, *Handbook of Action Research. Participative Inquiry and Practice* (London: SAGE, 2001), pp. 27–37.

Farias, I. and A. Wilkie, *Studio Studies: Operations, Topologies & Displacements* (London: Routledge, 2015).

Frisch, M., *Sketchbook 1966–1971* (New York: Harcourt Brace Jovanovich, 1974).

Garfinkel, H., 'Studies of the Routine Grounds of Everyday Activities', in H. Garfinkel, ed., *Studies in Ethnomethodology* (Englewood Cliffs, NJ: Prentice-Hall, 1967), pp. 35–75.

Guggenheim, M., 'Laboratizing and Delaboratizing the World: Changing Sociological Concepts for Places of Knowledge Production', *History of the Human Sciences*, 25.1 (2012), 99–108.

——'The Media of Sociology: Tight or Loose Translations?' *British Journal of Sociology*, 67(2012), 345–72.

Guggenheim, M., B. Kräftner, and J. Kröll, 'Creating Idiotic Speculators: Disaster Cosmopolitics in the Sandbox', in A. Wilkie, M. Rosengarten and M. Savransky, eds, *Speculative Research: The Lure of Possible Futures* (London: Routledge, 2016) pp. 145–62.

Guggenheim, M. J. Kröll, B. Kräftner, A. Martos, and F. Oberhuber, eds, *Die Wahr/Falsch Inc. Eine Wissenschaftsausstellung in Der Stadt* (Wien: Facultas Universitätsverlag, 2006).

Guggenheim, M., 'The Proof Is In the Pudding. On "Truth to Materials" in STS, Followed by an Attempt to Improve It', *Science Technology and Industry Studies*, 7.1(2011), pp. 65–86.

Hacking, I., 'The Looping Effects of Human Kinds', in, D. Sperber, D. Premack and A. J. Premack, eds, *Causal Cognition: A Multidisciplinary Approach* (Wotton-under-Edge: Clarendon Press, 1995), pp. 351–83.

Heintze, C., et al., 'Counseling Overweight in Primary Care: An Analysis of Patient-Physician Encounters', *Patient Education and Counseling*, 80.1 (2010), 71–75.

Hickey, A. M., et al., 'A New Short Form Individual Quality of Life Measure (seiqol-Dw), Application in a Cohort of Individuals with HIV Aids' *BMJ (Clinical research ed.)* (1996), 29–33.

Joas, H., *The Creativity of Action* (Chicago, Ill: University of Chicago Press, 1996).

Kräftner, B., and Xperiment!, 'What Is a Body/a Person? Topography of the Possible', in B. Latour and P. Weibel, eds, *Making Things Public: Atmospheres of Democracy* (Cambridge MA: MIT Press, 2009), pp. 906–9.

Kräftner, B., J. Kröll, and I. Warner, 'The Syndrome We Care for', in Xperiment!, A. Mol, I. Moser and J. Pols, eds, *Care in Practice. On Tinkering in Clinics, Homes and Farms* (Bielefeld: Transcript, 2010), pp. 301–22.

Latour, B., 'Drawing Things Together' in M. Lynch and S. Woolgar, eds, *Representation in Scientific Practice* (Cambridge, MA: MIT Press, 1990), pp. 19–68.

Law, J., Seeing Like a Survey, *Cultural Sociology*, 3.2 (2009), 239–56.

Law, J., and A. Mol, eds, *Complexities. Social Studies of Knowledge Practices* (Durham: Duke University Press, 2002).

Law, J., and J. Urry, 'Enacting the Social', *Economy and Society*, 33.3 (2004), 390–410.

Leavy, P., 'Performance-Based Emergent Methods', in S. N. Hesse-Biber and P. Leavy, eds, *Handbook of Emergent Methods* (New York: Guilford Press, 2008), pp. 343–57.

Lezaun, J., F. Muniesa, and S. Vikkelsø, 'Provocative Containment and the Drift of Social-Scientific Realism', *Journal of Cultural Economy*, 6.3 (2013), pp. 278–93.

Lury, C. and N. Wakeford, eds., *Inventive Methods: The Happening of the Social* (London: Routledge, 2011).

MacKenzie, D., and Y. Millo, 'Constructing a Market, Performing Theory: The Historical Sociology of a Financial Derivatives Exchange' *American Journal of Sociology*, 109.1 (2003), pp. 107–145.

Marres, N., '6 Experiment', in N. Wakeford & C. Lury, eds, *Inventive Methods: The Happening of the Social* (London: Routledge, 2012) pp. 76–95.

Meier, C. A., *Antike Inkubation und moderne Psychotherapie. Mit einem Geleitwort von C. G. Jung* (Zürich: Rascher, 1949).

Mol, A., *The Body Multiple: Ontology in Medical Practice* (Durham: Duke University Press, 2003).

Niewöhner, J., et al., 'Cardiovascular Disease and Obesity Prevention in Germany: An Investigation into a Heterogeneous Engineering Project', *Science, Technology, & Human Values*, 36.5 (2011), pp. 723–51.

Papin, D., *A New Digester, or Engine for Softening Bones: Containing the Description of Its Make and Use, Etc* (London: Malincroft Chemical Works, 1681).

Parisi, L., 'Speculation: A Method for the Unattainable', in C. Lury and N. Wakeford, eds, *Inventive Methods: The Happening of the Social* (London: Routledge, 2012), pp. 232–44.

Silverman, W. A., 'Incubator-Baby Side Shows', *Pediatrics*, 64.2 (1979), 217–141.

Whatmore, S. J., 'Mapping Knowledge Controversies: Science, Democracy and the Redistribution of Expertise', *Progress in Human Geography* 33.5 (2009), 587–98.

Wilkie, A., M. Rosengarten, and M. Savransky, eds, *Speculative Research: The Lure of Possible Futures* (London: Routledge, 2016).

4

TURNING CONTROVERSIES INTO QUESTIONS OF DESIGN: PROTOTYPING ALTERNATIVE METRICS FOR HEATHROW AIRPORT

Christian Nold

It is difficult for a measure to command public confidence when it effectively tells people living in places like Barnes, Fulham, Putney, Ealing, Chelsea, Stockwell and Windsor that they are not affected by noise because they live outside the Heathrow contour

Airportwatch 2013

INTRODUCTION

PUBLIC CONTROVERSIES ABOUT TECHNO-SCIENTIFIC ISSUES SUCH AS FOOD safety and environmental pollution have been extensively studied by scholars of science, technology and society. Classic work in this field has highlighted the political and epistemic aspects of such controversies, focusing on the ways in which knowledge becomes political when disagreements about seemingly technical issues like the above are made public through media reporting, activist mobilisation, court hearings, government consultations and so on (Nelkin 1997; Wynne 1992). More recently, authors such as Braun & Whatmore (2010) and Marres (2012) have insisted on the important role that materials and technologies play in the enactment of controversies about techno-scientific issues in social

94

and public life. Building upon this literature, this chapter offers methodological and theoretical reflections on the project of turning public controversies into occasions for and questions of design. These reflections are the outcome of a three-year-long research project that investigated and engaged with a controversy over aircraft noise at Heathrow airport in London (Nold 2017). I describe the process of coming to understand the infrastructures that were at stake in the Heathrow controversy, and of designing prototypes to support the formation of new socio-technical collectives around the issues. I argue that such design-led approaches have the potential not only to help us understand but also to intervene in public controversies about science and technology.

HEATHROW AS A CONTROVERSY

Heathrow is the world's third largest airport, with 73.4 million passengers passing through it every year (Heathrow Airport 2015), making London the city with the highest aircraft noise exposure in Europe (Mayor of London 2013). Yet there have been many calls to expand the air travel capacity in the south east of England, and in 2013 the Airports Commission was set up to establish which of the three London airports should be expanded. In 2015 the commission recommended the expansion of Heathrow with a third runway, and this was expected to generate £147 billion in additional Gross Domestic Product (GDP) over the next sixty years (Airports Commission 2015). Yet expansion would bring more flights and road traffic, and more people would be affected by aircraft noise. The issue of the airport's impacts is highly emotive, and it was and is being kept in the public eye by, among other means, ongoing media reporting of studies on air quality, health impacts and economic benefits. In many of these studies, the issue of Heathrow's expansion is framed in terms of a trade-off between addressing the 'annoyance and disturbance suffered by some local residents as a result of aircraft noise, while at the same time continuing to maximise the social and economic benefits that the airport delivers to the local community and the country as a whole' (Heathrow Airport Limited 2013: 7). While the Airports Commission has recommended the expansion of Heathrow, the government has repeatedly postponed its final decision, since it is seen as a 'toxic dilemma' (Kuenssberg 2015) that is likely to alienate large parts of the national electorate.

My own involvement with the Heathrow controversy started in 2012 in the context of an EU-funded engineering research project. This project distributed cheap environmental sensors to members of the public, who were encouraged to collect noise pollution data in response to the European Noise Directive (European Parliament 2002), which requires the production of EU-wide noise maps. Heathrow airport was one of the case study sites, and my role in the project was to facilitate the use of a smartphone app for gathering noise data with local residents, and to manage interactions with local groups. During the project both the participants and the researchers were frustrated by the usage-protocol of the smartphone application, which was not suited to capturing aircraft noise, and by the fact that the device was not sophisticated enough to generate results that would be comparable with the official noise data. When the project came to an end, I spent two years working in the area and, having become engaged by the issue of Heathrow expansion, I wanted to continue working with the controversy. During the EU-funded project, some of the stakeholders, such as the airport authorities, local councils and residents had requested static noise monitors that could be widely deployed across the area to track changes in flight patterns and produce data that could be compared with the official dataset. This request was not considered to be part of the EU project's goals, and was not fulfilled. However, it gave me a concrete starting point for my own research, as well as raising a number of challenging questions: who should I be designing noise monitors for? What exactly should the devices do, and what contribution should they make in relation to the noise controversy?

INFRASTRUCTURING CONTROVERSIES

Engaging with the Heathrow controversy through monitoring devices required a way of understanding it as a site for design. I therefore start this section by discussing work in participatory design that engages with social studies of science and technology and public controversies. Participatory design in the Scandinavian tradition defines itself as a shift away from designers as experts towards the wider participation of users in the design process (Ehn 1988). In this tradition, designers have sought inspiration from the STS concept of 'infrastructure' (Star and Ruhleder 1996), which moves away from mechanistic visions of technology as tubes and pipes, towards infrastructure as a connective resource that links people, organisations, standards and 'object worlds'. In this vision 'infrastructure is fundamentally and always a *relation,* never a thing' (Star and Ruhleder 1994: 253; emphasis in original). From this vantage point, building new infrastructures involves coordinating and facilitating the 'demands of multiple groups and making connections between them possible' (Neumann and Star 1996: 234). Infrastructure allows different practices to coexist: 'the cook considers the water system a piece of working infrastructure integral to making dinner; for the city planner, it becomes a variable in a complex equation' (Star and Ruhleder 1996: 113). Once built, infrastructure fades into the background, and it becomes the researcher's role to carry out an 'infrastructural inversion', to bring it back into the foreground, in order for it to become investigable.

Participatory designers have adapted this concept of infrastructure into an active method of 'infrastructuring' (Karasti and Syrjänen 2004; Ehn 2008; Björgvinsson et al. 2010; Hillgren et al. 2011; Björgvinsson et al. 2012; Le Dantec 2012; DiSalvo et al. 2014). This method embeds designers within a community in order to actively support this community over an extended period of time (Karasti 2014). Instead of the more clearly defined infrastructures of workplaces on which Star and Ruhleder's work focuses, the design method of infrastructuring targets social and political collectives assembling around issues, a focus inspired by Actor-Network Theory (Latour and Weibel 2005; Marres 2007). For example, Ehn (2008) talks about designing in order to target an object of concern, which would bring together a group of participants around an issue. Moreover, Disalvo et al. argue that design artefacts can 'expose and re-imagine constraints and parameters surrounding issues' (2014: 205), as well as function as 'scaffolds' for the 'affective bonds that are necessary for the construction of publics' (Le Dantec and DiSalvo 2013: 260). So, while Star and Ruhleder's notion of infrastructure is attuned to organisational and professional contacts, participatory designers are especially interested in infrastructure defined as a public and political affair. Yet I argue that participatory design has placed too much emphasis on the way infrastructures create connections between humans, and not enough on the way these infrastructures constrain and reinforce practices. For example, when creating a mobile phone communication system for a homeless shelter, the designers conceived the staff and residents as separate publics with different issues of concern (Le Dantec et al. 2011). At the end of the project, the designers discovered that their system had created two different issue outcomes. It had highlighted an issue of accountability for the staff, whilst for the residents it had organised their household chores. By choosing to situate the infrastructuring design process within an existing institution, it became difficult to transcend the underlying dynamics of the homeless shelter. In fact, the asymmetrical system the designers built seems to have reinforced the existing relations and distinctions between staff and residents. In order to turn controversies into questions of design, one needs to engage critically with the existing elements that comprise a controversy, and not only to build new relations.

In order to expand the notion of infrastructuring to address the composition of controversies, I turn to a concept of 'scaling' taken from early Actor-Network Theory (Callon and Latour 1981). This concept offers an alternative approach to the structure-agency distinction that assumes a hierarchy between a macro-actor such as the state and a micro-actor such as an individual. Callon and Latour argue that macro-actors are not innately large and important, but that their 'size' is the result of processes of enrolling many human and non-human actors in order to increase their size. In their words: 'we cannot distinguish between macro-actors (institutions, organisations, social classes, parties, states) and micro-actors (individuals, groups, families) on the basis of their dimensions, since they are all, we might say, the "same size", or rather since size is what is primarily at stake in their struggles it is also, therefore, their most important result' (Callon and Latour 1981: 279; emphasis in original). I argue that this concept of re-scaling actors through association adds three important points to the concept of infrastructuring social and political collectives.

First, it suggests that the size of an existing institution might be unrelated to its importance within a specific controversy. This means that participatory designers do not necessarily have to engage with existing institutions as gate-keepers for defining the scope or boundary of an issue. Second, it suggests that by assembling human and nonhuman actors into infrastructures, participatory designers are involved in a constitutive process of scaling that creates new onto-logical entities and realities in the world. Finally, the implication is that such an ontological approach changes the role of the designer, thus requiring them to make new kinds of choices. The role becomes one of 'immersing oneself in the networks described and searching for what is or can be achieved by new interlockings of artefacts and human work' (Berg 1998: 482). This brings with it what the anthropologist Mol calls an 'ontological politics' (1999) that involves identifying whether it is possible to build alternatives and develop ways to live with the infrastructures that cannot be changed. Designing thus involves political and ethical choices that will result in the inclusion and displacement of actors within the composition of new infrastructures.

THE INFRASTRUCTURE OF THE HEATHROW CONTROVERSY

How are these approaches and the concept of infrastructuring social and political collectives applicable to the Heathrow controversy? If one looks at this controversy through the lens of a 'material' definition of infrastructure, one sees only aircraft, acoustic pressure and measurement devices. If one looks through a purely 'political' lens, one sees politicians, industries and residents. By apply-ing the concept of relational infrastructure, however, one sees new connections across the material and political registers, such as techniques and metrics that mediate between the aircraft, local residents and the legislative authorities by measuring and governing the impact of the airport. A discussion of the issue of Heathrow noise pollution can help to make this clear.

Aircraft noise emerged as an issue at Heathrow with the introduction of turbo-jet aircraft in 1958, and it occasioned a survey of the impact of aircraft sound on humans (MIL Research Limited 1961). This was the first of three significant UK-based studies in which standardised interviews of residents were carried out and compared with the measurements of acoustic energy. Residents were asked how much the aircraft noise bothered them: 'very much, moderately, a little, not at all', and the responses were compared against local acoustic energy measurements. The data were used to create a dose-response relationship that was intended to predict community annoyance at increasing noise levels. While it is acknowledged that these metrics are poor predictors of individual or group annoyance, their goal is equity and a consistent noise policy for the 'general population' (Miedema and Oudshoorn 2001). The result of the 1961 study was the creation of the Noise and Number Index (NNI), a metric that has three threshold points denoting high, moderate and low community annoyance (Civil Aviation Authority 1981). Using models of sound dispersion, these threshold levels were then plotted on maps as exposure contour bands radiating out from the runways, effectively defining the people living within each contour as experiencing a set level of annoyance. The NNI metric was designed for 'estimating the total disturbance at the time of the surveys *and* a way of estimating the disturbance resulting from a change in the scale or pattern of airport operations' (Brooker et al. 1985: 1; emphasis in original). Its goal was thus as a policy instrument for forecasting annoyance, and for the last fifty years, the metric and its successor, LAeq, have been used as a calculative infrastructure to determine how many people are affected by the noise of Heathrow. People living within the modelled noise contour bands are defined as differently affected by noise in order to provide them with commensurate levels of financial compensation and subsidised sound insulation, while those living outside the bands are not compensated. Crucially, the number of affected people is also used as the basis for future decisions about the airport. The 2015 Airports Commission report (Airports Commission 2015) used the number of people within the 57 LAeq contour as the key indicator of local impact when comparing the different airport options and when it recommended building the third runway at Heathrow. This diagram describes the way noise metrics are assembled and function:

SURVEY RESPONSES + ACOUSTIC MEASUREMENTS =
ANNOYANCE CONTOURS > NUMBER OF PEOPLE AFFECTED
> GOVERNANCE DECISIONS

One way to understand the construction and function of community annoyance in scalar terms is by using the metaphor of the Leviathan as taken up by Callon and Latour (1981). The authors use this metaphor to describe the way collective capacities comes to be consolidated within a single entity. The Leviathan represents the power of a king, and is visually represented as a crowned giant that is physically assembled from the bodies of all his subjects. Callon and Latour proposed that this visual image of the Leviathan can be interpreted as an allegory for the constitutive power of macro-actors. In their words: 'The construction of this artificial body is calculated in such a way that the absolute sovereign is nothing other than the sum of the multitude's wishes' (Callon and Latour 1981: 278). However, while Callon and Latour use the metaphor to understand the capacities of social actors (such as scientists and engineers) I argue that community annoyance can be conceived as a Leviathan figure insofar as it acts as 'spokesman, mask-bearer and amplifier' for the collective of humans living under the flight path at Heathrow. Crucially, the local residents are extremely frustrated with the way community annoyance speaks on their behalf. Here is one resident's response to the Airports Commission: 'Heathrow are exploiting the 57dB noise threshold to make it look like there is a reduction in noise with an expanded airport. The reality of course is that noise continues to be hugely disturbing to many people considerably below that threshold, me included. Where I currently live, whilst better than Kew (hence I moved here) and just outside the 57dB contour is still disturbing enough to wake my children regularly' (Airports Commission 2013: 2).

We could say of this contested quality of the annoyance metric that it functions as an 'infrastructure' of the Heathrow controversy, since it connects aircraft, residents and politicians, and plays a key role in decision-making. Yet this connection is asymmetrical, since this annoyance spokesperson is used to dismiss individual resident's claims of affectedness and to disqualify them from being personally consulted. The 57dB threshold figures as an important actor in the narratives of the opponents to expansion, yet the metric is largely invisible within the broader public debate about the controversy. There was only a brief period in which the metric became a publically visible actor, and this was as a result of a controversy around a particular noise impact study. In 2007, the major, Government-sponsored ANASE study (cost £2,000,000) found that community annoyance started at much lower noise levels than identified in the 1985 study (Le Masurier et al. 2007). These findings suggested that the Heathrow annoyance contours should extend much further and envelop a much larger number of people. This was seized on by the media and opponents of the airport who argued that the 'true number affected by Heathrow operations is around 1m[illion] – four times the figure implied by the 57dB contour' (Airportwatch 2013: 3). The outcry increased when the ANASE study was officially dismissed for methodological discrepancies. Despite the fact that many high-profile politicians, local councils and pressure groups argued strongly against this dismissal, and pointed to the problems of the 57dB contour, the official legislative standard has remained at the level of the older 1985 study.

How is it possible that, despite the loss of public confidence in it, the metric has remained in place? The technical acoustics literature, from which this and related metrics are derived, is actually ambivalent about them, arguing that the variations among noise metrics are 'more a matter of convenience than any reflection on the strength of any assumed underlying dose-effect relationships' (Flindell 2003: 36). This quote suggests that these metrics are not simple empirical facts in or about the world, but pragmatic, or 'interested' tools that enable convenient management of the controversy. In the case of Heathrow, large amounts of data have been accumulated using a single metric, making comparisons between different operational proposals simple and convenient. While the above controversy around the ANASE study allowed the 57dB annoyance contour to briefly come to the foreground, the media's main focus is on the political choices that are presented as either ideological or pragmatic trade-offs between economic benefits and alienating certain voters. I suggest that the airport opponents' lack of success in challenging the metric may be due to the fact that they have been unable to politicise the lack of care involved in the way community annoyance has been measured.

Yet there are some interesting aspects to the dismissal of the ANASE study that point to an alternative method for intervening in the controversy. The official reason given for the rejection of the study cited specific procedures conducted during the interviews. The reviewers of the study discussed a number of methodological issues but focused on the interview process that took place in people's homes and included portable audio speakers. They argued that, 'the act of setting up and calibrating equipment would almost certainly have enabled respondents to deduce that the study was about attitudes to noise. Furthermore, the fact that the social survey sites selected were located away from other sources of noise may have enabled some respondents to conclude that the study pertained to aircraft noise' (Civil Aviation Authority and Bureau Vertias 2007: 16). The reviewers thus concluded that, 'there is a risk that the social survey results may have been contaminated by respondent bias. That is, respondents may have used the opportunity to voice their opinion on the Government's aviation policy and may have either deliberately or sub-consciously exaggerated their reaction to aircraft noise in the way they answered the question' (ibid.). The reviewers' argument is that the presence of the audio speakers triggered the respondents into thinking the study was about aircraft noise and aviation policy and that, because of this, the residents exaggerated their responses.

The ANASE authors published a report refuting these points. In regards to the loudspeakers they suggest these 'were not in fact used until after the key annoyance questions had been dealt with' (Ian Flindell & Associates and MVA Consultancy 2013: 12). Yet more broadly, they argue that the issue of the speakers is part of a broader disagreement with the reviewers about the reality of annoyance and how it should be staged. They argue that the 'review group's comments suggest a fundamental misunderstanding of the nature of noise annoyance, that it is somehow some kind of underlying and fixed physiological or neurological response to noise which is always the same regardless of any changes in attitudes and opinions in the people concerned' (ibid.). The authors suggest that it is impossible to isolate annoyance from the politics of aviation policy and that it would be 'impossible to ever find a "good" time to be able to carry out a supposedly unbiased aircraft noise questionnaire survey' (ibid. 11; emphasis in original). What is at stake is an ontological disagreement about different ways of staging community annoyance, as neurological and disembodied, on the one hand, or as pragmatically embodied with sound equipment and situated within political arguments, on the other. The controversy around the ANASE study reminds us that there are many practical choices to be taken when curating situations in which people can provide evidence of their experience. These include choices about the context in which residents are asked questions and the physical props that are present during the interview, as well as the manner in which the questions are asked. If we go along with the idea that the respondents were strongly affected by the mere presence of the speakers, then this suggests that the articulation of annoyance may be approached as a creative occasion for public experimentation, one in which a multiplicity of different elements might be introduced to generate new articulations of annoyance. The end effect would be that, rather than having a single way of defining and measuring annoyance, there would be multiple competing compositions.

This episode shows that there is not one but several controversies around noise at Heathrow: a media controversy focused on economic trade-offs, a failed political controversy about the number of people affected by noise, and an ontological controversy surrounding how to articulate annoyance as a matter of concern. Targeting the ontological controversy raises the question of how a more suitable annoyance metric could be created, what elements it should consist of, and how such a design process could be publicly legitimated. Interestingly, a number of acousticians who have worked with social survey methods for decades are now proposing a shift towards spontaneous self-reporting of complaints by residents as a way of bringing back transparency and legitimacy into noise governance. Fidell argues that noise complaints were abandoned in the 1970s because they 'were difficult to process and systematically compare, largely inaccessible to researchers, and generally awkward to interpret' (Fidell 2003: 3012). He argues that the growing use of distributed, networked computing devices is making it possible for geographically tagged noise complaints to function as a new metric. Adopting such a system would shift annoyance from a given neurological concept-measure into an active process of resident participation. The key aspect of this shift in register is that it turns annoyance into a phenomenon partly dependent on curation processes, and hence involving questions of design, which invariably raises a multitude of practical questions around how to stage annoyance.

INFRASTRUCTURING HEATHROW

My investigation of how to turn the Heathrow controversy into a site for participatory design has, then, yielded an answer to the question of who to design for. Instead of setting out to create a project for a particular group of residents or an institution handling the issue, my aim was to carry out participatory design with the infrastructure of the controversy itself. Rather than being accountable to a human client, my task was to become responsive to the issue itself. My research also provided me with a design target in the form of the annoyance metric, as well as a methodology, namely that of infrastructuring social-political collectives by using 'micro/macro prototyping' techniques (Nold 2015). My goal was to build an alternative Leviathan, one that differed in crucial respects from how the annoyance metric composed the public. My alternative 'body politic' would be composed of new entities and would ideally be able to compete with the existing metric in a kind of robot battle over who has the right to wield the authority of collective experience. To begin this process of re-composition, I decided to create a series of design prototypes consisting of custom hardware and software to test with the interested parties.

My prototypes were intended as material-semiotic devices that are simultaneously *things* as well as *concepts* in order to set up new propositions about the relationship between aircraft, residents and governance. Each prototype was a composition that proposed different ways in which the noise issue might be handled by inserting or removing material, symbolic or computational elements. The prototypes have names that identify the specific propositions they present, and this reinforces the notion that each prototype is a unique actor with its own distinct voice. The aim of the prototypes was not to seek approval for the designs but to allow the participants to experience and articulate new infrastructural compositions and to build alternative networks of human and nonhuman actors that might challenge the existing annoyance metric. I took the four initial prototypes to potential partners who might want to join the process, such as the airport administration, local councils and residents. During the meetings and workshops, the prototypes were used as props and demonstration devices. The following vignette describes one of these workshops at a community centre located under the Heathrow flight path, with nine residents who did not know each other beforehand. During the workshop, planes could be heard overhead at regular intervals.

PROTOTYPE 1: 'I SPEAK YOUR FEELINGS'

The first prototype (Fig. 4.1) samples the voltage sensed by a microphone and translates this into a phrase displayed on a LCD screen. Instead of decibel numbers, the screen displays sound level using a scale of emotive words: quiet, audible, loud, very loud, extremely loud, and painful. The words on the screen

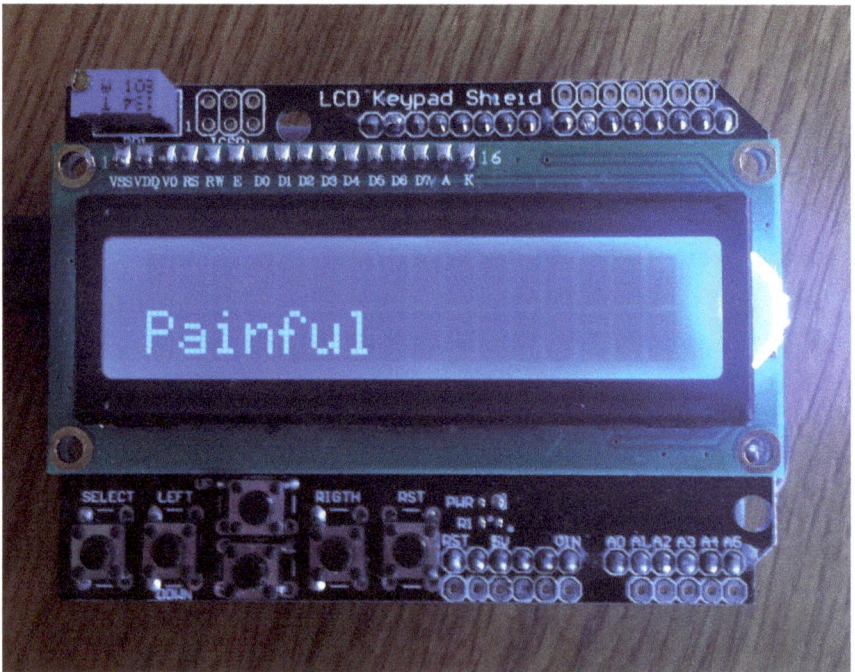

FIG. 4.1 Photograph of the 'I speak your feelings' prototype (photo: Christian Nold)

change continuously in response to sudden sounds. The prototype uses the dose-response logic implied by the community annoyance metric and turns it into a tangible object that can be placed on a coffee table. The machine experiences sound pressure on behalf of humans, which is transformed into an emotive language without people being involved. The prototype is designed to performatively highlight the simplistic relationship between measured acoustic pressure and annoyance level that the current metric relies on. This diagram represents the composition and function of the prototype:

SOUND SENSOR > TRANSLATION INTO ANNOYANCE WORDS
> LCD DISPLAY

When the device was presented to the workshop group it acted as a catalyst for the participants to talk about the way noise affects them in their daily lives, such as, 'I don't want to cut myself off, which is really what noise is about, it is cutting you off'. They identified elements that the current LAeq metric does not capture, such as the interval between flights and the harmonics of noise, with someone arguing that 'it's not just decibels, there is something else in there as well'. The participants discussed 'a more complex device which will analyse the sound and tell you about the interesting element of the sound harmonics and different pitches'. In addition, some suggested alternative ways of providing evidence of their experience, such as by measuring their physiological responses to noise. Yet two of the participants seemed frustrated: 'I think it would be completely chaotic if you just had people's feelings about it. What would you do with that data? You have got to have an objective reference'. Their argument was that 'for the purposes of any kind of campaign it's got to be objective. So, its amounts of particles per million, it's got to be measurable rather than [...] smelling'. At this point another participant interjected that social policy uses anecdotal stories as evidence in conjunction with statistical data.

During the workshop, the reductive emotive words displayed by the proto-type seemed to spur the participants into describing the limitations of the current noise metrics when it comes to their ability to encompass their experience of noise. This triggered a process of reflection on different ways of evidencing the impacts of noise. While it was widely agreed that evidence was needed, there was disagreement as to which method or technology would provide the greatest political legitimacy for campaigning. Yet the participant who was most vocal about the need for an objective reference said, 'is it really worth debating this? I mean people have different opinions, why don't people contribute what they contribute from their perspectives'. He followed this with an enthusiastic exclamation of 'take it all'. The main observation I took from this prototype interaction was the pragmatic suggestion of combining different evidential methods in order to build a cohesive collective around the issue.

PROTOTYPE 2: 'I DISPLAY NOISE PUBLICLY'

The second prototype (Fig. 4.2) consists of a mock-up of a large noise meter display mounted on the exterior walls of a building. The device illuminates when a specified noise level is exceeded. The prototype investigates where the issue of noise should be located and whom it should address. It is based on the observation that the geographical area around Heathrow looks like many other suburban areas in Britain, with the built environment not providing any visual reference to the noise overhead. Many of the residents I had been in contact with talked about aircraft noise in the context of their private homes, and described its effects in a solitary and personal way. As a provocation, this prototype locates the issue of noise outdoors within public space. In the workshop, I introduced the prototype as something that could be mounted on the participants' houses as a way of engaging their neighbours, and I described a scenario in which a plane coming in to land at night would see the ground light up as it flew overhead. The composition and logic of the device is as follows:

SOUND SENSOR > OUTDOOR WARNING DISPLAY
> ADDRESSING A PROXIMATE PUBLIC

During the workshop, it quickly emerged that the participants were excited by the device, yet no-one wanted to fix it onto their own home. Instead they suggested

FIG. 4.2   Image mock-up of the 'I display noise publicly' prototype (photo: Christian Nold)

that it should become a 'norm' to have it installed on public buildings such as offices and schools. One of the participants suggested that mounting it on one's own house could have negative consequences: 'I don't want to be a downer on this, but we do have to bear in mind that people think that campaigning and emphasising the noise problem is giving them a problem. Because it affects the value of their house and they might want to sell their house and they don't want to be labelled as a problem area. And we have found that schools have quite remarkably low levels of interest because they get money out of the airport for various activities and they don't want to be seen as the wrong school to send your child to' (Others nodded and voiced agreement). This interaction clearly identified an aspect of the prototype that I had not considered. Placing the device on one's own home would characterise the immediate area as affected by noise and would make the resident personally identifiable as a campaigner, which could have direct negative effects for that person.

The prototype identified a tendency to privatise the issue of noise pollution, namely, to locate noise within individual people's homes and to not define it as a collective problem. This atomisation of the issue is reinforced by the remedial measures that the airport offers, which focus on noise insulation for individual homes rather than public spaces. This effect can also be seen in the telephone hotline infrastructure the airport has set up to allow individuals to make complaints. What is absent are public platforms that allow local residents to engage with the noise controversy collectively. Taking into account the participants' responses highlighting the dangers of public campaigning; this prototype interaction suggested to me a need for a sound-monitoring network that could discreetly connect individuals' homes and institutions.

PROTOTYPE 3: 'I MAKE SOMEONE RESPONSIBLE'

The third prototype (Fig. 4.3) is programmed to send an SMS text message to a mobile phone whenever a peak decibel level of 90dB is exceeded. The prototype is based on conversations with residents in which I felt there was a lack of clarity as to who or what is responsible for noise pollution. Whole ranges of entities were identified, including local and national government and its agencies, the airport, individual airlines, and capitalism. The provocation of the prototype is to choose a single entity that might be held directly responsible. The logic of the device is as follows:

SOUND SENSOR > SMS ALERT > TARGET AN INDIVIDUAL ENTITY

When I introduced the prototype, I showed the workshop participants the source code of the micro-controller, and mentioned that the mobile number could be changed to anybody's phone number. Suddenly a dramatic change of atmosphere occurred, with all the participants laughing loudly, as they understood the implication of inserting somebody else's number into the source-code. The participants excitedly discussed a range of potential entities that could have their number inserted, including airport complaint phone-lines, institutional

FIG. 4.3 Photograph of the 'I make someone responsible' prototype (photo: Christian Nold)

bodies, politicians in favour of airport expansion, and the Prime Minister. Whilst a range of entities was discussed, there was no consensus about who should be held accountable. During the workshop, whenever voices were raised or a plane flew overhead, the prototype would send an SMS message that would be received with loud bleeps, and the group would respond with laughter. It was interesting to observe the way the prototype held the participants' visual attention and tightly focused the discussion on technical interventions. Some participants were highly engaged by the confrontational approach of the prototype, and extended its logic by talking about an event when loudspeakers had been installed outside a politician's house to wake them up with the noise of the early morning flights. Others in the group felt that the targeting logic of the prototype was too personal: they wanted to make the SMS messages more 'public' by redirecting them to a Twitter stream or automated hotlines, 'I think tweeting may well be a more acceptable way of doing that and it's in the public domain so you can see there have been 80 tweets at that time in the morning and it's not going to a direct person'.

From my perspective, the prototype allowed the group to experience a new relational infrastructure that created a direct connection between a noise event and an actor who is regarded as responsible for it. This bypassed the technical mediators who currently deal with noise data. Instead of the sanctioned infrastructure of the annoyance metric that traces long-term patterns, the prototype is a technical hack that uses the decibel data to act like a shouted complaint at a politician in the street. The prototype triggered a group discussion about the strategies and tactics that a noise-monitoring network should adopt. Should it force new political connections by holding individuals accountable, or should it focus on building a data repository that is more acceptable to the current logic of the airport's data practices? At stake were different ways of staging annoyance. Yet the diversity of reactions among the workshop participants made it clear that any infrastructure designed for this collective could not adopt a single way of staging annoyance, but would have to support a multiplicity of approaches.

PROTOTYPE 4: 'I TURN NOISE INTO NUMBERS'

This prototype (Fig. 4.4) uploads sound pressure measurements at regular intervals to an online repository, where it is presented as a time series. The noise of passing aircraft can be identified as visual spikes on the online graph. The prototype directly addresses the requests by residents for a static monitoring device that can be placed in their own home to provide evidence of their noise exposure. The composition and function of the device is as follows:

SOUND SENSOR > DECIBEL DATA > ONLINE DATA ARCHIVE

FIG. 4.4 Photograph of the 'I turn noise into numbers' prototype (photo: Christian Nold)

During the workshop, this prototype triggered the least discussion and provoked no disagreement among the group. The residents asked practical questions about where it could be located in their home and whether future versions could be made more accurate. Compared with the previous prototypes, this one is the most similar in function to existing, official noise meters, which produce decibel numbers as their output. The innovation of the device is that its low cost would allow the participants to carry out their own data gathering by choosing where and how they monitored noise, whilst still allowing a connection to the existing data infrastructure of the airport. Yet at a conceptual level, the prototype was not challenging and seemed to be largely familiar to the participants. Despite the fact that it was not clear exactly what data would be collected, or what would be done with it, the prototype was treated as a tool that could be used, rather than a provocation that needed to be discussed. At the end of the workshop I asked the participants if they wanted to borrow any of the prototypes, and half of the group excitedly asked to take this prototype home with them.

INFRASTRUCTURING A NOISE MONITORING COLLECTIVE

The main results from the workshop were that a number of people were now enthusiastic about participating in a noise-monitoring network, and I learnt a huge amount about the way noise and noise metrics function in the local area. I had identified a prototype that people wanted to use, and gathered insights for future prototypes. I installed the 'I turn noise into numbers' prototype in one of the participant's homes, where it was in operation for three months. During this time, one of the other workshop participants informed me when the device temporarily stopped sending data, so I knew that at least some people were paying attention to the data feed. This encouraged me to continue the process and build a new device that would incorporate the insights from the workshop. I tried to enrol additional actors to put together a loose team to develop and test the prototypes as well as gather financial support for the hardware. Over a period of a year, I assembled a network that included a charitable foundation that funded the hardware, a local council that agreed to co-locate a prototype alongside their noise monitors, a noise pressure group who provided strategic advice as well as individual local residents, and sound artists and academics working on noise and biodiversity. The hardware and software were created as a loose collaboration with the sound artists, an academic and a Heathrow resident who is a programmer. It was not only the issue of Heathrow noise that encouraged people to join the network, but also the practical development of the device, which became a tangible focal point for the gathering of this network. During a follow-up workshop at which the group met to work on the programming, one of the members spoke about their surprise at the mix of collaborators involved with the prototype, which included personal friends, family members and local residents, as well as institutions and pressure groups.

PROTOTYPE 5: 'I QUANTIFY AND BROADCAST'

This final prototype (Fig. 4.5) uses a Raspberry Pi computer and a calibrated measurement microphone, which were chosen for their measurement accuracy,

FIG. 4.5 Photo of the 'I quantify AND broadcast' prototype (photo: Christian Nold)

low unit cost and availability for the foreseeable future. The key feature of the device is that it sets up two parallel infrastructures and ways of dealing with sound. The first treats voltage changes at the microphone as acoustic pressure, which is converted into the LAeq official noise metrics of the airport. A script on the Raspberry Pi samples, filters and uploads the data to an online repository where it is viewable as a time-series graph and historical data. The second approach treats the voltage changes at the microphone as a soundscape, and creates a sound stream that is available as a real-time internet radio station. A computer program continuously encodes the microphone data and posts it to a public server where listeners can experience the soundscape. These two infrastructures are intended to materialise the diversity of actors involved in the assembly of the monitoring prototype and the opinions articulated during the workshops. The device relies on an ontology of noise as decibel measurement in order to enrol existing institutional actors such as the airport, but also adds an ontology of sound as audio broadcast that is alien within the context of Heathrow noise pollution monitoring. While at a conceptual level this doubling up seems contradictory, at a material and technical level it is perfectly normal to run multiple software scripts simultaneously. In fact, virtually all computer systems run hundreds of scripts as part of their operating system. Using a design approach to deal with the ontological controversy about how to stage annoyance allows an additive methodology: devices can stack multiple ontologies on top of each other rather than having to replace one logic with another. The aim of the two infrastructures is not just to represent diversity but also to enable a multiplicity of sound practices that support each other. During the EU-funded research project, our sound-monitoring activities had received the criticism that residents were measuring spikes caused by other noise sources and not just aircraft. By synchronising the sound and data feeds, this prototype can verify the source of a spike, as well as allow people to visually identify and listen to particularly loud or quiet parts of the soundscape. In this way, the two ontologies of the prototype start to overlap and mutually support each other.

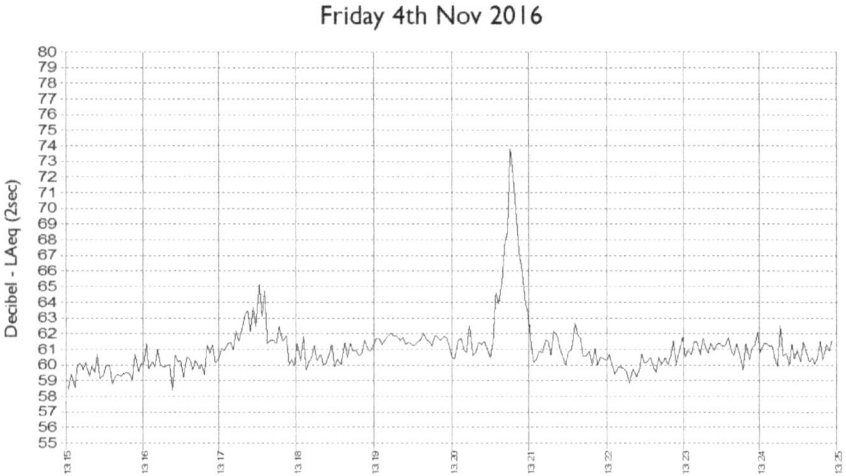

FIG. 4.6 Windsor prototype data being used to make a noise complaint about an off-track aircraft

At the time of writing, in November 2016, three prototypes have been installed, with the oldest, in Windsor, having collected more than a year's worth of data. The Windsor device is 6.5 km west of the Heathrow runways; another is in Hanwell, 9.5 km east of the runways; and the last is in Camberwell, 24 km from the runways. Based on these installations, it has been possible to make some observations about the sound practices they have enabled. The Windsor device is hosted in the garden of a member of the development team who is skilled in data analysis. He has used the data to identify particularly disruptive flights by correlating noise peaks with third party aircraft data as evidence for making complaints to the airport (Fig. 4.6). In his complaint he writes, 'on Fri 4th Nov at 13:20, BAW17 directly overflew, my house at 73.8db LAeq2s. It was off track and should have been 1km further north. The usual noise level of outbound flights going north is around 60–65db. Please discipline the pilot. Please contact me to confirm this complaint. I attach screen clips of noise level and track'. The prototype functioned like this:

SOUND SENSOR > DECIBEL DATA ARCHIVE > DISRUPTIVE SOUND EVENT >
EVIDENCED COMPLAINT TO AUTHORITIES

The host of the Windsor device also used the prototype to try and determine whether 'Heathrow [is] getting better or worse and how fast'. He built custom software to track noise exposure episodes at different decibel levels to identify long-term trends in the airport's operation. What is interesting about this approach is that it steps beyond the logic of individual complaints to focus on the creation of longitudinal data models that until now had been the reserve of the airport. In its public literature, the airport continually makes the claim that 'Heathrow is getting quieter' (Heathrow Airport Limited 2013: 14) based on graphs showing shrinkage in the annoyance contour. Yet based on a visualisation of thirteen months of data from the Windsor prototype, it has been possible to demonstrate that at this site and over this duration, the noise has remained remarkably constant (Fig. 4.7). This visualisation thus presents situated evidence that can interrogate the claims of the airport. What is key about this long-term visualisation is that it starts to rescale the prototype into a spokesperson that can stand alongside the official noise metrics and begin to challenge the airport's Leviathan. I suggest that this approach points the way towards a model for staging annoyance based on situated empirical data collected by residents rather than aggregated social surveys. The dataset has also been shared with the Aviation Forum and the environmental officers of the local council, and presents a new way for residents to collaborate with the local authorities in holding the airport to account. The prototype thus enacts the following infrastructure:

SOUND SENSOR > DECIBEL DATA ARCHIVE > LONG TERM METRIC TO
MONITOR CHANGES IN AIRPORT OPERATION

The internet radio station part of the prototype has also enabled two public art installations that were attended by over 1200 people. These installations allowed visitors to see the data feeds, read an account by one of the prototype hosts and listen to the live soundscapes at Windsor and Camberwell in order to compare them (Fig. 4.8). The hosts of the prototypes were present to talk to members of the public about their own experience with noise, as well as the wider issue of Heathrow. While the visitors expected aircraft noise in Windsor,

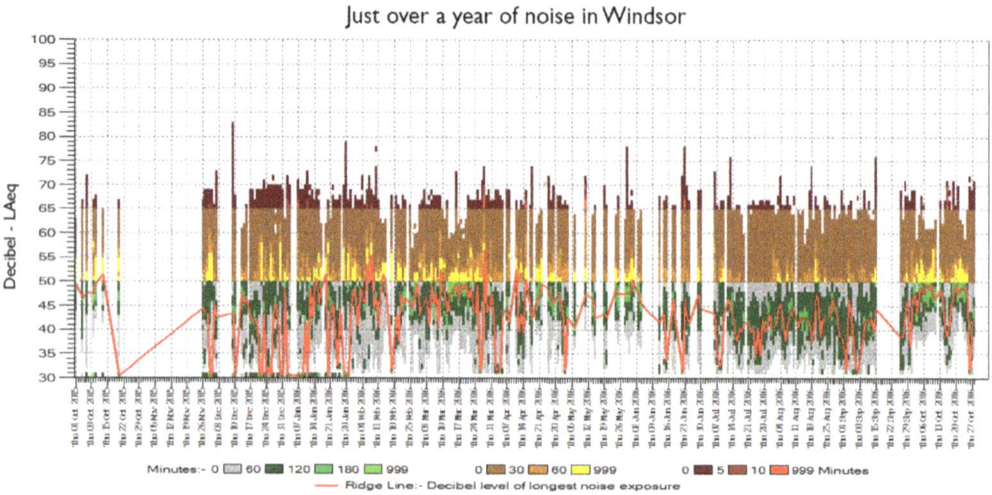

FIG. 4.7 Visualisation of thirteen months of data from the Windsor prototype. Each day is represented by a vertical line with yellow indicating many loud episodes above 50dB LAeq2s. The red line indicates the noise trend

the frequent and loud aircraft in Camberwell, which was 24 km from the runways and outside the annoyance contours, shocked them. This was the first time that many visitors had paid active attention to aircraft noise and noted the different sonic qualities of the aircraft and their effects on wildlife. When I was present, I would draw people's attention to the way birds seemed to screech in shock from the aircraft. Even after a jet passed, it was possible to hear the lingering effect on the birds as they continued to squawk. Despite the fact that the visitors were listening remotely, the sound installation created a tangible experiential connection to Heathrow. In this deployment, the prototype had the following infrastructure:

SOUND SENSOR > ONLINE RADIO STATION > PUBLIC SOUND INSTALLA-
TION > VISITORS EXPERIENCE HEATHROW NOISE

These multiple functions of the prototype as noise complaint, monitoring device and sound installation have demonstrated the versatility of the device. The prototype has enabled a variety of different infrastructures that engage existing participants in the controversy, such as the local councils and airport authorities, but has also made a connection to a broader audience of people who did not have any specific personal relation to the issue of Heathrow. The project is ongoing and growing, as there are other Heathrow residents waiting to install prototypes at their homes. The plan for this loose prototype collective is to support the deployment of a dozen devices and continue developing functionality that could enable programmatic sound

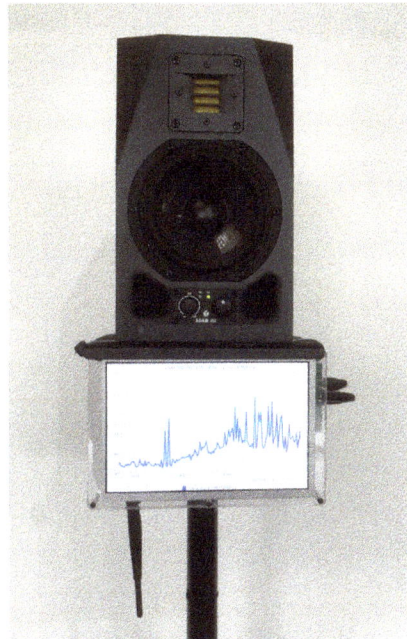

FIG. 4.8 Detail of the 'Prototyping a new Heathrow Airport' sound installation

identification of birds in order to demonstrate the broad impact of aircraft noise on living entities at Heathrow.

DISCUSSION

This chapter has added to the existing literature on controversies by out-lining an approach to turning controversies into questions of design, and by presenting preliminary results of my project to prototype the Heathrow noise pollution controversy. Key to my approach are the metaphors and methods of infrastructure and infrastructuring. My project sought to extend these using a method of scaling in order to identify and challenge the existing infrastructure of the Heathrow controversy. The combination of these two metaphors – infrastructure and scale – has highlighted the importance of the community annoyance metric as a key socio-technical device that con-nects aircraft, residents and governance, and one that has the capacity to structure decision making on the third runway. The metric functions as a spokesperson that speaks on behalf of residents about their experience of noise, yet acts against their wishes. The issue of Heathrow pollution actually consists of three different controversies: a media controversy around eco-nomic trade-offs, a failed political controversy about the number of people affected by noise, and an ontological controversy about how to stage annoy-ance. Yet the opponents to the airport extension have so far not made use of this ontological controversy. This case study presents a way of turning the ontological controversy of Heathrow into a space for participatory prototyp-ing. The prototype devices explored different ways of staging annoyance, and identified a need for multiple ways of providing evidence for the impact of noise. The prototyping process also resulted in the gathering of a loose col-lective focused on building a sound-monitoring network that could use the logic of sound measurement to allow targeted complaints and to develop a new metric that could challenge the airport's claims, as well as allow a new public to experience and discuss the impact of Heathrow by listening remotely. This object-centred design approach made it possible to stack multiple ways of staging annoyance within a single device and collective. The device points the way towards building alternative *spokespeople* that can act on behalf of local residents and speak about the impact of noise in multiple ways. This case study has demonstrated the unique qualities of a design approach that not only analyses a socio-technical controversy but also allows experimentation and intervention in it. It is worth speculating how many other controversies might benefit by being turned into questions of design.

ACKNOWLEDGEMENTS

This research was made possible through collaboration with Andrew Hall, Grant Smith, Max Baraitser Smith and Matthias Stevens. The research was part of the Hubbub project investigating rest and its opposites, supported by the Wellcome Trust [103817/Z/14/Z]. Thanks to Noortje Marres, Alex Wilkie and Daniela Boraschi for their feedback on the chapter.

REFERENCES

Airports Commission, *Airports Commission: Final Report* (London, 2015) < https://assets. publishing.service.gov.uk/government/uploads/system/uploads/attachment_ data/file/440316/airports-commission-final-report.pdf> [accessed 30 April 2018].
——'Member of the Public 16: Noise Discussion Paper' (London, 2013) <https://www. gov.uk/government/publications/stakeholder-responses-to-airports-commission- discussion-papers> [accessed 15 December 2015].
Airportwatch, '2M Group of Councils Call for New Study into Attitudes to Aircraft Noise', *Airportwatch* (2013) <http://www.airportwatch.org.uk/2013/09/2m- group-of-councils-call-for-new-study-into-attitudes-to-aircraft-noise/> [accessed 4 December 2013].
Berg, M., 'The Politics of Technology: On Bringing Social Theory into Technological Design', *Science, Technology & Human Values*, 23 (1998), 456–90.
Björgvinsson, E., P. Ehn, and P. A. Hillgren, 'Agonistic Participatory Design: Working with Marginalised Social Movements', *CoDesign*, 8 (2012), 127–44.
——'Participatory Design and "Democratizing Innovation"', in *Proceedings of the 11th Biennial Participatory Design Conference* (New York: ACM, 2010), pp. 41–50.

Braun, B., and S. J. Whatmore, eds, *Political Matter: Technoscience, Democracy, and Public Life* (Minneapolis: University of Minnesota Press, 2010).

Brooker, P., J. B. Critchley, D. J. Monkman, and C. Richmond, *Aircraft Noise Index Study: Main Report* (London, 1985) <https://publicapps.caa.co.uk/docs/33/ERCD 8402. PDF> [accessed 30 April 2018].

Callon, M., and B. Latour, 'Unscrewing the Big Leviathan: How Actors Macro-Structure Reality and How Sociologists Help Them to Do So', in K. D. Knorr-Cetina and A. V. Cicourel eds, *Advances in Social Theory and Methodology: Toward an Integration of Micro- and Macro-Sociologies* (New York: Routledge, 1981), pp. 277–303.

Civil Aviation Authority, *The Noise and Number Index* (London, 1981) <https://publicapps.caa.co.uk/docs/33/ERCD7907.pdf> [accessed 30 November 2012].

Civil Aviation Authority, and Bureau Vertias, *Attitudes to Noise from Aviation Sources in England Non SP Peer Review* (London: Department for Transport, 2007).

Le Dantec, C. A., 'Participation and Publics: Supporting Community Engagement', in *Proceedings of the SIGCHI Conference on Human Factors in Computing Systems* (New York: ACM, 2012), pp. 1351–60.

Le Dantec, C. A., and C. DiSalvo, 'Infrastructuring and the Formation of Publics in Participatory Design', *Social Studies of Science*, 43 (2013), 241–64.

Le Dantec, C. A., et al., 'Publics in Practice: Ubiquitous Computing at a Shelter for Homeless Mothers', in *Proceeding CHI '11 Proceedings of the SIGCHI Conference on Human Factors in Computing Systems* (New York: ACM, 2011), pp. 1687–96.

Department for Transport, *Heathrow Airport Year 2014 Actual Modal Split Average Summer Night Leq Noise Contours, GOV.UK* (2014) <https://www.gov.uk/government/publications/noise-contours-on-os-maps> [accessed 8 December 2015].

DiSalvo, C., et al., 'Making Public Things: How HCI Design Can Express Matters of Concern', in *CHI 2014: Conference on Human Factors in Computing Systems* (New York: ACM, 2014), pp. 2397–406.

Ehn, P., 'Participation in Design Things', in *Proceeding PDC '08 Proceedings of the Tenth Anniversary Conference on Participatory Design 2008* (Indianapolis, IN: Indiana University, 2008), pp. 92–101.

——*Work-Oriented Design of Computer Artifacts, Stockholm Arbetslivscentrum* (Stockholm: Arbetslivscentrum, 1988).

European Parliament, *The Environmental Noise Directive (2002/49/EC)* (2002) <http://eur-lex.europa.eu/legal-content/EN/TXT/?uri=CELEX:32002L0049> [accessed 30 April 2018].

Fidell, S., 'The Schultz Curve 25 Years Later: A Research Perspective', *The Journal of the Acoustical Society of America*, 114 (2003), 3007–15.

Flindell, I. H., 'Do Public Inquiries for Noise Control Serve a Useful Purpose? – An Acoustic Consultant's View', *Noise & Health*, 5 (2003), 31–38.

Flindell, I., and Associates, and MVA Consultancy, *Understanding UK Community*

Annoyance with Aircraft Noise: ANASE Update Study (2013) <http://www.aef.org. uk/uploads/understanding_uk_community_annoyance_for_2m_group.pdf> [accessed 30 April 2018].

Heathrow Airport, 'HeathrowFacts and Figures' (2015) <http://www.heathrowairport. com/about-us/company-news-and-information/company-information/facts-and-figures> [accessed 29 May 2015].

Heathrow Airport Limited, *A Quieter Heathrow* (London, 2013) <http://www.heathrow. com/file_source/HeathrowNoise/Static/a_quieter_heathrow_2013.pdf> [accessed 30 April 2018].

Hillgren, P. A., A. Seravalli, and A. Emilson, 'Prototyping and Infrastructuring in Design for Social Innovation', *CoDesign*, 7 (2011), 169–83.

Karasti, H., 'Infrastructuring in Participatory Design', in *PDC '14 Proceedings of the 13th Participatory Design Conference: Research Papers – Volume 1* (New York: ACM, 2014), pp. 141–50.

Karasti, H., and A-L. Syrjänen, 'Artful Infrastructure in Two Cases of Community PD', in *Proceedings of the 37th Annual Hawaii International Conference on System Sciences, 2004* (New York: ACM, 2004), pp. 20–30.

Kuenssberg, L., 'Heathrow Airport Expansion: A "Toxic Dilemma" for Ministers', *BBC News*, 19 October 2015 <http://www.bbc.co.uk/news/uk-politics-34568530> [accessed 23 October 2015].

Latour, B., and P. Weibel, eds, *Making Things Public: Atmospheres of Democracy* (Karlruhe and Cambridge, MA: MIT Press, 2005).

Marres, N., *Material Participation: Technology, the Environment and Everyday Publics* (Chippenham, UK: Palgrave Macmillan, 2012).

——'The Issues Deserve More Credit: Pragmatist Contributions to the Study of Public Involvement in Controversy', *Social Studies of Science*, 37 (2007), 759–80.

Le Masurier, P., et al., *ANASE: Attitudes to Noise from Aviation Sources* (2007) <http://www.airportwatch.org.uk/wp-content/uploads/anase-report-2007.pdf> [accessed 30 April 2018].

Mayor of London, *Airports Commission Discussion Paper 05: Aviation Noise The Mayor of London's Response* (2013) <https://www.tfl.gov.uk/cdn/static/cms/documents/ airport-commission-discussion-paper-05-noise-mayor-of-london-response.pdf> [accessed 26 May 2015].

Miedema, H. M. E., and C. G. M. Oudshoorn, 'Annoyance from Transportation Noise: Relationships with Exposure Metrics DNL and DENL and Their Confidence Intervals', *Environmental Health Perspectives*, 109 (2001), 409–16.

MIL Research Limited, *Aircraft Noise Annoyance around London (Heathrow) Airport* (London, 1961).

Mol, A., 'Ontological Politics: A Word and Some Questions', in J. Law and J. Hassard, eds, *Actor Network Theory and After* (Oxford and Malden, MA: Blackwell Publishers, 1999), pp. 74–89.

Nelkin, D., ed., 'Controversy: Politics of technical decisions' (3rd ed.), Sage focus editions, Vol. 8. Controversy (Thousand Oaks, CA, US: Sage Publications, Inc., 1992).

Neumann, L. J, and S. L. Star, 'Making Infrastructure: The Dream of a Common Language', in *Proceedings of the Fourth Biennial Participatory Design Conference (PDC'96)* (Palo Alto: Computer Professionals for Social Responsibility, 1996), pp. 231–40.

Nold, C., 'Device Studies of Participatory Sensing: Ontological Politics and Design Interventions' (PhD Thesis, University College London, 2017).

——'Micro/macro Prototyping', *International Journal of Human-Computer Studies*, 81 (2015), 72–80.

Star, S. L., and K. Ruhleder, 'Steps Toward an Ecology of Infrastructure: Design and Access for Large Information Spaces', *Information Systems Research*, 7 (1996), 111–34.

——'Steps Towards an Ecology of Infrastructure: Complex Problems in Design and Access for Large-Scale Collaborative Systems', in *Proceeding CSCW '94 Proceedings of the 1994 ACM Conference on Computer Supported Cooperative Work* (New York: ACM, 1994), pp. 253–64.

Wynne, B., 'Misunderstood Misunderstanding: Social Identities and Public Uptake of Science', *Public Understanding of Science*, 1 (1992), 281–304.

5

DESIGNING AND DOING: ENACTING ENERGY-AND-COMMUNITY

Alex Wilkie, Mike Michael

INTRODUCTION

IN THIS CHAPTER, WE REPORT ON AN INTERDISCIPLINARY PROJECT — COMbining expertise in science and technology studies (STS) and design – that explored, amongst other things, the ways in which community can be 'made' through energy. Thinking of energy as a heterogeneous assemblage that entailed, in this instance, energy policy, funding opportunities, social and technological innovations, and information flows, as well as the 'stuff' of energy (e.g. photons, electrons, ground heat, wind-power), we begin to trace the emergence of distinct 'communities' and their interrelations. However, we do not see this as a simple representational project in which we charted this emergence. Rather, the research we conducted self-consciously contributed to this process of emergence. Indeed, we designed a technological device – the Energy Babble – to fold into this emergence, to interject a certain playfulness that, hopefully, affords this process of emergence new or unexpected avenues and openings. On this score, we see our methodology as performative. However, the performativity in which we have engaged is one that, rather than close down the enactment of the social (the community) aspires to open up, or invent that 'social'.

In what follows, we provide a brief review of the project and its empirical backdrop. We go on to note that this project was performative, and specify our particular version of performativity: in particular, we suggest that many methods can be regarded as probabilistic in that they close down the empirical by reinforcing particular frameworks of analysis, that is, of re-producing existing problems. By comparison, we stress that our project aspired to be possibilistic insofar as it aimed to open up – to reframe – the issues at stake, specifically how to understand the interconnections between community and energy. We illustrate this possibilistic dimension of making the social through an examination of the design of the Babble. We follow this with an extended reflection on the ironies of the project and the Babble – how its possibilistic intent was, in multiple ways, not always realised. The chapter ends with a discussion of some of the more general implications of possibilistic research.

ENERGY COMMUNITIES

Between 2011 and 2012 the UK Departments of Energy and Climate Change (DECC), and Enterprise, Trade and Investment (DETI), the Welsh Government and Sciencewise-ERC (an organisation promoting public dialogue between policy, science and technology) provided £10 million to fund the exploration of twenty-two low carbon 'test-bed' communities through the Low Carbon Communities Challenge (LCCC). The objective of the project was to fund and learn from local community-based approaches to the implementation of low carbon technologies and measures in achieving energy demand reduction, and to explore sociological models of behaviour (notably the notion of 'nudge') to trigger so-called 'behaviour change' amongst the communities. According to the evaluation report (DECC 2012), the LCCC project saw the delivery of 8206 low carbon measures, including but not limited to the installation of low energy light bulbs, boiler jackets, biomass district heating systems, solar photovoltaic (PV) installations, air source heat pumps, wind turbines, triple glazing and smart energy monitors, as well as community evaluation and infrastructure projects including low carbon vehicles and car clubs, home visits and energy assessments, community hub buildings, advice sessions, open days and conferences. The initiatives and measures deployed as part of the LCCC implicated a wide range of 'stakeholders' as constituents of energy communities. Accordingly, (energy) community, in this sense, can be seen as an object and instrument of UK government policy with which to cut across and include a diverse range of local actors and settings involved in energy demand reduction, such as local authorities, third sector organisations, local enterprises, households, individuals, energy companies, social interest groups, resident associations, transition groups and so on. The overall ambition of the LCCC was to inform and contribute to the UK government target (DECC 2009) of delivering a 34% reduction in carbon emissions by 2020, as well as an energy supply target of 15% sourced from renewables (30% of electricity), also by 2020.

In the direct aftermath of the LCCC, and as a means to further build on and sustain the many concrete initiatives that emerged as part of the programme, the Research Councils UK (RCUK) led a further programme of research into energy communities as part of its Energy Programme.[1] This initiative, led by the Economic and Social Research Council (ESRC) and the Engineering and Physical Sciences Research Council (EPSRC), funded seven projects that aimed to assess, evaluate and report on the communities that participated in the LCCC, as well as explore further developments with community-based carbon reduction and environmental action. One project within this initiative, and the focus of this chapter, was the project 'Sustainability Invention and Energy Demand Reduction: Co-designing Communities and Practice' (ECDC). Here, ECDC specifically responded to the call for projects to 'work directly with communities to examine how individuals and communities use, and manage energy, and help them find ways to reduce energy demand'.[2] Furthermore, and (with some circumspection) drawing on Wenger (1998), the project aimed to address communities of energy demand reduction practice and how such practices raised issues about the nature of social and technical practices, notably demand reduction and resource management – a key objective of UK energy policy through measures such as the replacement of fifty-three million domestic gas and electricity meters with so-called smart energy monitors and In-Home Displays (IHDs) by 2020 (DECC 2013: 6).

If this formed the backdrop to the project, it soon became apparent that the efficacy of feedback and monitoring technologies, as well as the very premise of behaviour change (Dietz et al. 2009), was subject to considerable dispute, not least in the following ways. First, the introduction of smart monitors in the home is part of a broader UK environmental policy objective to effect behaviour change in the home, where a benign informational nudge is considered an effective intervention into routine energy consumption practices (Burgess and Nye 2008; Darby 2006). Through empirical evidence, however, recent scholarship has begun to refute the effectiveness of behavioural intervention. Feedback technologies, and energy-saving technologies more broadly, have been seen to give rise to the 'boomerang effect' (Schultz et al. 2007), where perceived savings lead to an actual increase in energy use or little or no change (Buchanan, Russo, and Anderson 2015). Second, the preoccupation with behavioural intervention as a means to address energy consumption side-lines, or simply ignores, the sociotechnical settings of energy consumption practices (Shove 2003; Hargreaves, Nye, and Burgess 2010) and the sophistication of energy consumers (e.g. Strengers 2013). As such, recent scholarship has begun to question how individuals-as-energy-users are configured as calculative actors capable of reflecting on and making rational decisions about energy consumption irrespective of the situated complexities of energy demand. Indeed, as Noortje Marres (2012) notes, drawing on Michel Callon (2009), carbon accounting technologies, notably smart meters, 'co-articulate' the simultaneous enactment of multiple registers, including politics, economics and innovation. That is to say, such technologies elicit and mediate environmental action, political engagement and domestic comfort simultaneously. Taken alongside Elizabeth Shove's emphasis on social practices which similarly embeds the energy user within a nexus of technological, cultural and corporeal relations, it is clear that there are emerging alternatives to the economisation of the energy user, with its focus on the rational, calculative individual of energy demand reduction. In this context, it is unsurprising that the literature on feedback technologies that purportedly reduce energy demand calls for a more nuanced, 'thicker', understanding of the energy user as constitutively situated within a sociotechnical assemblage. Such a view can also be set alongside a longstanding preoccupation within STS with the development and deployment of energy-related technologies, and the more or less problematic attempts to enrol users figured into particular innovation initiatives. For instance, we can point to such classic studies as the (failed) development of electric cars (Callon 1986), the prospective users of a mass transportation system (Latour 1996), the ambivalence of villagers to be enrolled as citizens by way of electricity meters in the Ivory Coast (Akrich 1992), and the role of interpretive actors in constructing the meaning of electric light bulbs (Bijker 1995).

With all this in mind, the ECDC project set out to avoid narrowly conceived assumptions about what constitutes a community, not least one that is composed of the rational, calculative energy users figured in energy policy and much supporting literature. In so doing, the approach taken was shaped by the particular interests and make-up of the project team, notably a combination of HCI approaches to ludic design (Gaver 2002) and speculative design (Michael 2012; Wilkie, Michael, and Plummer-Fernandez 2015) – where designed artefacts are deployed to explore the prospects of technology and everyday life – and sensibilities in STS attuned to the empirical study of social processes involving heterogeneous mixtures of human and non-human actors. As such, the ECDC project set out to question, challenge and explore core assumptions at play in energy policy and the associated literature, namely the instrumentalised characterisation of communities as morally responsible collectives of rational citizens (see Rose 2000). Such communities can be understood as novel objects of policy that sit between measures for disciplining the conduct of individuals and broader policy instruments, such as the cap-n-trade economies of market-based emissions trading. In contrast, the mixture of design and STS that comprised ECDC was sensitised to both rational and non-rational meaning and practices, as well as to collectives that did not privilege or reduce communities to human actors, let alone human actors of a particular sort. So while we began with a view that communities are constructed (e.g. Cohen 1985), we regarded their construction to be a heterogeneous process, one in which technological practices could be seen to be constitutive of 'hybrid communities' (Callon 2004). However, as we discuss in the next section, the character of our methodology went beyond the mere documentation of such constructive heterogeneity: as we discuss in the section, we as researchers were intimately implicated in this constructive process.

METHOD AND METAPHYSICS

As a collaborative project that spanned social science and design, ECDC can be understood in numerous ways. From a social scientific perspective, it is a speculative approach that assumes the performativity of its methods in making its objects of study. This view of method has become a commonplace, perhaps best articulated in the work of John Law (2004). For Law, reality is in flux, characterised by emergence, relationality and multiplicity. In trying to study such a reality, one is necessarily performing or enacting it, and, in some ways, fixing it. Rather than method, Law prefers the notion of 'method assemblage': this enables us to address the fact that any methodological engagement entails, on the one hand, many levels (e.g. affective, pragmatic, political as well as epistemic aspects), and, on the other, a partial process of rendering relations – relations which both reflect the flux and complexity of that reality and necessarily delimit that reality. There is, as Law remarks, a 'crafting of a bundle of ramifying relations that generates presence, manifest absence, and Otherness' (Law 2004: 45). Nevertheless, the notion of 'method assemblage' allows us to 'imagine more flexible boundaries, and different forms of presence and absence' (ibid. 85). In particular, we can also begin to imagine this as a process whereby these different forms of presence and absence are partially constitutive of the researchers themselves. That is to say, the method assemblage (which includes the researchers, of course), in its multiple relationality with the world-in-flux, is itself subject to emergence.

This argument can be approached through the notion of the event. Drawing on the process metaphysics of Whitehead, Deleuze and Stengers, the event is an 'actual occasion' that comprises social/material, micro/macro, human/

non-human, and cognitive/affective elements (or prehensions). These 'concresce', in Whitehead's (1978 [1929]) terms, to yield a momentary durability or 'satisfaction'. Crucially, one can regard this concrescence less as a matter of interacting elements (which retain their identity) and more as one of intra-action (Barad 2007) in which prehensions mutually change, co-become, or become-with one another. Assuming that a method assemblage is a part of the concrescence that makes up the 'research event' (which can range from a single interview to an extended period of participant observation, or a multi-sited ethnography), then it too can co-become with other elements (e.g. human and non-human participants). This also raises the intriguing spectre that what is happening is not research but something rather different. No longer is it simply a matter of a research question being addressed, but rather the grounds of the empirical engagement begin to shift.

This account of the research event borrows heavily from Isabelle Stengers' (2005) cosmopolitical proposal. Accordingly, when political actors interact, they can co-become, in the process reformulating not only their own interests, but also the very point of the cosmopolitical event. In other words, instead of seeking answers to a pre-existing question, issue or problem, the question or issue or problem has itself shifted. With such a shift comes the prospect of formulating a more interesting issue, or posing better, more relevant questions, that is of engaging in, as Mariam Fraser (2010: 78) puts it, 'inventive problem-making'. Two challenges arise here. First, how can (energy demand) problems be induced to express their relevance in and to the research event, something we address in what follows in the literal form of a designed research device. According to Fraser (ibid.), the '(ethical) obligation here, in other words, is not to solve a problem, or to explain it away but rather to try to enable it to "speak" or to pose it in terms that enable it to play itself out in productive ways'. Second, and given the researchers' constitution in the research event, how to speak about the event without explaining it away as if from nowhere (Haraway 1988: 581)? In other words, how to be situated in the research event and contribute to its becomings and problem articulation?

One upshot, and response to the challenges posed above, is that the research event, by virtue of both making and being made by its objects of study, can take on a more speculative tenor. As social scientists, we need not address ourselves to a shifting reality in which we are methodologically embroiled and epistemically emergent, in terms of our usual analytic frameworks. Perhaps we can take a more speculative tack and re-envision the research event, and imaginatively reformulate the issues at stake in it. Following Stengers (2010: 57), we might wish to develop an approach that 'affirms the possible [...] actively resists the plausible and the probable targeted by approaches that claim to be neutral'.

One might be tempted to read into this phrase an opposition between the possible and the probable. We often see these as tendencies that range over a no-doubt multi-dimensional spectrum, and as such we prefer to use the terms *probabilistic* and *possibilistic*. Indeed, as we shall see below, the relation between these is rather more topological, with what is to count as possibilistic or probabilistic being an emergent and relational property rather than something that can be measured against external criteria (Lash and Lury 2007). For the moment, however, we want only to note that our methodological entrée into the empirical field, which we briefly summarised in the preceding section, was a multivalent one, though our focus and that of our participants was mainly upon the speculative device of the Energy Babble (see next section). In other words, within our method assemblage, there was a battery of elements. These included devices such as cultural probes (Gaver, Dunne, and Pacenti 1999) and the project website, engagements such as probe workshops and site visits, re-scripting workshops to trace and interrogate the geographies of delegation (Akrich 1992: 206) materialised by existing feedback devices, experimental and evaluative prototypes, individual relations (though these born as much out of the contrast with other projects in the programme and the government funding regimes to which the communities were connected), and so on. While our focus remains on the Babble, what the Babble 'is', and what it lures and co-becomes with, is multiple (Mol 2003) in the sense of being variously probabilistic and possibilistic. Phrased in the language of 'inventing the social', our method assemblage of devices, engagements, bodies, and so forth stands in the topological enactment of energy-and-community as at once marked by inventive problems and standardised questions.

THE ENERGY BABBLE:
A DESIGN DEVICE AND THE POSSIBLE

At the beginning of the project it was not evident that the interdisciplinary team of designers and social scientists (of which we were part) would design a research device in the form of a 'product' or appliance. However, through an engagement with and exploration of the problem space of community-scale energy demand reduction – including but not limited to ethnographic and designerly contact with seven existing energy communities, an investigation of environmental and energy demand reduction technologies, a review of energy literature and policy, as well as design propositions in the form of design workbooks (Gaver 2011) – the design team began to focus on the design of a device that would itself playfully mediate the problem space of energy demand reduction.[3] In part, this approach was inspired and informed by four pronounced design directions that gained traction during the project: 1) *Energy Tourism*: how sustainability changes our relation to visible energy infrastructures; 2) *Insistent Activism*: how to re-situate and reformat discourses of the environment and sustainability in unfamiliar, unpredictable or inappropriate ways and settings (e.g. apart from formal community meetings) and how to open up discourses that have hardened around known problems and solutions (e.g. behaviour change and off-the-shelf green industry technologies such as PV installations); 3) *Energy Awareness*: how to support communities of practitioners in sharing their experiences, expertise and successes (or failures), and; 4) *Cosmopolitical Energy Communities*: who or what are the members of energy communities, and what are their dynamics? Here, the increasingly salient role of the internet and social media in mediating environmental discourse and action as well as community initiatives sensitised us to the emergence of novel practices and energy actors such as Bots (Wilkie, Michael, and Plummer-Fernandez 2015).[4]

As these interests coalesced and concretised (over the period of a year), we formulated a design brief to synthesise our examination of the design space and to precipitate the design of the research device: '*Design an Energy-Babble system that displays material, collected from some combination of individual, community and publics sources, to open and promote constructive affect and involvement in energy reduction issues and orientations. More specifically, the system should support understandings of, and practices related to, energy demand reduction'.*

Over the next eighteen months, the team designed what became the Energy Babble (Fig. 5.1, below), which took the form of (or parodied) a networked audio information appliance – to be given to community members – that vocalises (quite literally speaks out using software based synthetic voices) internet-sourced and community contributed content. Needless to say, this involved much aesthetic and technological expertise and work, including a combination of graphic, product, sound, software and electronics design.

The resulting design and system consisted of twenty-eight individual devices, the audio content of which was produced and managed by an online server-based content scraping, audio generation and distribution system featuring algorithmically sourced and generated environmental and energy-related content.

The Energy Babble device combined a Raspberry Pi computer, a loudspeaker, a Wi-Fi card, a soundcard, a memory card (for the OS) as well as two blown-glass sections, an injection-moulded main enclosure and microphone handset, a 3D printed volume knob and internal support structures, and a large-diameter cable

FIG. 5.1 The Energy Babble (photo: Alex Wilkie)

to connect the microphone handset to the main enclosure. The server software, which provides and manages the audio content of the babble, included software routines and algorithms to retrieve web-based content including:

- Scraping Twitter feeds from a range of pre-identified energy-related feeds, including the communities, local and national government, the energy and green industries, and activists and other implicated actors.
- Querying Twitter for the occurrence of particular search terms, such as 'climate change', 'energy bills', and 'renewable energy'.
- Querying Twitter for the occurrence of tweets that include the text string 'switched off the...' and returning a list of things (broadly put) reportedly having been turned off.
- Scraping textual content from URLs that are returned in tweets as part of Twitter queries.
- UK National Grid status updates, including current energy demand and carbon intensity, as well as the ratio of sources (coal, combined cycle gas turbines, nuclear, wind).[5]

In addition, the server software also managed the input of content from the community members who used the device, including a variety of questions and prompts that were sporadically spoken through the device. This was, in part, a means to invite users to contribute content by using the microphone handset to communicate with others using the system.

Lastly, and notably, the system featured a Markov Chain algorithm, which used the corpus of content generated from the above routines to probabilistically produce new and often locally intelligible (to the systems collection) text strings. In other words, the Markov function takes the words of others (human or non-human) and produces new content, sometimes appreciable, at other times nonsense.

When running, the Energy Babble system provided a sporadic interplay of spoken statements, evocative of talk radio, drawn from the pool of content provided by the sourced content, the algorithms and community inputted messages. Each message was cued by a short jingle, indicating and segmenting the spoken feeds. In the main, the content comprised energy and environmental news, reports of energy practices, and other matters relating to sustainability. Often, though, other content and topics entered into the speech, originating from the source and the Markov-generated interjections.

In total, twenty-one Energy Babble devices were deployed to members of the seven energy communities we had engaged, each community receiving three to four devices, and often handing over the device to other community members after a period of use. The handing-over of the devices was conducted at pre-organised community events, events organised specifically for the handover, or to individual, typically prominently active, figures, where appropriate. The deployment continued for approximately six months, during which time members of the team repeatedly visited the communities and listened to the ensuing content using a device set up in the team's studio or at home.

At base, the Energy Babble (the combination of the networked devices and the server-based system) was a research device designed to reveal how local communities engage with energy matters (news, views, practices, experiences, demand) as well as live with and include an energy-related and consuming technology as part of their everyday practices. On the one hand, the Energy Babble sought to mediate and explore how the seven communities share information and experience its multiplicity, utility or otherwise. On the other hand, the device also sought to occupy and actively articulate (by expressing and connecting) the problem space of energy demand and carbon reduction by scrambling, interjecting and provoking, or inviting, responses. How might the communities react to the presence of, or participate with, the Babble with all its idiosyncrasies and playfulness in what are, after all, issues of the utmost urgency? Rephrased in the terms of the preceding section, the Babble was designed to nurture a 'possibilistic research event' in which the users might begin to co-emerge with the Babble and thus pose more interesting questions about energy demand reduction, about the nature of community and its embroilments with energy, and about the meanings of energy information and its movements (not least through and across communities).

In what follows we consider some of the ironies of the implementation of the Babble. While in this section we have gone into detail about the design intent and effort that went into the Babble, the Babble does not stand alone. It is part of a method assemblage in which it arose amongst existing relations to the communities (and particular figures within those communities) and to a series of enactments of energy politics by both the communities and the members of the research team. As such, while we reflect on some of the reactions to the Babble on the part of community members, we mainly focus on those aspects of the method assemblage that militated against a possibilistic research event. Put another way, we begin to trace how the inventiveness of the invention of the social through the research process, despite the best of intentions, can become diluted.

ASSEMBLING ENERGIES, COMMUNITIES AND IRONIES

The team's initial contact with energy communities came about through a one-day event organised on behalf of the RCUK energy programme for all the award holders at a hotel in Central London. A key aim of this event, as it turned out, was to introduce and, preferably, match communities to research teams, and thus to initiate longer-term research engagements. This was done by way of presentations and posters (summarising each project), which the research groups brought to and displayed on the walls of the conference room. Representatives of LCCC communities, present at the event, were invited to approach research teams whose research interests matched their local efforts, initiatives and interests. The vivid yellow poster for ECDC described our research process in three stages (investigation, batch production of speculative devices, and ethnographic engagement) and portrayed, using photographs, two previous research devices (i.e. Gaver et al. 2010; Gaver et al. 2011) in order to communicate what was, in contrast to other projects, a more unusual approach. Both here, and during the follow-up meetings with the communities that approached the team during the event, it became apparent that many community members viewed ECDC as a curiosity in that it did not promise a technological fix, clear solutions or epistemic assurances. Despite, or perhaps because of, the lack of utilitarian or instrumental expectations, however, the communities were drawn to the prospect of hosting and living with an exploratory device as part of their routine energy practices (neither we nor they knew exactly what the device would be, beyond being a discrete product-like appliance). We surmised at the time that the relative popularity of the ECDC project lay not only in its novelty, but in its contrast to standard social methods – methods that the energy communities had long been exposed to as, or so we were told, one of the most researched populations in the UK (e.g. Clark 2008).

Notwithstanding the team's seemingly successful efforts to frame the initial expectations of the communities, during the handover of the Babble to the community members – approximately two years after the first meeting – the expectations elicited again relied upon or required the device to address utilitarian demands. Upon receiving the device, G, from the Meadows, for example, exclaimed, 'We thought we were going to get a gizmo to save energy'. Another Meadows member asked if DECC was going to receive a Babble so that they could complain directly to the UK Government about an ongoing dispute with British Gas. A retired engineer from Rye Harbour, near Hastings, asked, 'How does this improve the social operational wellbeing of the people who use it? If I make an investment, how do I get a payback?' and continued: 'I wanted it to solve a problem'. At Woodlands Valley Farm (an organic farm and conservation and sustainability activity centre), in Ladock, members of the Ladock Grampound Road Transition Group were initially perplexed, though curious, when introduced to the Babble. Their expectations were altered, however, by an electrician who interceded as an impromptu spokesperson for the Babble. The electrician quickly realised that the Babble used a Raspberry Pi, a 'British' technology which he was already using at the heart of his home-made low-powered home media centre, and that the Babble could be repurposed (a common response across the communities) as a way to report on and broadcast the state of his experimental car-battery-operated home electricity system. In doing so, he also quelled the members' concerns over the Babble's energy consumption, and advocated the pedagogic prospects of the Raspberry Pi, suggesting that it could help members undertake their own experimental projects. J, from Sidmouth, echoed the impulses of the electrician to reconstruct the Babble by suggesting that it could use the internet connection of a mobile phone and be powered by a car to allow for some kind of mobility.

Similarly, when deployed to the members of Energise Hastings, during a routine meeting at which representatives of Hastings Borough Council were present, the Babble was first likened to a smart monitor and its adoption was framed in terms of extending or integrating with existing feedback technologies. Crucially, it was also viewed as a device that could be enrolled for marketing purposes; as one member put it, 'That is a very powerful sales tool'. Latterly, however, the views of the members changed, typified by one member's response: 'It's a new type of thinking, you don't know what you'll get, it might just be chaos'. Thus, at Hastings, and at Reepham and at Sidmouth, the Babble became construed, in part, as a device that could be enrolled to play a role in community outreach and awareness activities and thus operate to persuade people to become involved in sustainable issues and practices, as well as to interest prospective community members.

This instrumentalised view of the Babble does not simply reflect the practical interests of these members of energy communities. It is also partly a response to the way that we presented the Babble. The process of implementing a specu-lative device involves presenting it as something strange or novel – however, this strangeness and novelty cannot be so extreme as to be threatening (as opposed to promising – see Michael, in press): as such, ironically, the temp-tation is to temper the novelty or strangeness by suggesting that the device also has practical uses. In other words, the research event was affected by the ways in which we as researchers transmitted mixed messages that per-formed our speculative device (the Babble) as simultaneously speculative and instrumental. We can see the contortedness of our enactment of the Babble in the ways in which it is described in Figure 5.2 (an article on the Babble in the November 2013 issue of *Reepham Life*). On reading the article, and Bill Gaver's account, one is left with a sense of quasi-instrumentality, to coin a phrase: there are hints at the Babble's oddness but also at its utility, though these are never quite clear. On reflecting on our own practices of implementa-tion – especially on how we described the Babble to our energy community participants – we detect a similar ironic contortedness of trying to express both the strangeness and utility of the device, to at once excite and reassure its prospective users.

Despite these observations, we can nevertheless note the variety of ways in which the Babble was instrumentalised: as an energy saving gizmo, a means of direct communication, a problem solver, a model use of Raspberry Pi, and as a marketing tool. Indeed, we suggest that these cumulative instrumentalisations imply a possibilistic opening up of the very idea of the instrumental in relation to energy demand reduction. In other words, there is a second-order irony at play here. Especially if these accounts of instrumentality were circulated via the Babble, there is a possibilistic prospect of speculative reflection on – that is, asking more interesting questions about – the meaning of what counts as instrumental (and this includes cognate terms such as practical, utility, or problem-solving). Moreover, there arises the possibility of using the Babble to

FIG. 5.2 The Energy Babble, held by project member Matthew Plummer-Fernandez, as featured in the November 2013 issue of *Reepham Life* (Reepham Community Press)

pose more interesting general questions about the complex practical purposes that might attach to communities-and-energy.

By contrast to (the ironies of) this highly instrumentalised view of the Babble, other rationalities or sensibilities were also evident across the communities. For example, D from the Meadows announced that she would name the device 'Finnegan' in reference to James Joyce's literary stream of consciousness style. An artist, also from Meadows, who was somewhat engrossed by an experimental form of sustainable living in a low-energy eco home, designed with her husband (an architect) and built on industrially polluted land, characterised (perhaps unsurprisingly) the device as an intercom-like 'Art Babble'. Soon after receiving a Babble, J from New Cross sent an SMS: 'It's amazing! I love it so much already. The messaging system reminds me of the barbed wire telephone system in Wild West. Seriously – Google it. Thanks guys :)'. On first reading, this might suggest that the instrumental can also be side-lined and the aesthetic privileged. However, the ease of such a categorisation (at least amongst some participants) might, ironically, imply a closing down or probabilistic enactment of the Babble's speculative role. So, insofar as it can be categorised as an aesthetic other it might leave untouched the probabilistic, instrumentalised business-as-usual of the communities-and-energy.

So far, we have looked at the initial reception received by the Babble. We now reflect on how it was enacted over the course of its implementation in various private and public spaces. As above, there was a marked ongoing appreciation of the Babble as an aesthetic artefact as well as a novel technical device. R, from Reepham, described the device as beautifully well made in hand blown glass, and P from the Meadows called it a 'really nice object'. However, here we concentrate on the varieties of instrumentalisation of the Babble, not least with regard to the utility of the information which it broadcast. It was clear that there were two key issues here, the first of which related to the type of information involved. Thus, during use, the germaneness of the internet-sourced content that the Babble recurrently uttered was called into question, although what counted or was construed as appropriate varied across communities and members. J, from the Meadows, who used the Babble in her office at the local social club, suggested that the device could have a 'filter' (reporting on government and community rather than oil and gas) since it vocalised much extraneous information. M, from Hastings, who viewed the content as a reflection of the complex milieu of community energy demand, related how the repetitiveness of the content suppressed the relevance of the Babble (a view shared by J from Ladock). At the same time, M noted the similarities between the Babble's information and the content of conversations on and around the topic of carbon reduction. Second, germaneness was also shaped by the timeliness of the Babble's broadcasts. Here, J remarked how the Babble would not speak on cue, and that once spoken, messages could not be retrieved. Neither of these observations should come as much of a surprise: we would expect that an instrumental enactment of the Babble would focus on the content and timing of its messages. However, more intriguing was the ways in which the instrumentalisation of the Babble spun out to take in other elements of its milieu within the communities-and-energy.

To put this another way, the eventuation of the utility of the Babble brought into play a series of other elements. These can be summarised as the siting or placement of the Babble, the timing of its installation, and its connectedness to other issues and concerns. With regard to siting, the previously discussed article in Reepham Life (Fig. 5.2), features the Reepham Green Team, who invite suggestions for further installation sites for Babble. With regard to timing, R, at St Leonards said, 'if you had given this now, then it might have been more useful to me'. R reported using the device as part of the energy initiatives he was involved in, such as an energy advice event at Bexhill which, he claimed, attracted four hundred people, most of whom wanted advice on their energy bills. R also used the Babble in efforts to partner with a Dutch energy supplier in order to market and sell community tariffs to individuals. Most notably, R made repeated reference to the recent emergence of Community Energy South – a meta-community of sorts – that is itself a partnership of energy community groups across the south of England. The Babble could have been instrumental in this process had its timing been better. With regard to connectedness, the Babble's utility was also played out as an aspect of proximity to other energy issues. In Ladock, for example, J spoke of how the Babble echoes her involvement with Christian Aid and Credit Unions, where energy issues are associated with issues of poverty (which overspill often parochial UK concerns with the environment and technology). The Babble also connected, according to J, to the relation between energy and the agricultural sector (in which individuals are employed and with which communities are engaged).

Taking all this together, we see how the typical problem of instrumentalising the Babble in pursuit of the probabilistic enactment of community-and-energy (business as usual, as it were) also shades into a possibilistic eventuation of community-and-energy. For example, the various attempts to make the Babble useful suggest that interesting problems can be posed about what counts as community-and-energy. What we see in the above brief examples are attempts to make the Babble informative – attempts that draw on the Babble's spatial and temporal setting and its issue connectedness. Along the way, we also glimpse a more possibilistic rendering of community-and-energy in which the spatial, temporal and substantive (i.e. content-full) parameters of a community are questioned. The sorts of questions that come to mind might include, Where are the 'right sites' for the Babble, sites which recreate or challenge a sense of a discrete community-and-energy? How does the Babble evoke other versions of community-and-energy (e.g. around international poverty) and how do these fuse with, or become differentiated from, the local community-and-energy where the Babble is installed'? 'How does the timing of the arrival and installation of the Babble affect the ongoing enactments of a particular community-and-energy, as some of its members forge connections into other collectives?

CONCLUDING REMARKS

In this chapter, we have attempted to trace out how a particular design and social scientific interdisciplinary project might speculatively engage with communities-and-energy. The key methodological intervention – the Energy Babble – was designed to enable people playfully to explore the character of energy demand reduction and thus the character of those communities themselves. As such, our aim was, via the Babble, to 'invent a social' that was possibilistic – that opened up an unforeseen or not-as-yet version of the social (more specifically, the communities-and-energy). As it turned out, and partly as a result of certain tacit enactments of Babble by the research team (i.e. the de facto focus on the possible utility of the Babble) and the responses of the participants, we were faced with many instances of how the Babble was variously instrumentalised. However, rather than simply see these as probabilistic enactments of the Babble in which communities-and-energy emerged more or less unaffected (engaged in business as usual), we also detected more possibilistic dimensions to these processes. In particular, we suggested that in the attempt to render the Babble straightforwardly instrumental for the community, the very meanings or parameters of instrumental and community became open to more interesting questions.

Finally, there is a broader lesson to be drawn here, a speculative reflection on speculative method itself. If our interdisciplinary methodology was geared to accessing the possibilistic, it clearly provoked the probabilistic. We hoped to see an exploration of the possible in relation to community-and-energy; that is, an enactment of the social that was open and unfolding. Instead, we found a probabilistic enactment – an instrumentalisation – of our key methodological tool (the Energy Babble) that seemed to reinforce the existing performances of the social. And yet in this very process there were hints of a possibilistic enactment of community-and-energy. The anti-speculative responses to our speculative enactments ironically yielded a tacit speculation. Speculative method might thus be speculative, not because of its speculative character or intent, but in spite of it.

ACKNOWLEDGEMENTS

This chapter draws upon research conducted under the project 'Sustainability Invention and Energy Demand Reduction: Co-designing Communities and Practice' funded by the RCUK and led by the EPSRC (project code ES/1007318/1). The authors would like to thank members of the project team including Andy Boucher, Bill Gaver, Tobie Kerridge, Liliana Ovalle and Matthew Plummer-Fernandez. Thanks are also due to all the participants who gave so generously of their time.

NOTES

1 See http://www.rcuk.ac.uk/research/xrcprogrammes/energy/. Accessed 11th May 2015.

2 See http://www.esrc.ac.uk/research/major-investments/energy-and-communities-collaborative-venture.aspx. Date accessed 12th May 2015.

3 The communities that were engaged as part of the ECDC project were a mixture of 'first mover' (recognised by policy actors as exemplars of carbon reduction initiatives) and 'second mover' (showing clear evidence and commitment to cutting carbon emissions and implementing sustainability measures) communities (DECC 2012: 10) and included: Energise Hastings; Greening Goldsmiths; Low Carbon Living Ladock; Meadows Partnership Trust (Nottingham); Reepham Green Team; Sid Valley Energy Action Group; and Transition New Cross.

4 We are paraphrasing Gaver et al. (2015), who provide a complimentary discussion of the design process which gave rise to the Energy Babble.

5 See http://www.gridwatch.templar.co.uk for an example of online National Grid status.

REFERENCES

Akrich, M., 'The de-scription of technical objects' in W. Bijker and J. Law, eds, *Shaping Technology/Building Society: Studies in Sociotechnical Change* (Cambridge, MA: MIT Press, 1992), pp. 205–24.

Barad, K., Meeting the Universe Halfway: Quantum Physics and the Entanglement of Matter and Meaning (Durham, NC: Duke University Press, 2007).

Bijker, W. E., Of Bicycles, Bakelites, and Bulbs: Toward a Theory of Sociotechnical Change (Cambridge, MA: MIT Press, 1995).

Buchanan, K., R. Russo, and B. Anderson, 'The Question of Energy Reduction: The Problem(s) with Feedback', *Energy Policy*, 77 (2015), 89–96.

Burgess, J., and M. Nye, 'Re-materialising Energy Use Through Transparent Monitoring Systems', *Energy Policy*, 36 (2008), 4454–59.

Callon, M. 'The Sociology of an Actor-Network: The Case of the Electric Vehicle' in M. Callon, J. Law and A. Rip, eds, *Mapping the Dynamics of Science and Technology* (London: Palgrave Macmillan,1986), pp. 19–34.

——'The Role of Hybrid Communities and Socio-Technical Arrangements in the Participatory Design', *Journal of the Center for Information Studies*, 5.3 (2004), 3–10.

——'Civilising Markets: Carbon Trading between In Vitro and In Vivo Experiments', *Accounting, Organizations and Society*, 34.3–4 (2009), 535–48.

Clark, T., '"We're Over-Researched Here!" Exploring Accounts of Research Fatigue within Qualitative Research Engagements', *Sociology*, 42.5 (2008), 953–70.

Cohen, A., *The Symbolic Construction of Community* (London; New York, NY: Ellis Horwood & Tavistock Publications,1985).

Darby, S., 'The Effectiveness of Feedback on Energy Consumption: A Review for DEFRA of the Literature on Metering, Billing and Direct Displays', Environmental Change Institute: University of Oxford 22 (2006), 1–21.

Department of Energy and Climate Change, 'The UK Low Carbon Transition Plan: National Strategy for Climate Change', HM Government (2009), 1–220.

——'Low Carbon Communities Challenge: Evaluation Report', London: Department of Energy and Climate Change (2012).

——'Quantitative Research into the Public Awareness, Attitudes, and Experience of Smart Meters', Department of Energy and Climate Change (2013).

Dietz, T., et al., 'Household Actions can Provide a Behavioral Wedge to Rapidly Reduce US Carbon Emissions', *Proceedings of the National Academy of Sciences*, 106.44 (2009), 184–52.

Fraser, M., 'Facts, Ethics and Event', in C. B. Jensen and K. Rödje, eds, *Deleuzian Intersections: Science, Technology and Anthropology* (New York, NY: Berghahn, 2010), pp. 57–82.

Gaver, W., 'Designing for Homo Ludens', *I3 Magazine*, 12 (2002), 2–6.

——'Making Spaces: How Design Workbooks Work', Proceedings of the 2011 Annual Conference on Human Factors in Computing Systems (2011), 1551–60.

Gaver, W., M. Blythe, A. Boucher, N. Jarvis, J. Bowers, P. Wright, 'The Prayer Companion: Openness and Specificity, Materiality and Spirituality', *Proceedings of the 28th International Conference on Human Factors in Computing Systems* (Atlanta, GA: ACM, 2010), 2055–64.

Gaver, W., A. Boucher, J. Bowers, M. Blythe, N. Jarvis, D. Cameron, T. Kerridge, A. Wilkie, P. Roberts, P. Wright, 'The Photostroller: Supporting Diverse Care Home Residents in Engaging with the World', *Proceedings of the SIGCHI Conference on Human Factors in Computing Systems* (New York, NY: ACM, 2011), 1757–66.

Gaver, W., T. Dunne, and E. Pacenti, 'Design: Cultural Probes', *Interactions*, 6 (1999), 21–29.

Gaver, W., et al., 'Energy Babble: Mixing Environmentally-Oriented Internet Content to Engage Community Groups', *Proceedings of the 33rd Annual ACM Conference on Human Factors in Computing Systems* (New York, NY: ACM, 2015),1115–24.

Haraway, D. J., 'Situated Knowledges: The Science Question in Feminism and the Privilege of Partial Perspective', *Feminist studies*, 14.3 (1988), 575–99.

Hargreaves, T., M. Nye, and J. Burgess, 'Making Energy Visible: A Qualitative Field Study of How Householders Interact with Feedback from Smart Energy Monitors', *Energy Policy*, 38.10 (2010), 6111–19.

Lash, S., and C. Lury, *Global Culture Industry: The Mediation of Things* (Cambridge: Polity Press, 2007).

Latour, B., *Aramis, or the Love of Technology* (Cambridge, MA: Harvard University Press, 1996).

Law, J. *After Method: Mess in Social Science Research* (Abingdon; New York, NY: Routledge, 2004).

Marres, N., 'The Costs of Public Involvement: Everyday Devices of Carbon Accounting and the Materialization of Participation', *Economy and Society*, 40.4 (2012), 510–33.

Michael, M., '"What Are We Busy Doing?": Engaging the Idiot', *Science, Technology & Human Values*, 37. 5 (2012), 528–54.

——'Speculative Design and Digital Materialities: Idiocy, Threat and Com-promise', in E. Ardevol, S. Pink and D. Lanzeni, eds, *Designing Digital Materialities: Knowing, Intervention and Making* (London: Bloomsbury. in press).

Mol, A., *The Body Multiple: Ontology in Medical Practice* (Durham, NC: Duke University Press, 2003).

Rose, N., 'Community, Citizenship, and the Third Way', *American Behavioral Scientist*, 43.9 (2000), 1395–411.

Schultz, P. W., et al., 'The Constructive, Destructive, and Reconstructive Power of Social Norms', *Psychological Science*, 18.5 (2007), 429–34.

Shove, E., *Comfort, Cleanliness & Convenience* (Oxford; New York, NY: Berg, 2003).

Stengers, I., 'The Cosmopolitical Proposal' in B. Latour and P. Weibel, eds, *Making Things Public* (Cambridge, MA: MIT Press, 2005), pp. 994–1003.

——*Cosmopolitics I* (Minneapolis, MN: University of Minnesota Press, 2010).

Strengers, Y., Smart Energy Technologies in Everyday Life: Smart Utopia? (Basingstoke: Palgrave Macmillan, 2013).

Wenger, E., *Communities of Practice: Learning, Meaning and Identity* (Cambridge: Cambridge University Press, 1998).

Whitehead, A. N., *Process and Reality: An Essay in Cosmology* (New York, NY: The Free Press, 1978 [1929]).

Wilkie, A., M. Michael, and M. Plummer-Fernandez, 'Speculative Method and Twitter: Bots, Energy and Three Conceptual Characters', *The Sociological Review*, 63.1 (2015), 79–101.

FIG. 6.1 Barcelona Pavilion, above and below ground (photos and composition: Andrés Jaque, 2012)

6

OUTING MIES' BASEMENT: DESIGNS TO RECOMPOSE THE BARCELONA PAVILION'S SOCIETIES

Andrés Jaque

ARCHITECTURAL PRACTICES ARE MEANT TO ENGAGE SOCIALLY THROUGH transformation of the social – whether by bringing in non-existing possibilities or reexamining old ones. Yet the field of architecture has often struggled with conceptualising the role of architectural practices within the processes by which associations rearticulate, particularly when dealing with the so-called masterpieces of modern architecture, whose exceptionality is often described as the outcome of their capacity to transcend the mundane. Among these masterpieces stands the Barcelona Pavilion, the 1986 reconstruction of the German National Pavilion, which was designed for the 1929 Barcelona International Exhibition by Ludwig Mies van der Rohe and Lilly Reich, major figures of the twentieth-century German architectural avant garde. After decades of influencing architecture, the 1929 Pavilion still stands, with its almost complete lack of furniture, as an exemplar of formal minimalism. In 1929, journalists could read its features as evidence of the Pavilion's detachment from the ordinary. Rubió i Turudí described it as 'metaphysical architecture' that uses technique to 'abandon the realm of physics' and 'detach itself from the social forces that originated it in the first place' (Turudí 1929). This metaphysical interpretation has played an important part in shaping architectural critics' understanding of the Pavilion. For instance, in 1979, Manfredo Tafuri described the Pavilion as a radically empty architecture available for whatever reality one could occupy it with (Tafuri 1979). This reading of the Pavilion is the one that most Mies-admirers participate in; the current daily management of the reconstructed Pavilion, which since its opening has functioned as an architectural monument open to visitors, has been designed to be perceived by visitors as metaphysical. This requires a great many design adjustments that must be imperceptible so as to make it seem that the Pavilion has always been read this way and, therefore, that the Pavilion does not seem designed at all. The following text provides an account of a number of architectural redesigns temporarily carried out in the Pavilion that were meant to challenge its daily management. All of them were effective to a certain extent in exposing the Pavilion's daily life as a constructed process, rather than as something that occurred naturally, and its architecture as a momentous actor in the making of the milieu of associations the Pavilion exists by.

MIES-KNOWING SOCIETY

Figure 2 is difficult to identify, but it was shot inside one of the best known and most photographed examples of modern architecture, the Barcelona Pavilion (built in 1986 according to designs of the architects Cristian Cirici, Fernando Ramos and Ignasi de Solá Morales). The Pavilion was conceived as a reconstruction of the *Reich Repräsentationspavillon* (the German National Pavilion), designed and built under the direction of Ludwig Mies van der Rohe and Lilly Reich as part of the 1929 Barcelona International Exhibition. According to the Fundació Mies van der Rohe, the public foundation that manages the building and its image rights, the Barcelona Pavilion caters to four main functions: (1) To be open to the public from 10am to 8pm daily, with a 10 euro ticket cost. Visiting the Barcelona Pavilion is a cultural activity that people interested in arts and architecture would plan when travelling to Barcelona. It is part of the informal curriculum most architectural students from European, American and Japanese schools of architecture are expected to be familiar with. (2) To be available for temporary rental. Parties, commercial photo-shoots, cultural happenings, product launches, and wedding receptions are some of the events hosted in the Pavilion that contribute to the building's economic feasibility. (3) To serve as a location where town hall officials take visiting decision makers to provide them with evidence of what Barcelona is about, its capacity to successfully engage on international projects and its belonging to the historical making of modernity.[1] (4) To be periodically photographed as a key piece of Mies van der Rohe's work and to be included in publications circulated on- and off-line.

All four functions that the Pavilion performs play an important role in the making of what could be called 'the distributed societies of *Mies-knowing*. This refers to the collective way that societies constituted by Mies' buildings – as they currently exist, have existed, are reconstructed, or as originally envisioned by the various architectural offices and student groups Mies directed – associate with the fabrication, sorting, archiving, publication, distribution, surveying, exhibiting, celebrating, fictionalising or criticising of Mies-related entities. The participants in this conversation are the many people who are enthusiastic about Mies (who I will call 'Mies-knowers' from now on).

THE BASEMENT

Although visits, events, official tours and photographs are usually experienced as spontaneous registries of the 'whole of the building', they are actually the result of careful adjustments in the material constitution of the building itself, and of its daily maintenance, style and management.

The 1929 *Reich Repräsentationspavillon* only had a small underground receptacle, no larger than 5 m², but its 1986 reconstruction included a 1050 m², 2.4 metre-high mostly underground basement. The basement is not part of the visitor's *parcour*. Until recently, it has never been included in the numerous circulating photographs of the Pavilion; nor has it ever been discussed by any of the many architectural historians, critics or theoreticians who have written about the building. Cirici, Ramos and de Solà-Morales initially conceived the basement as the place where the plumbing and the filtering equipment – which reclaims the water of the two ponds located aboveground – could be accommodated and reached for periodical maintenance, thus avoiding having to do work on the upper floor, which would affect the building's visitors and events. However, the basement ended up performing many other functions as well. The broken tinted glass in Figure 6.2 was removed from the Pavilion's aboveground floor when it was accidentally broken. In the same way, broken travertine marble slabs (Fig. 6.1) and ripped white-leather cushions that once were part of the upper floor's decor are stored down in the basement once they are no longer pristine – to be replaced by identical-looking new ones, so that the upper floor never manifests the existence of accidents, breaking or ripping. Figure 3 shows a velvet curtain faded by the sun. It was removed, replaced by a new one, and put in the basement once it lost its uniform red color, in case its presence on the upper floor reminded anyone that the Pavilion has aged, and also to avoid any dissimilarities from photographs taken of the *Reich Repräsentationspavillon* on its opening on the morning of 27 May 1929, when only new materials where in evidence.[2]

The bottom of one of the ponds was initially covered with black acrylic panels that warped unexpectedly within a few months. They were replaced by glass panels and stored in the basement (Fig. 6.3). One of the stainless steel frames of the Pavilion pivot doors deformed due to its weight and eventually broke at its upper hinge. The whole door was replaced by one with a lighter frame and stored in the basement. Evidence of trial-and-error tentative material development are concealed in the basement, so that the upper part of the Pavilion can be acknowledged as resulting directly from Mies' mind and thoughts.[3]

The basement also shapes the Pavilion's association with different kinds of life. Early in the morning, before the Pavilion is opened to the public, Fanny Nole, a staff member (Fig. 6.6), removes the algae growing in the rainwater that accumulates in the holes of the travertine paving slabs, using for this purpose a Kärcher machine, which injects pressurised water into the holes, and then a vacuum cleaner. Both machines are placed in the basement before visitors are allowed in (Fig. 6.5). The basement is also the place where Nole has lunch, puts on her working clothes and rests. Figure 9 shows the hidden-in-the-basement machinery that filtrates and dilutes chlorine into the Pavilion's two ponds. Figure 7 shows the place where the cat Niebla (Fig. 6.8) sleeps, eats and defecates. Niebla is taken to the upper floor every night to help prevent rodent infestation.

FIG. 6.3 Broken travertine slabs and remaining pieces of Alpine marble stored in the basement of the Barcelona Pavilion (photo: Andrés Jaque, 2012)

FIG. 6.4 Fading velvet curtain stored in the basement of the Barcelona Pavilion (photo: Andrés Jaque, 2012)

FIG. 6.5 Hoses, Kärcher machine, vacuum cleaner and mop in the basement of the Barcelona Pavilion (photo: Andrés Jaque, 2012)

FIG. 6.6 Fanny Nole (photo: Andrés Jaque, 2012)

FIG. 6.7 Niebla's cat space in the basement of the Barcelona Pavilion (photo: Andrés Jaque, 2012)

FIG. 6.8 Niebla, the cat of the Barcelona Pavilion (photos and composition: Andrés Jaque, 2012)

Specific spatial, technological and performative design arrangements are carried out within/by the basement to remove algae and rodents from spaces where crowds use the Pavilion. To effect this, presences like the Kärcher, the vacuum cleaner, Nole and Niebla are convened to realise specific daily performances by which they engage with the Pavilion's ongoing production. These performances thus include the temporary confinement of the Kärcher, Nole and Niebla in the basement, which helps to conceal from visitors the processes and performances by which the presences and absences of the rodents and algae – and of the Kärcher, Nole and Niebla themselves – are distributed and effected. One result of this is that visitors experience the appearance of the Pavilion as a given, one whose association with living beings is embodied in its design and not dependent on practices such as the ones that the Kärcher, Nole and Niebla perform daily.

Two architectural elements connect the basement with the aboveground part of the Pavilion, neither of which is suitable for human circulation: a spiral staircase and a dumbwaiter. The stairway's headroom clearance fails to comply

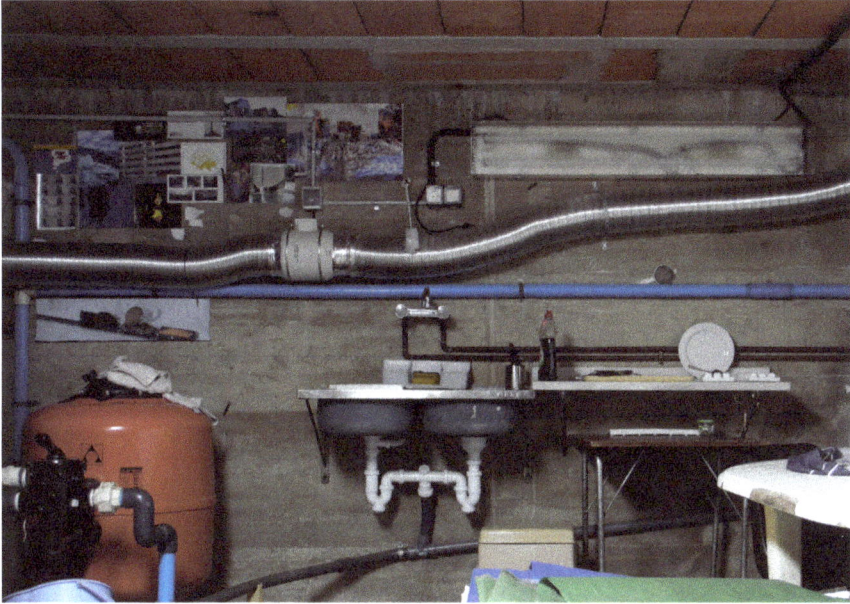

FIG. 6.9 Filtering system in the basement of the Barcelona Pavilion (photo: Andrés Jaque, 2012)

FIG. 6.10 Removed plexiglass cladding in the basement of the Barcelona Pavilion (photo: Andrés Jaque, 2012)

with architectural regulations and, together with the lack of a fire escape, makes the basement unsuitable for an occupancy permit. This could be seen as a design flaw, but it was actually an intentional decision taken by the architects to make it unlikely that in the future the Pavilion's visitor tours would expand into the basement. Consequently, visitors' unawareness of the basement was, so to speak, built into their relationship with the Pavilion.[4]

Carpets, lights, cables, microphones, chairs and other equipment used when space is rented out at the Pavilion is hidden in the basement when not in use (Fig. 6.12).

According to Víctor Sánchez, the Pavilion's manager, no visitor has ever asked about the basement: 'Visitors coming here already have a relationship with architecture and design.[5] They already know the Pavilion. They know what it is that they come to see. They know what to expect. They do not ask, "What is going on?" or "What is it?" They just come, sit down on the benches. Some of them spend three hours like that. [...] Our visitor is one that knows Mies, and one who knows that comes to see "nothing"'.[6]

FIG. 6.11 Broken door in the basement of the Barcelona Pavilion (photo: Andrés Jaque, 2012)

FIG. 6.12 Events equipment in the basement of the Barcelona Pavilion (photo: Andrés Jaque, 2012)

This 'nothingness' is the Pavilion itself, not as the all-above-ground-building that ages, breaks and fades, with spontaneously evolving aquatic ecosystems, mice and rats, produced in a tentative process of material experimentation, but as a two-storey building that is part of and contributes to producing a society of people, books, historiographies, and the performance of visiting the Pavilion itself. Thus visitors photograph it the way it is expected to be photographed, and photograph themselves within the interior of the Pavilion's upper floor – all of them ignoring the existence of[7] its basement, by which certain presences, and certain performances, are promoted and others evacuated. In this way the basement determines the Pavilion's aesthetics and therefore the way its social dimension is sensed. It distributes visibilities and hides the evidence that prove the Pavilion's materiality to be the result of an iterative experimental development affected by contingency and uncertainty, and evolving in time through processes of aging, accident and emergency.

SPOTTING THE FLAW AS HIERARCHY-MAKER VERSUS SOCIAL MULTIPLICITY

The performance of interrogating the material configuration of the *built Pavilion*, in regards to the constructed-in-the-circulating-documents *known Pavilion*, when visiting the built Pavilion, produces a hierarchy among different ways of being a Mies-knower. Mies-knowers visiting the Pavilion often engage in a sort of 'spot the difference' activity that provides opportunities to acknowledge the superior competence of those capable of recognising small differences. The capacity to spot features – such as the fact that it was not the Philips-head screws of the 1986 reconstruction that were used in the 1929 Pavilion, or that the butterfly-like disposition of the onyx's veins shows that it is not the one used in the 1929 construction – identifies particular Mies-knowers and specific ways of performing as a Mies-knower as *advanced* Mies-knowers. Hierarchy makes it possible for the Mies-knowing societies to avoid reading those differences as evidence of the impossibility of detaching the materiality of the Pavilion from the social dependencies and contingencies that shape it. Rather, differences are presented among Mies-knowers as mistakes (mistakes caused by a lack of knowledge or capacity to connect knowledge with design and construction on the part of the architects who reconstructed the Pavilion in the 1980s).

This way of assessing architects' authority by their competence to recognise the reconstruction's similarity or dissimilarity with the 1929 Pavilion played an important role in the decision-making process during the construction of the Barcelona Pavilion. In response to a scarcity of onyx in the last stages of the Pavilion's construction in 1986, one of the architects proposed replacing that rare mineral with a large printout of photographed onyx. The architect's supposed lack of engagement with what is generally considered to be the truthful materiality of the 1929 Pavilion is recurrently narrated in conversations as an evidence of his lack of 'knowledge' about Mies' material sensitivity (Reuter and Schule 2008). As I interviewed different people involved in the daily running of the Pavilion, I was often told about this infamous architect's cladding proposal, and was advised to discount anything this person might tell me related to my project.

In 1938, Mies van der Rohe patented, with Walter Peterhans, a 'Method for the production of large photographs and negatives', with the intention of using wall-sized photographs of precious materials as architectural components. This fact being a lesser-known aspect of Mies' trajectory, most Mies-knowers are not aware of it. It would have been perfectly possible to recognise the discredited architect as a Mies-knower participant of an alternative Mies-knowing society, but this would have eliminated the hierarchy's capacity to deny multiplicity among the Mies-knower societies.

The evaluation of the capacity to 'find authenticity flaws' among Mies-knowers – understood as their capacity to express disappointment when confronted with differences between the Pavilion as a circulating and discussed reality and the built Barcelona Pavilion – is performed by Mies-knowers as a means to collectively agree on how roles are distributed among different ways of performing as a Mies-knower and also as a multiplicity resulting from different ways of constituting Mies-knowing societies.

OTHER MIES-KNOWERS FOR OTHER MIES-KNOWING SOCIETIES

The Pavilion is simultaneously part of many different social enactments. People often access the building trying to find a place to relax or talk after partying in Montjuïc. There are numerous cases of drunk youngsters trying to dive into the 30 cm-deep pond. There are also people who engage in gay cruising at night in its back garden, and others who enter the Pavilion searching for shelter from the rain. Homeless people use it as a place to sleep. Stray cats sneak in to drink from the ponds. A number of realities neither associated nor registered with/by the publications, the photographs, the narrations, the archives and the performances of the previously mentioned Mies-knowing societies are themselves enacting alternative ways of knowing Mies by registering it and visiting the built Pavilion, contributing to other possible Mies-knowing societies.

FIG. **6.13** *Phantom. Mies as Rendered Society* (photo: Andrés Jaque, 2012)

FIG. **6.14** *Phantom. Mies as Rendered Society* (research and drawings: Office for Political Innovation. Graphic design: David Lorente and Tomoko Sakamoto)

FIG. 6.15 *Phantom. Mies as Rendered Society* (photo: Andrés Jaque, 2012)

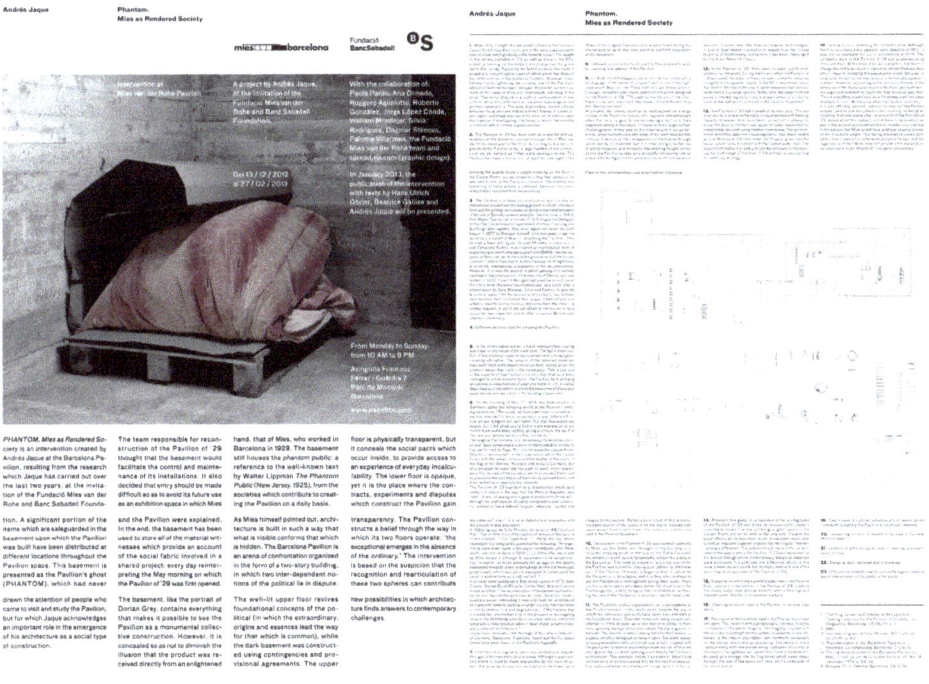

FIG. 6.16 *Phantom. Mies as Rendered Society* (research and drawings: Office for Political Innovation; graphic design David Lorente and Tomoko Sakamoto)

TAKING THE BASEMENT CONTENTS UPSTAIRS

In 2011, the architectural office I direct, the Office for Political Innovation, was invited to intervene in the Barcelona Pavilion through a temporary architectural installation. Our intervention, called *Phantom. Mies as Rendered Society*, was programmed from December 13 2012 to February 27 2013. It consisted of two strategies: (1) Distributing a great selection of objects usually stored in the basement around the ground floor. Faded curtains, pieces of broken glass, broken travertine slabs, chlorine bags, the acrylic panels removed from the bottom of the pond, the Kärcher and vacuum-cleaner, event chairs, Niebla's litterbox, and so on were set in the most visible parts of the Pavilion's upper floor (Figs. 6.13, 6.14, 6.15), confronting the main axes of visitor movement in that area. (2) Maps of the installation were piled at the entrance and offered to visitors. The maps exposed the material histories of twenty-three objects (or groups of objects) taken from the basement to the upper floor, as well as the objects' participation in extended social interactions (Fig. 6.16).

Three periods can be distinguished in the way the Pavilion's societies evolved following the intervention. During the first weeks it was mostly Mies-knowers who responded to the intervention. Their reactions manifested the technologies and practices by which they engaged with the Pavilion, and this made it possible to track the networks that the built Pavilion is part of.

The intervention was temporarily 'the most popular story' in several design-oriented blogs (Fig. 6.17). The stories related to the twenty-three objects were not published online, but photographs of the intervention itself were published. The first reactions, prompted by photographs, were followed by fleshed-out reviews in architectural media by well-known critics, who contextualised the intervention within a number of specific architectural and artistic traditions[8]

The intervention succeeded in redistributing Mies-knowers visiting the Pavilion as participants in specialised Mies-knowing groups.

Group 1. A great number of visitors, not informed of the intervention, conspicuously complained of the way unexpected presences disturbed the experience they had anticipated, as an exacerbated version of the 'spot the difference' practice. In their complaints, *Phantom* was described as a 'mistake' and the

ze en **Dezeen** @Dezeen
An intervention at the Barcelona Pavilion was our most popular story
yesterday: dezeen.com/2013/01/04/pha...**andres-jaque/**
Ver resumen

Ashraf Osman @archimemory
Barcelona Pavilion as you've never seen it before: filled with junk
from its basement | dezeen.com/2013/01/04/pha...**andres-jaque/**
via @dezeen
Seguido por ExStam
Ver resumen

Chenoe Hart @chenoehart
Andrés Jaque clutters the Barcelona Pavilion with objects from its
own history. bit.ly/ZZpLmY via @Dezeen
Seguido por Semana Diseño 2014 y otros 12
Ver resumen

ze en **Dezeen** @Dezeen
Reader comment: "For the first time I'm glad **Mies** is dead"
dezeen.com/2013/01/04/pha...**andres-jaque/**
Ver resumen

FIG. 6.17 Comments in Dezeen reacting to *Phantom. Mies as Rendered Society*

result of a lack of competence on the staff's part in their capacity to assess how to manage the Pavilion. As a result of their confounded expectations, a number of visitors, according to the testimonies of the Pavilion's staff, engaged in actions that challenged the authority of the Pavilion's custodians, such as refusing to pay to enter the Pavilion, or insulting them. The use of photographic cameras, however, often helped those same visitors construct their expected image of the Pavilion. By trying to find points of view in which the main features of the building could be photographed without including any of the objects added by the intervention, these visitors were obliged to experience the building in ways divergent from the usual visitor's tour, in a kind of tactical displacement. The work of finding the place from which the expected image could be reconstructed through photography became a reconstructive performance itself, one that turned the 'spotting the difference' practice into a 'removing-the-difference' one, rendering uninformed Mies-knowers as constructors of the Pavilion as one coupled with its expanded Mies-literate accounts.

Group 2. This group comprised followers of architectural blogs who rapidly incorporated the intervention as part of the Pavilion's temporary online social life. Reviews and images of the intervened Pavilion encouraged them to revisit it. They accepted the intervention as an extension of the Pavilion-knowing society of which they were a part.

Group 3. A number of interactions within online platforms frequented by Mies-knowers had the effect of expanding the intervention's strategy and mobilising unnoticed parts of the Pavilion's enactment. Many comments hosted information on accidents, unknown events or artists' guerrilla works on the Pavilion. Outraged Mies-knowers, who considered the intervention to be misaligned with Mies' 'essentiality', satirised the intervention by distributing images of compositions of what they would consider non-Miesian disgraceful technologies (including buckets, mops or Hello Kitties); they identified these technologies as disconnected to their shared notions of what Mies' essence could mean, but by publishing these images they also made them visible, thus inadvertently creating a collective archive of the counter-Miesian.

ALTERING LABOUR ASSESSMENT

The relocation of a number of needed technologies on the ground floor, such as the vacuum cleaner, the Kärcher machine and the pesticides used by the Pavilion's gardeners, transformed some of the Pavilion's daily routines. Usually, the distinction between the custodial staff and the floor staff is clearly marked: there is a time for the custodial staff (before the Pavilion opens to the public, mainly consisting of cleaning) and a time for the floor staff (after the cleaning has ended). The two staff sections are also hired in different ways: the custodial staff is hired through a subcontracted company, which makes their jobs less durable and more sensitive to daily assessment, while the floor staff is hired directly by the Fundació Mies van der Rohe. The Foundation's endorsement by both the municipal and the regional government means that the employment situation of the floor staff is more durable and less dependent on daily assessment. The intervention's displacement of cleaning objects such as the vacuum cleaner, the Kärcher machine and pesticides rearticulated the way decisions were taken in regards to the way visitors experienced the Pavilion. Nole's knowledge was needed in deciding where the machinery could be safely exhibited to visitors, and in weighing the risk of exhibiting pesticides within visitors' reach. The presence of previously segregated agents in locations where they would have the opportunity to interact with visitors implied/required a redistribution of the roles played by individual staff members. If this could be seen as an opportunity for subcontracted employees to remain vital and enliven their jobs, it also worked the other way around. According to Nole's testimony, a large part of her job was perceived by others as easy to do, whereas in fact she considered it tough and risky. She was responsible for the care of precious materials, and if things were damaged, she would likely be the one to take the blame. Due to the usual time divide between her job and the rest of the staff, others had never witnessed her working. When Nole's work became transparent, any accidents that might occur – and according to her, 'accidents are inevitable' – would likely lessen her chances of retaining her job.[9]

THE STINKY WATER DILEMMA

The displacement of objects made it more difficult to treat the pond water in the usual way. The water stopped being raked, and after several weeks leaves had accumulated and the water started to lose its clarity. Even though the intervention was originally met with great resistance among the directors of the Foundation, the support of art-interested board members, the media impact and the increased flow of visitors attracted by the media attention eventually caused the directors to celebrate the project. Once the pond was filled with objects from the basement, it became too difficult to rake the water. Most of the intervention's transformations remained unnoticed by the Foundation's directors, but there was concern that the water would start to smell, which obliged acknowledgement of the capacity for the intervention to result in actual, as opposed to merely symbolic, ecosystemical transformation. The Foundation perceived the smelly water as a problem that would unnecessarily deter prospective event-location seekers. But since the intervention had been officially presented as a culturally valuable art work, any action to remove the installation would make it seem as if the Foundation was not being supportive in its cultural program, and could even jeopardise its partnership with donors such as Fundació Banc Sabadell that had specifically supported the intervention. Two of the Foundation's sources of income (rental of space and sponsorship) were jeopardised by incompatible versions of the built Pavilion's ecosystems. The Foundation's directors were paralysed by the impossibility of making a decision that would resolve the dilemma. The installation, for those Mies-knowers informed of its context within contemporary art, was already part of a Mies-knowing society, the one in which previous interventions in the Pavilion sponsored by the Fundació Banc Sabadell were already participating in a superadvanced Mies-knowing society. In a step towards a further layering of the Mies-knowers' societies, for other groups of Mies-knowers the accumulation of leaves in the pond was turning the pristine Pavilion into what they would consider a non-Miesian swamp. No decision was taken, so the leaves accumulated until the day the installation closed. Once it was dismounted, the elements brought to the upper floor were taken back to the basement.

Whereas the 1929 German National Pavilion, as one of the preeminent masterpieces of modern architecture, has often been explained by architectural critics, such as Rubió i Tudurí and Tafuri, as an autonomous material entity operating beyond the mundane and the contingent, the role played by the basement of the Pavilion's 1986 reconstruction shows the Pavilion as a socially distributed assemblage, one produced by the association of the building with humans, books, and documents circulating online. The design of the actual experience of visiting the Pavilion plays a key role in both stabilising the extended assemblage and enacting the process by which the evidence of its mundanity is excluded, hidden or policed as external to the assemblage or discredited as 'mistaken'. The durability of this *metaphysically-perceived* assemblage depends on its capacity to keep its constructed condition hidden, a task that relies heavily on the basement's performance.

The intervention *Phantom* subverted the long-running relationship between the basement and the upper floor of the Pavilion by exposing the way that the Pavilion, rather than transcending the mundane and deploying a capacity to accommodate the social, is itself the social and contributes to the making of the social. The intervention enabled this contribution to gain new layers of multiplicity by allowing the Pavilion's assemblages to divide and increase, not least by drawing attention to the participation of the building itself. The intervention also forced the detachment of previously important contributors, such as Fanny Nole, from the Pavilion's assemblage; for instance, in the way Nole's involvement in the *sensibility* of the assemblage was challenged. Including the Kärcher and Niebla in the Mies-knowers' aesthetics, therefore making accessible Nole's performance, eventually excluded her from the assemblage. The dilemma of the stinky leaves shows the impossibility for design of delivering universal enrolment, and also demonstrates the role aesthetics can play in the daily competition between self-excluding assemblages, each based on alternative ways of sensing propriety (in this case, those based on the value of cultural experimentation versus those dependent on notions of celebration based on stereotypical sensorial comfort).

NOTES

1 This practice started soon after the 1986 Barcelona Pavilion began construction, in the years that Pascual Maragall was the mayor of Barcelona. Cristian Cirici, architect and co-author of the 1986 Barcelona Pavilion in audio-recorded conversation with Andrés Jaque, 2011.

2 With the only exception of *Der Morgen*, a 1925 bronze sculpture by Georg Kolbe, that was considered the only 'artistic content' of the 1929 Pavilion. It is part of a two-piece installation, 'Der Morgen und Der Abend', placed at the *Ceciliengärten* at Tempelhof-Schöneberg, Berlin. It was temporarily included in the Pavilion and brought back to *Ceciliengärten* soon after the Pavilion's dismantling.

3 'When it comes to take decisions about the Pavilion we try to put ourselves in the architect's head [in Mies' head]'. Marius Quintans, architect in charge of the Pavilion's maintenance, in audio-recorded conversation with Andrés Jaque, 2011.

4 Isabel Bach, on-site architect during the construction of the Pavilion and the architect in charge of the maintenance after its opening, in audio recorded conversation with Andrés Jaque, 2011.

5 For those not familiar with the historiography of modern architecture, it is important to understand the relevance of the 1929 building and its circulation through all kinds of media in the construction of a shared discussion among most Western-educated architects. Photographs and plans of the Pavilion were included in the 1932 exhibition 'Modern Architecture: International Exhibition' at the Museum of Modern Art in New York, which was remarkably influential in the formation of the modern canon. A black-and-white photograph of the Pavilion illustrated the front page of the catalogue of the 1947 exhibition that the Museum of Modern Art dedicated to the work of Mies van der Rohe, a

catalogue that, according to most Mies' historians, consolidated his image as it is currently known among many architects, and promoted Mies, by means of numerous technologies, as a 'master' of the modern architectural movement. The most relevant researchers of the work of Mies van der Rohe, including Beatriz Colomina, Caroline Constant, Michael K. Hays, Henry-Russell Hitchcock, Philip Johnson, Franz Schulze, Manfredo Tafuri and Wolf Tegethoff have all considered that the extensive circulation of photographs, drawings, models and literary descriptions of the Pavilion, since its construction to the present, has made it the most quoted and the most influential of Mies' works, a game-changing design that anticipates the work developed by him in different parts of the world after he moved to the US in 1937, and a formal and constructive model in the development of corporative, cultural, educational and residtential modern architecture since the 1960s.

6 Víctor Sánchez in audio-recorded conversation with Andrés Jaque, 2011.

7 '[Visitors] always make sure to have the building as a background in their photographs. Like it is happens in this case [pointing to a couple giving instructions to another visitor about the way to include a sculpture and a green marble wall as the background to the photograph the other visitor is taking of the couple]. It is often difficult to achieve, specially in the stairs. [...] I guess it is the normal way for them to "access" a place like this'. Alejandro Raya in audio-recorded conversation with Andrés Jaque, 2011.

8 Axel N. (n.d.) and Pohl, E.B. (2013).

9 Fanny Nole in conversation with Andrés Jaque, 2012.

REFERENCES

Axel, N. (n.d.), 'Architecture and/of the Other. PHANTOM. Mies as Rendered Society by Andrés Jaque', *Quaderns*, <http://quaderns.coac.net/en/2013/03/phantom-jaque/> [accessed 30 April 2018].

Pohl, E. B., 'Il valore dell'infra-ordinario', domus (23 January 2013), <http://www.domusweb.it/it/architettura/2013/01/23/il-valore-dell-infra-ordinario.html> [accessed 30 April 2018].

Reuter H., and B. Schule, *Mies and Modern Living: Interiors, Furniture and Photography* (Ostfildern: Hatje Cantz, 2008).

Rubió i Tudurí, N. M., *Cahiers d'Art*, 29 (1929), 409–11.

Tafuri, M., *Architecture and Utopia: Design and Capitalist Development* (Cambridge: MIT Press, 1979).

SECTION TWO

ESSAYS

7

EARTH, FIRE, ART: PYROTECHNOLOGY AND THE CRAFTING OF THE SOCIAL

Nigel Clark

INTRODUCTION: INSIDE OUT, OUTSIDE IN

CELEBRATED FOR HIS DEPICTION OF ATMOSPHERIC EFFECTS, THE PAINTER J. M. W. Turner is often regarded as a predecessor of impressionism or even abstract expressionism. Philosopher Michel Serres takes a different angle, proposing that the artist is a 'proper realist' (1982: 57). With deadly accuracy, proclaims Serres, Turner reveals a social order being transformed by fiery energy. He is first amongst artists to truly capture the changes under way in the early nineteenth century, as a way of life pushed along by wind, water-flow and muscle submits to a world propelled by steam. While the forms of trains, boats and bridges may still be visible amidst elemental upheaval, what Turner's paintings actually show, Serres insists, are the thermochemical reactions taking place *inside* the industrial heat engine: 'Turner no longer looks from the outside [...] he enters into the boiler, the furnace, the firebox' (1983: 56). While the boiler envelops and harnesses the forces of the cosmos, so too does the whole universe begin to appear in the guise of the blazing energetic metamorphoses occurring within the steam engine:

the engine dissolves into the world that resembles it. [...] Heaven, sea, earth, and thunder are the interior of a boiler which bakes the material of the world [...]. Hotter and hotter, less and less confined by a boundary (1983: 60).

As Serres would have it, Turner's canvasses show us not merely an energetic societal transition in process, but the emergence of a whole new way of relating to and understanding the earth and the universe: a cosmology mediated by machines whose primary purpose is to convert heat into work. But perhaps it is the late twentieth-century philosopher who is as much the visionary as his early Victorian subject. Serres' article on Turner was first published in 1974, in the midst of an energy crisis but well in advance of the rise of global concern over climate change. As climate scientists would soon be telling us, the energetic reactions taking place *inside* the boiler, the turbine and the motor were indeed transforming the world on the *outside*. The industrial heat engine's impact was being felt far beyond the bounds of its metallic casing: its cumulative carbon emissions were quite literally baking the material of the world, rendering the earth hotter and hotter.

Climate change has quickly emerged as an imperative – perhaps unprecedented in scale and urgency – to reinvent the social. Successive international forums, reports and manifestos have called for new and binding international legislation, novel political architectures, technological and infrastructural transition, new economic instruments, and even complete socioeconomic system change. If the semantic core of invention, as Jacques Derrida reminds us, is the Latin *venire* – to come (2007: 6; Caputo 2012: 28), so too is climate change – in the most literal sense – an incoming, an arrival, an event.

Recent research points to an eventual sea level rise of around 2.3 meters for each degree of warming – an irreversible advance of salty and increasingly acidic water into the low-lying coastal zones where our species now clusters in vast numbers (Montaigne 2013). Along with these more-or-less calculable changes comes a host of possible but defiantly unpredictable outcomes: nonlinear shifts in climatic systems, ecosystem collapses, extreme weather events. Shorthanded in the Anthropocene concept is the proposition that thermo-industrially induced changes in atmospheric composition are one of the main drivers pushing the entire earth system into a new state, a possibility that would afford humankind – or part thereof – the status of geological agent (Crutzen 2002; Zalasiewicz et al. 2008; Clark 2014).

At the 2015 UN Climate Change Conference in Paris, representatives of 195 nation states agreed in principle that the prevention of dangerous climate change requires some 80% of known reserves of fossil hydrocarbons to remain in the ground. One way or another, Turner's world of irrupting fiery energy – which is still in many ways our own energetic cosmos – must undergo yet another transformation. A pressing question now is whether the productivity, mobilities and levels of consumption attained through combusting the fossilised biomass of ancient geological epochs can be sustained using alternative energy sources, or whether there needs to be a fundamental shift in the kinds of social existence that we are trying to power (see Urry 2013). A related and no less important question is whether we should be thinking in terms of social groups and formations with heavy carbon footprints renouncing their geological agency, or whether it might be more fruitful to consider what other forms or modalities of collective 'geological being' might be explored and developed (see Yusoff 2013). To ask, in other words, what kinds of geological agents we might yet become.

In this way, it is not only social futures but entire planetary futures that now seem to be at stake. From the point of view of social agency, however, the sheer scale of such issues – encompassing at once the spatial extensivity of the whole earth and the temporal span of past, present and possible geological epochs – can feel numbingly distant from lived experience and collective purchase (Jasanoff 2011: 237–38). It is in this sense that I want to come back to Serres' twist on Turner, and his elegant idea of turning outsides in and insides out. What Serres' depiction of the industrial heat engine as an enfolding of the forces of the earth might offer us is a means of moving between scales. His image of an envelopment, a concentration and intensification that in turn opens outwards to transform the world, can take us from the tangible scale of single enclosed space to the vastness of the planet, and back again. More than just a way of getting our *heads* around planet-sized problems, Serres' folding/unfolding logic points to how we might get our *hands* involved in the crafting of social and planetary futures.

The idea of enfolding a section of the world's turbulence and forcefulness so that it is modestly enough scaled to actually do some work, I want to suggest, could help us imagine spaces conducive to collective experimentation with geological agency.

While Serres offers us an alluring entry point to the folding-in-and-out theme, it is Gilles Deleuze and Félix Guattari (1987) who have more systematically explored the fold as a worldly operation or practice that brings new things into being. Borrowing the idea of 'creative involution' from Henri Bergson (1998), they propose that the most surprising and generative changes in the world tend to come not from following a single line of development (*evolution*) but from an enfolding or *involution* of an outside that is composed and structured very differently from the interior into which it is drawn. 'Becoming is involutionary, involution is creative', Deleuze and Guattari argue (1987: 238, see also pp. 46–7). Such creative involution might include previously distinct human technologies coming together or the conjoining of unrelated life-forms, but so too might it include human or other living things reengaging with the whole geological substratum in some new way (De Landa 1997: 25–8). But Deleuze and Guattari also make it clear that capturing and incorporating elements from a completely different layer or stratum of existence is inherently risky, precisely because it involves a new intimacy with an entire domain of potent and unfamiliar forces (1987: 502–03).

What interests me in this chapter is how – in the context of changing climate and shifting earth systems – we might reinvent the social and ourselves as social beings by transforming the way we tap into, enfold and incorporate the planet's geological strata. What I am not going to do is to try and map out the precise forms that such a geological renegotiation – a geologic *involution* – might or ought to take. Instead, I want to take an extended run up, and ask what the contemporary challenge of constructing novel geo-social futures might be able to learn from a long and rich history of prior social engagements with geological strata.

That early industrial moment that Serres (with the help of Turner) depicts so evocatively was far from the beginning of the enclosure and setting to work of the earth's fiery energies. In order to utilise the potent, condensed energy of fossilised hydrocarbons, the inventors of modern heat engines required a wealth of collective experience in working with fire or combustible matter. More specifically, they needed to be able to contain and control intense combustion in an enclosed space. This ability, I argue, emerged gradually over countless generations from diverse and widely distributed practices involving the use of concentrated heat in ovens, kilns and furnaces: a set of arts or techniques that has been described as 'pirotechnia' or more recently, 'pyrotechnology' (Biringuccio 1990; Wertime 1964, 1973; Rehder 2000). Scholars of the deep history of tech-nological innovation have spoken of 'a single, complex pyrotechnic tradition' spanning some ten thousand years, that includes the ceramic, metallurgical and glass-making arts (Wertime 1973: 676). But whereas modern heat engines are centred on the use of heat to produce force or do 'prime-moving' work, these fiery arts are focused on the transformation of a whole range of materials into novel forms, structures and objects.

In a quite literal fashion, pyrotechnology generated many of the materials out of which sedentary – some would say 'civilised' – social existence has been composed. But it is as much the process as the products that concern us here. Pyrotechnology can be seen as a multi-millennial spree of experimentation – one that involved a whole new enfolding of the geological domain into the social world. It is in this sense that we might ask what lessons, insights and inspira-tions the pyrotechnic arts offer for any current social renegotiation with the geologic. And in particular, what role fire might come to play in the invention of novel social worlds if it were to be set to tasks other than burning fossilised hydrocarbons.

FIERY ARTS AND THE INVENTION OF THE SOCIAL

Revisiting Turner two decades after his first engagement with him, Serres speaks of the painter's 'pyrotechnical canvases' (1997: 2), a phrase that gestures at once to the fiery themes of his artwork and to the more general way in which new modes of combustion were then transforming the very fabric of nineteenth-century society. But Turner, his art suggests, is no cheerleader of industrial revolution. His is a profoundly ambivalent vision of the turbulent new world. And he is not alone. For all their innovations in putting fossil hydrocarbons to work, northwest Europeans have been deeply equivocal about the whole business of combustion-driven industrialism – and *en masse* they have rarely mourned its outsourcing to other regions. Then again, Europeans are not particularly enamoured with open-air fire either (Pyne 2001: 168–70; Clark & Yusoff 2014: 209–10).

By planetary standards, Europe is 'an anomalously fire-free patch', as environmental historian Stephen Pyne puts it (2001: 168). This is partly an effect of Europe's perennial coolness, dampness and corresponding lack of a defined fire season, though it also reflects the intensity of agriculture that can be supported by its recently glaciated soils (Pyne 1997: 18–20). In such a densely gardened region, there is simply not much of a niche left for burning, and not a lot of enthusiasm for letting flames claim a share of biotic productivity. Whereas most cultures worldwide have tended to appreciate the value of open fire or 'broadcast burning' for enhancing the productivity of grassland, scrub and forest, Pyne observes, modern Europeans and their cultural progeny have developed a pronounced tendency to associate blazing fire with disorder and wastefulness. They have come to see open flame as a signal of bad farm management or societal breakdown rather than as a medium of regeneration and new life, a tool of insurgents and 'firebrands' rather than a means of crafting communal bonds or caring for the landscape (Pyne 1997: 162–68; 2001: 145–46; see also Marder 2015). And this tendency to dwell on fire's destructive side seems to be exacerbated by the highly publicised impact of combusting fossil fuels on the global climate.

European discomfort with anything other than fully domesticated flame is paralleled by a marked marginalisation of fire in Western scientific and philosophical thought, as Gaston Bachelard has noted (1987: 2–3). 'In the twentieth century,' adds sociologist Johan Goudsblom, 'social scientists have tended to follow their colleagues in the natural sciences and have dropped the subject of fire from their agenda' (1992: 3). That fire does not have its own science is remarkable when we consider that Earth is the only planet in the solar system on which fire occurs, that *Homo sapiens* is the earth's only fire-manipulating species, and that over the last million or so years the genus *Homo* has deployed fire with such prodigiousness as to have transformed most of the planet's surface (Pyne 1994; 1997: 3). Fire, as Pyne (2015) would have it, is not so much an element or a substance as a reaction that brings together the earth's other elements – synthesising air, water, and earth into a single event. This too is how we might see the role of fire in crafting social worlds. Not only do flames transform the very stuff of the world, but fire also has a special role in simmering, fusing, melding, alloying and annealing the heterogeneous elements of social life into workable unity. To which must be added fire's omnipresent capacity to unravel and obliterate the very order it has helped bring into being (Derrida 1991: 43–4, 57; Clark 2012).

How humans first came to an understanding of fire's transformative effects on vegetation, flesh, wood, bone, stone and clay is largely a matter of speculation. It is with the development of agriculture and more sedentary settlement patterns shortly after the end of the last Pleistocene glaciation – some 10 to 11,000 years ago – that evidence mounts of the systematic use of heat to transmute the structure of inorganic matter (Wertime 1973). There is broad agreement amongst pyrotechnic scholars that ceramics was the first real pyrotechnology, emerging most likely as an offshoot of the ovens whose intense heat rendered grains and other agricultural products palatable (Wertime 1973: 676; Rehder 2000: 42). While the oven itself might appear to be no more than a stepwise development of the open cooking hearth, there is another sense in which we might view these novel enclosures of fire as a new kind of human geological agency, and as such one of the most 'geo-socially' significant innovations since the capture and propagation of fire by early hominids.

With advances in kiln technology in the ancient world came the gradual ascent of a ladder of heat intensity. Higher temperatures enabled an ever-greater range of materials to be subjected to transformation, from the baking of clay starting at around 500 °C through to the 1400 – 1600 °C required to smelt iron and fuse it with carbon (Wertime 1973; Rehder 2000: 6–7). More than a quantitative shift along the thermal spectrum, chambering allows skilled agents to set up and modulate the environment in which combustion occurs – a level of control that could never be achieved with the multiple variables at play in any 'open air' combustive event. And it is in this sense that we might see fire's 'creative involution' into contained spaces not simply as a human achievement, but as a transitional moment in the very trajectory of terrestrial fire that would make it a significant event in the earth's own history (see also Pyne 1994: 889).

A recurrent theme in pyrotechnical scholarship is that the impulse toward heat-induced metamorphosis of earth materials cannot simply be read off the uses eventually found for its outputs. As metallurgist and materials scientist Cyril Stanley Smith observes, 'the making of ornaments from copper and iron certainly precedes their use in weaponry, just as baked clay figurines come before the useful pot' (1981: 242). It is not only that beauty and adornment so often precede – and exceed – utility, but that the very process of discovery seems to resist cause-effect relations (Clark 2015). It has often been noted that many of the thermo-chemical reactions discovered by ancient artisans involve changes too dramatic to have been intentional. How it came to be known that crumbly ores could transmute into lustrous metals or powdery oxides into translucent glazes, it is surmised, could only have come about by accident or some kind of open-ended experimentation (Childe 1942: 85; Forbes 1950: 201). What metallurgical historian R. J. Forbes – one of Deleuze and Guattari's key sources – has to say about his own field would seem to apply to pyrotechnology more generally: 'the early metal worker was not pushed along the path of progress because he had no idea it was a path at all' (1950: 12).

But discoveries indeed settled into pathways, both figuratively and literally. 'Although they might have been launched as innocent and isolated skills,' observes archaeometallurgist Theodore Wertime, 'the pyrotechnic crafts in the years between 10,000 B.C. and 2000 B.C. became formidable industrial "disciplines," entailing the most severe chemical controls on daily operations' (1973: 670). So too were pyrotechnic products channelled into particular uses, both practical and symbolic (Forbes 1950: 11). As the objects fired and fashioned by artisans were set to work, many of them came to play their own formidable disciplining role in the operations of daily life. As metallurgist and historian J. E. Rehder sums up, '[t]he material fabrics of nearly all settled civilisations have by and large consisted of things that exist only because of pyrotechnology

(2000: 3). Or as we might say in another register, the oven, the kiln and the furnace helped forge and weld together an entire 'order of things' (See also Foucault 1989).

In the context of burgeoning sedentary life – as human beings convened in unheard of numbers and unprecedented proximities – the outputs of the artisanal oven came to play a vital role in the ordering of time and space. Just as they could collect and channel flows of water, impound seeds or grains, or store and portion out foodstuffs, pyrotechnic products could also help to distribute and direct living bodies. Kiln-fired materials lent substance and durability to the built environment, a hard-baked rigidity that served to regulate 'the movement of human flesh' (De Landa 1997: 27–8). So too, from out of the artisan's furnace arrived eye-catching adornments and sumptuary objects, to be used in 'visual displays of identity' that signalled where and when bodies belonged in ever-more complex urban spaces (Roberts et al. 2009: 1019). And not least, from the ancient foundries came standardised and portable mediums of exchange: gleaming metallic tokens that both aided the circulation of other objects and provided hitherto unthinkable possibilities for hoarding wealth (Wertime 1973: 680; Goudsblom 1992: 63).

As Bruno Latour noted some time ago, one of the key characteristics that distinguishes human societies from those of other complex organisms is their propensity to extrude, sediment and concretise social interactions into durable objects (1996, 2002). But, as Latour continues, the objects, materials and techniques that we enrol as the mediators of our social transactions rarely function in a neutral and predictable manner: 'They do not transmit our force faithfully,' he muses, 'any more then we are faithful messengers of theirs' (1996: 240). While the proliferation of the pyrotechnic arts across much of ancient world effected an irruption of artefactual quantity, diversity and durability, it is only in retrospect that anything like a coherent story can be pieced together of the contribution these productions made to emergent social orders and formations. Latour's attention to the transmission of force is pertinent, and it might be added that it is not only the power or potentiality of the *objects themselves* that is at stake, but the way these objects actualise and express the forces of *an entire stratum*. For what both the products and the processes of the pyrotechnic arts encapsulate,

I suggest in the following section, is something of the very forcefulness of the earth itself. And it is the experiential breadth and depth of this enfolding of the geologic into the social that makes the ten thousand-year pyrotechnic adventure so relevant for any renewed negotiation with the stuff of the earth.

ENFOLDING GEOLOGY

Excavations of the Neolithic town of Çatalhöyük in southern Anatolia have revealed a remarkable mural featuring a dappled orange mound foregrounded by a black and white grid-like formation (Schmitt et al. 2014). Some researchers refer to the image as the earliest documented landscape painting; others consider it the world's oldest warning sign. Though interpretations abound, the favoured reading is of a volcano spewing effluvia over a townscape. It has been proposed that the twin peaks of the frescoed mountain represent the double volcanic cones of Hasan Dağı, located seventy miles north-east of Çatalhöyük. Adding heft to this hypothesis, volcanologists recently confirmed that Hasan Dağı erupted around 9000 BP (Before Present), a date just prior to the estimated execution of the wall painting (Schmitt et al. 2014).

Widely regarded as the largest and best-preserved Neolithic settlement, Çatalhöyük is also the site of some of the oldest known pottery works. Excavated kilns, featuring thick walls, built-in covers, and flues to regulate air supply are again dated at around 9000 BP (Rehder 2000: 9; Joseph 1999: 1–2). Çatalhöyük is also one of the earliest sites with plentiful copper artefacts and clear evidence of working with metal. The ceramic-copper concurrence may be more than coincidental. Copper was most likely the first terrestrial metal that artisans learnt to smelt, a process entailing the use of heat and a reducing agent to trigger a chemical reaction that separates metal from its ore. The smelting of copper calls for temperatures of around 1100 °C, well within the thermal range of the pottery kilns found in the Anatolian settlement. The reduced or oxygen-poor atmosphere required to fire the red or black clay used by the potters of Çatalhöyük would also have produced the conditions required to melt copper ores (Joseph 1999: 2). Moreover, azurite and malachite, two of the ores of copper, are known to have been introduced into the firing processes in the form of pigments used in the decorative glazing of ceramics, leading to speculation about the accidental discovery of smelting in the course of ceramic production (Aitchison 1960: 40).

Whether this adds up to evidence of very early copper smelting in Çatalhöyük, or whether the metalwork recovered from the excavations relied upon naturally occurring – hence unsmelted – copper, is still debated (Birch et al. 2013). Even more speculative is the existence of any clear connection between pyrotechnic breakthroughs and proximity to volcanic activity, though it is well established that the active plate tectonics of this region – a belt of folding and thrust where the Eurasian and Arabian plates meet – results in crustal stresses that squeeze out exceptionally rich and visible fluxes of metallic ores (Yener 2000: 1–2). But direct causal linkages need not concern us here. What I want to explore is a more general line of inquiry that contextualises pyrotechnic innovation within an expanded field of geological eventfulness and potentiality.

Both the well-documented climatic volatility of the Pleistocene and the possibility of an unstable Anthropocene have served to accentuate the stability of the Holocene. This exceptional spell of climatic quiescence is often credited with providing the preconditions for agriculture and sedentary life. It is important to note, however, that the exit from the last Pleistocene glacial maximum was anything but smooth. Between 15,000–6,000 BP, a span that includes the early Holocene and takes us into the heart of the pyrotechnic developments in question, sea levels rose by 120–130 meters (Nunn 2012). Not only were coastlines drowning and new alluvial flats forming, there is strong evidence that the crustal stresses caused by changing ice volumes triggered an intensification of volcanic activity. As geophysicist Bill McGuire and his colleagues demonstrate in a study of the eastern Mediterranean, despite the distance of the volcanic edifices from the melting ice sheets, there is a significant correlation between rapid sea level rise from 17,000–6,000 BP and enhanced frequency of explosive activity of volcanoes (1997).

For their human witnesses, such geological upheavals can be experienced as both threat and incitement, as Immanuel Kant (2005: 75–6) ventured in the latter 18th Century. Philosopher Elizabeth Grosz puts a more Deleuzean spin on this intuition. Grosz sets out not from any Kantian sense of the innate powers of the human subject to rise above the chaos of the cosmos, but from the idea that human practical and creative capacities are ultimately an extension of the dynamism and self-differentiating structure of the universe itself (2008: 19). For her, *art* – understood in the broadest sense – is the propensity of human and nonhuman life to express itself in ways that exceed immediate need or utility:

> Art is an agent of change in life, a force that harnesses all the other forces of the earth, not to make sense of them, not to be useful, but to generate affects and to be affected, to affect subjects, but also objects and matter itself (2011: 189).

These same inhuman forces of the earth and cosmos that threaten to overwhelm us, Grosz argues, also provide 'the excess of colors, forms, materials' that are taken up, extended and elaborated upon in creative processes (2008: 9). But this is not a matter of plunging unprotected into the fire, the volcano, or the tumult of biological life – which would be more than most of us could endure. Drawing on Deleuze and Guattari's creative involution theme – and their injunction to experiment cautiously – Grosz speaks of the need to extract, isolate and envelop something of the forcefulness of the earth in order to bring it down to human scale. Just as 'the living produce a barrier, a cell, an outline, a minimal space or interval that divides it from its world', any other creative agent must find a way to calve off a more hospitable interior from a vast and potentially hostile exteriority (Grosz 2011: 38).

Though Grosz does not explicitly engage with the pyrotechnic arts, her logic of an extrapolation on the forces of the earth played out on a manageable scale would seem to be exemplified by the walling of fire in a robust chamber, the control of atmospheres of combustion, and the application of heat to metamorphose matter. Which is to say that we might conceive of the oven, the kiln, the furnace as means to 'temporarily and provisionally slow down chaos enough to extract from it something not so much useful as intensifying, a performance, a refrain, an organization of color [...]' (Grosz 2008: 3). Or as Michel Serres puts it, in a related sense, 'The furnace is the engine for going back toward chaos'

(1983: 61). Mythopoeic accounts of pyrotechnology are, of course, replete with volcanic imagery. But Grosz's diagramming of the creative impulse, with its reference to specific physical forces – 'the relation between fields, strata, and chaos', 'the geology of the earth' – invites a more literal interpretation (2011: 45; 2008: 45). Such a reading would take seriously the rise and fall of sea levels, climatic turbulence, and volcanic and seismic activity.

Not merely a backcloth or context, nor even an object of representation like the Çatalhöyük mural, *the geologic* manifests itself in the pyrotechnic arts as process or force. Rehder points out that as ancient artisans improved their pyrotechnic skills, their kilns and furnaces regularly achieved levels in excess of 1200–1300 °C. This, he reminds us, is the temperature that volcanologists believe to be the maximum heat of molten lava (Rehder 2000: 54). And indeed, excepting only lightning, this is the highest temperature naturally occurring anywhere on the surface of the planet. Across much of the ancient world, then, wherever pyrotechnology emerged or spread, human settlements forged themselves around and through heat intensities rivalling those of the most powerful 'inhuman' forces on earth.

We might say that what the pyrotechnic arts do is to introduce the igneous and metamorphic processes of the earth itself into the very core of social existence. In short, pyrotechnology installs the transformative power of volcanism and other geologic forces in the space of the village, on the street corner, in the rhythms of everyday life. And this is much more than just a diffusion or multiplication of force. Over the generations, artisans attempted to transmute nearly every conceivable mineral element. They explored spaces of possibility that included compounds, variations and embellishments as yet unrealised by the earth itself. Many of the resulting products have a beauty and exuberance that still enchants contemporary audiences, while the skills that were acquired are often credited with being vital precursors of the scientific knowledge and industrial techniques of the modern world (Smith 1981: 242, 203–06; see also Childe 1942).

In retrospect, we can track continuities between the chambered fire of the ancient world and the heat engines that powered the eighteenth and nineteenth-century industrial revolution. Without the experience of controlling heat in robust chambers, and without the metals and the metalworking skills to construct these casings, there would have been no blazing boilers, no steam-powered machines, no internal combustion engines. But the emergence of industrial machinery fuelled by buried hydrocarbons is by no means a necessary end-point of pyrotechnical innovation. This is no simple progression, no 'path of progress' – to recall Forbes' point about metallurgy. What is vital to remember is that the chambered fire of the pyrotechnic artisan is intended to transmute the structure and properties of heterogeneous materials into new forms. For the firebox of the modern era, on the other hand, metamorphosis is simply the means to an end. The contained fire of the industrial heat engine is primarily devoted to the conversion of fuel into regular and replicable motive or kinetic functions. From the point of view of the power these new machines unleash, they represent a massive *expansion* on the exertions of their predecessors. But from the perspective of their metamorphic or transformational capacities, the application of chambered fire to prime moving or mechanical work can be seen as an equally momentous *contraction* (Clark & Yusoff 2014: 212; Clark 2015). From being 'the great transmuter' (Pyne 2001: 120), fire has been reduced to pushing and shoving.

It is in this sense – rather than in any notion of pure aestheticism or art for art's sake – that we might reconsider the open-endedness and experimentality of the pyrotechnic arts in our own era. As we have seen, the current environmental predicament is beginning to prompt industrialised social formations to turn away from their dependence on fossilised hydrocarbons. Both conventional economic logic and ecological critique, in this context, exhort us to do more with less, to tighten and close the circuits of matter-energy. But the carbon descent question can also be posed in terms of what other geological strata, what other forces of the earth, we might turn to. Put differently, we might ask what else energy or matter is for, and what else we might do with fire. Such questions do not neces-sarily eschew efficiency or renounce restraint. What they can do, however, is to draw us away from the preoccupation with how much work we can get out of available energy, and turn us toward all the other possibilities that still inhere in the geological strata. These are questions, practical challenges, that bring us to the potentiality of the earth itself – to the field of forces, processes and properties that, as Deleuze or Grosz would insist, is far in excess of whatever humans or other forms of life have yet been able to make of it.

And it is this sense of the virtuality of the earth exceeding its actuality that invites renewed mineral-energetic probing, new variations on igneous and metamorphic themes, and further elaboration on the rhythms and singularities of the earth, experimental modes that are likely to be as least as much aesthetic as techno-scientific or managerial (Clark 2015). So too, as we enter an era of possible destabilisation of earth systems, is it important to keep in mind that the pyrotechnical innovations of the early–mid Holocene may have responded, in some indeterminate and irrecoverable way, to the provocations of geologic and climatic unrest. It would be unfortunate if this were to be taken as a call to aestheticise or dramatise geophysical catastrophe. But what it might do is to help attune us to the ways in which the earth explores its own possibilities, crosses its own thresholds, enacts its own experiments. And to remind us that this very unruliness is what we will need to reach into, enfold and take hold of in order to perform our versions of experimentation.

FUTURE EARTH AND PLANETARY CONVENTIONS

By tracking the chambering of heat back to its primordial moments, and in characterising pyrotechnic origins as an experimental involution of the geological substrata, I have sought to salvage a genre of inventive engagements with the earth from the dense accretion of functions and purposes it later accrued. This is not to ascribe an originary purity to artful genesis, or to assume that all functionality is a fall from grace. If artistic expression is indeed an extrapolation of the excessive forces of an inhuman earth, there is no guarantee of beneficent creation. As Elizabeth Grosz reminds us, 'art is also capable of that destruction and deformation that destroys territories and enables them to revert to the chaos from which they were temporarily wrenched' (2008: 13). Or in the words of Cyril Stanley Smith, reviewing the long history of craft production, 'aesthetic creation suggests things that may, if widely adopted, cause disruptive change' (1981: 346). And if fire is the medium of our creative ventures, that capacity for destruction or disruption will never be far away. It will be as near as a stray spark, or a flicker of inattention.

To play on the theme of primordial pyrotechnology is not to imply that we can or should dis-assemble subsequent developments and start anew from some baseline of raw, uncommitted artisanal potentiality. But it is to suggest that any pathway out of the 'new and burning society' we have composed for ourselves will need to engage on the same excessive and unstable plane. Just as our species has gradually learnt how to isolate, encapsulate and intensify the unruly forces of the cosmos, so too will we have to learn to enfold, enclose and elaborate on the chaos that our own activities have added to the earth's inherent turbulence.

We should be mindful too that any call for a new societal involution of earth processes quickly comes up against complications or tensions that inhere in the very idea of invention. Deleuze and Guattari are insistent that destratification – the reworking of the earth's constitutive strata – needs to be undertaken with caution. It calls for trial runs, a slow accumulation of skill and experience, a safety net of fallow spaces and uncommitted resources to fall back on if things go wrong (1987: 161). Such provisos suggest that, for all their affirmation of surprise and open-endedness, Deleuze and Guattari's bid 'for a new earth and people that do not yet exist' (1994: 108) requires a carefully modulated play of difference and repetition, exuberance alloyed with restraint: 'It is through a *meticulous* relation to the strata', they contend, 'that one succeeds in freeing lines of flight' (Deleuze & Guattari 1987: 161. My emphasis).

This tempering of 'unheard-of becomings' with circumspection and care – what we might see as an originary complication of inventiveness – is more explicitly analysed by Derrida. For Derrida, as for Deleuze and Guattari, a creative event implies a rupture with the known and the familiar, and thus an inevitable degree of disturbance and transgression: 'An invention always presupposes some illegality, the breaking of an implicit contract; it inserts a disorder into the peaceful ordering of things, it disregards the proprieties' (Derrida 2007: 1). At the same time, to make any real difference to its world – to have a future – an invention must also entail a certain *conventionality*: it must abide by the rules or habits by which new things are admitted into their social context, passed on and disseminated:

It will only receive its status of invention, [...] to the extent that th[e] socialization of the invented thing is protected by a system of conventions that will at the same time ensure its inscription in a common history, its belonging to a culture: to a heritage, a patrimony, a pedagogical tradition, a discipline, a chain of generations. Invention begins by being susceptible to repetition, exploitation, reinscription (Derrida 2007: 6).

While we might now trouble Wertime's assumption that pyrotechnic crafts began as *innocent* skills, his observations about their developments into *disciplines* is well made, not just with regard to the technical aspects of controlling matter, but also in the sense of the complex customs, codes and ritual through which knowledge has been both protected and transmitted. Indeed, the very propensity of socio-material processes and techniques to transmit their effects 'unfaithfully' depends, ultimately, on the presence of more or less effective modes of uptake, transmission and iterability.

To affirm such logics of invention – with their indissociability of eventful rupture and conventionality – is to raise questions about the distinctiveness of generative processes in the stratum that is recognisable as 'ours'. However much the creative involutions of other strata give rise to novel structures, assemblages, and operational possibilities, and however much the forces of the 'inhuman' strata might energise, summon or provoke our own becomings, there are limits to how far we might wish to stretch the idea of conventionality. Though other sites or modes of creativity 'provide [...] the ground and support for human invention,' Derrida notes, 'no one has ever authorized himself to say of animals that they invent' (2007: 25), a verdict we can assume he would extend to other nonhuman creatures and to the geologic. So too do we need to recall that for all their affording of ontological dignity to the articulations of all strata, Deleuze and Guattari acknowledge specific cultural-linguistic capacities that help merit human productions a stratum of their own.

Today, as evidence of intensifying planetary heating provokes increasingly urgent demands for the reinvention of human socio-material relations with the rest of the earth, the tension between the advent of the wholly new and the conventions through which novelty is re-inscribed flares with especial intensity.

'Even a summit of all the nations of the earth, preceded by the most strident media campaigns, could not digest an issue so intractable and so enmeshed in contradictory interests as this one', remarks Latour of the current deadlock in climate change politics (2010: 228–9).

On the one hand, this impasse appears to issue from the limitations of unfathomably complex and interminable deliberation. Global forum after global forum seem at best only to generate new conventions, but never an inventive rupture with existing socio-material orders. On the other hand, the procedural commitment to fairness, inclusion and consensus to which many climate negotiators ascribe is increasingly haunted by the possibility of new kinds of grand scale physico-material intervention: geoengineering schemes or climate modification experiments that vaunt their inventiveness while threatening to circumvent deliberative processes (Clark 2013). In short there appears the disconcerting spectacle of two extremes: convention bereft of invention, and invention untethered from convention.

Under the current compulsion to invent – to contrive new legislation, techniques, products – Derrida detects a further paradox. In the context of political economic competition and national rivalries, it is increasingly seen as necessary to pre-order and institutionalise creative change. Not only is the logic of attempting to programme the unforeseeable inherently contradictory, Derrida contends, but the demand for incessant innovation soon becomes tiresome and draining:

> A closer analysis should show why it is then the word "invention" that imposes itself [...]. And why this desire for invention, which goes so far as to dream of inventing a new desire, remains, to be sure, contemporary with a certain experience of fatigue, of weariness, of exhaustion (2007: 23).

Climate change – a topic Derrida himself barely broached – couples the almost universal exhortation to innovate with the enervation attending interminable effort in a world of diminishing resources. As philosopher Michael Marder notes, the consequence of intensifying industrial combustion is burnout, 'the breakdown and exhaustion we experience when we run out of the mental and physical resources to be expanded at an ever-accelerating rhythm of self-incineration'

(2015: 94). Burnout, Marder insists, is at once a planetary and a personal predicament. Under such pressure, even the ardent affirmation of creativity in radical visions might come to seem world wearying. While broadly sympathetic to Deleuzoguattarian notions of becoming, ethical philosopher John Caputo eventually draws breath and confesses, 'I find it too exhausting, all this outpouring and overflowing, all this firing away of forces night and day' (1993: 53), a lament we might imagine the earth itself echoing.

Given conditions of compounding emergency and exhaustion, it is small wonder that the planet-scaled task of reinventing the social threatens to overwhelm. Faced with the daunting prospect of crafting what we might refer to as new 'geosocial formations' (Clark & Yusoff 2014: 224), the deep history of pyrotechnology offers no answers, though it may offer hints, clues and prompts about how we might 'learn to be affected' by the matter-energy of the earth (see Latour 2004). The key to the success of the emergent pyrotechnic complex seems to have been its ability to corral, enclose and insulate; to downsize vast and intimidating forces to an intimate level; to sublimate inhuman forces into everyday spaces. Attuned to accidents, perhaps enamoured with chance and surprise, pyrotechnic knowledge was also enframed in lore and convention, though its inscription into the social frequently took forms we would hardly wish to revisit.

That the work of reinventing the social in a turbulent world might respond to the allure of matter and flame, that critical practice might coalesce around palpable workings with the grit and grain of proximate materials, points towards social sciences with a more sensuous touch and an expanded toolkit. Our focus on the *longue durée* of artisanal practice serves as a reminder that metaphors of forging, shaping, moulding or constructing social worlds have literal traces, and in turn hints at the distance that has opened up between modern social thought and what was once the everyday work of manipulating matter-energy to make useful and beautiful things (see Ingold 2013; Guggenheim et al., this volume). More than simply admonishing would-be earth system engineers for their circumvention of socio-political procedures, it might be time for social thinkers to seek out modes of geotechnics and material-energetic experiments more to our liking. It should also be kept in mind that there are likely many more pathways along which the materials of the earth might be coaxed than have yet been pursued, though neither should we downplay looming doubts about whether we still have time or energy enough to craft whole new social worlds out of the intransigent forces of the earth.

REFERENCES

Aitchison, L., *A History of Metals, Volume 1* (London: MacDonald & Evans, 1960).

Bachelard, G., *The Psychoanalysis of Fire* (London: Quartet, 1987 [1938]).

Biringuccio, V., *The Pirotechnia* (New York: Dover Publications, 1990 [1540]).

Bergson, H., *Creative Evolution* (Mineola, NY: Dover Publications, 1998 [1911]).

Caputo, J., *Against Ethics* (Bloomington, Indiana University Press, 1993).

——'Teaching the Event: Deconstruction, Hauntology, and the Scene of Pedagogy' in C. Ruitenberg, ed., *Philosophy of Education 2012* (Urbana, IL: Philosophy of Education Society, 2012), pp. 23–34.

Childe, G., *What Happened in History* (Harmondsworth: Penguin, 1942).

Clark, N., 'Rock, Life, Fire: Speculative Geophysics and the Anthropocene', *Oxford Literary Review* 34.2 (2012), 259–76.

——'Geoengineering and Geologic Politics', *Oxford Literary Review*, 34.2 (2013), 259–76.

——Geo-Politics and the Disaster of the Anthropocene, in M. Tironi, I. Rodriguez-Giralt, and M. Guggenheim, eds., *Disasters and Politics: Materials, Experiments, Preparedness* (Oxford: Blackwell, 2014), pp. 19–37.

——'Fiery Arts: Pyrotechnology and the Political Aesthetics of the Anthropocene', *GeoHumanities* 1.2 (2015), 266–84.

Clark, N., and K. Yusoff, 'Combustion and Society: A Fire-Centred History of Energy Use', *Theory, Culture & Society*, 31.5 (2014), 203–26.

Crutzen, P., 'Geology of Mankind', *Nature* 415.6867 (2002), 23.

De Landa, M., *A Thousand Years of Nonlinear History* (New York: Swerve, 1997).

Deleuze, G., and F. Guattari, *A Thousand Plateaus: Capitalism and Schizophrenia* (Minneapolis: University of Minnesota Press, 1987).

——*What is Philosophy?* (London: Verso, 1994).

Derrida, J., *Cinders* (Lincoln and London: University of Nebraska Press, 1991).

——*Psyche: Inventions of the Other* (Stanford, CA: Stanford University Press, 2007).

Forbes, R. J., *Metallurgy in Antiquity* (Leiden: E. J. Brill, 1950).

Foucault, M., *The Order of Things: An Archaeology of the Human Sciences* (London: Routledge, 1989).

Goudsblom, J., *Fire and Civilization* (London: Allen Lane the Penguin Press, 1992).

Grosz, E., *Chaos, Territory, Art: Deleuze and the Framing of the Earth* (Durham, NC: Duke University Press, 2008).

——*Becoming Undone: Darwinian Reflections on Life, Politics, and Art* (Durham & London: Duke University Press, 2011).

Guggenheim, M., B. Kräftner, and J. Kröll, 'Incubations: Inventing Preventive Assemblages', in N. Marres, M. Guggenheim and A. Wilkie (eds.), *Inventing the Social* (Manchester: Mattering Press, 2018), pp. 65–93.

Ingold, T., *Making: Anthropology, Archaeology, Art and Architecture* (Abingdon, Oxon: Routledge, 2013).

Jasanoff, S., 'A New Climate for Society', *Theory, Culture & Society*, 27.2–3 (2010), 233–53.

Joseph, G., *Copper: Its Trade, Manufacture, Use, and Environmental Status* (Novelty, OH: ASM International, 1999).

Kant, I., *Critique of Judgement* (Mineola, NY: Dover Publications, 2005 [1790]).

Latour, B., 'On Interobjectivity', *Mind, Culture, and Activity*, 3.4 (1996), 228–45.

——'Morality and Technology: The End of the Means', *Theory, Culture & Society*, 19.5–6 (2002), 247–60.

——'How to Talk About the Body? The Normative Dimension of Science Studies', *Body & Society*, 10.2–3 (2004), 205–29.

McGuire, W., et al., 'Correlation between Rate of Sea-level Change and Frequency of Explosive Volcanism in the Mediterranean', *Nature*, 389 (1997), 473–76.

Marder, M., *Pyropolitics: When the World is Ablaze* (London: Rowman & Littlefield, 2015).

Nunn, P., 'Understanding and Adapting to Sea Level Rise', in F. Harris, ed., *Global Environmental Issues*, 2nd edn (Chichester: John Wiley & Sons, 2012), pp. 87–107.

Montaigne, F., 'Leaving Our Descendants a Whopping Rise in Sea Levels', *Yale Environment 360* (2013) <http://e360.yale.edu/feature/leaving_our_descendants_a_whopping_rise_in_sea_levels/2675/> [accessed 18 April 2018].

Pyne, S., 'Maintaining Focus: An Introduction to Anthropogenic Fire', *Chemosphere*, 29.5 (1994), 889–911.

——*Vestal Fire* (Seattle: University of Washington Press, 1997).

——*Fire: A Brief History* (Seattle and London: University of Washington Press, 2001).

——'The Fire Age', *Aeon*, 5 May 2015 <http://aeon.co/magazine/science/how-our-pact-with-fire-made-us-what-we-are/> [accessed 18 April 2018].

Rehder, J. E., *The Mastery and Uses of Fire in Antiquity* (Montreal & Kingston: McGill-Queens University Press, 2000).

Roberts B., C. Thornton, and V. Pigott, 'The Development of Metallurgy in Eurasia', *Antiquity*, 83 (2009), 1012–22.

Schmitt A., et al., 'Identifying the Volcanic Eruption Depicted in a Neolithic Painting at Çatalhöyük, Central Anatolia, Turkey', *PLoS ONE*, 9.1 (2014) https://doi.org/10.1371/journal.pone.0084711 [accessed 27 April 2018].

Serres, M., 'Turner Translates Carnot' in J. Harari and D. F. Bell, eds, *Hermes: Literature, Science, Philosophy* (Baltimore: John Hopkins University Press, 1982), pp. 54–62

——'Science and the Humanities: The Case of Turner', *The Journal of the International Institute*, 4.2 (1997) http://hdl.handle.net/2027/spo.4750978.0004.201 [accessed 27 April 2018].

Smith, C. S., *A Search for Structure: Selected Essays on Science, Art, and History* (Cambridge, MA: MIT Press, 1981).

Urry, J., 'A Low Carbon Economy and Society', *Philosophical Transactions of the Royal Society A*, 371.1986 (2013), 1–12.

Wertime, T. A., 'Man's First Encounters with Metallurgy', *Science*, 146.3649 (1964), 1257–67.

——'Pyrotechnology: Man's First Industrial Uses of Fire', *American Scientist*, 61.6 (1973), 670–82.

Yener, K., *The Domestication of Metals: The Rise of Complex Metal Industries in Anatolia* (Leiden: Brill, 2000).

Yusoff, K., 'Geologic Life: Prehistory, Climate, Futures in the Anthropocene', *Environment and Planning D: Society and Space*, 31.5 (2013), 779–95.

Zalasiewicz, J., et al., 'Are We Now Living in the Anthropocene?', *GSA Today*, 18 (2008), 4–8.

8

HOW TO SPOT THE BEHAVIOURAL SHIBBOLETH AND WHAT TO DO ABOUT IT

Fabian Muniesa

IN A REMARKABLE PAMPHLET TITLED *THE WESTERN ILLUSION OF HUMAN NATURE*, Marshall Sahlins wrote the following:

> Time and again for more than two millennia the people we call "Western" have been haunted by the spectre of their own inner being: an apparition of human nature so avaricious and contentious that, unless it is somehow governed, it will reduce society to anarchy. The political science of the unruly animal has come for the most part in two contrasting and alternating forms: either hierarchy or equality, monarchical authority or republican equilibrium: either a system of domination that (ideally) restrain people's natural self-interest by an external power; or a self-organizing system of free and equal powers whose opposition (ideally) reconciles their particular interests in the common interest. Beyond politics, this is a totalised metaphysics of order, for the same generic structure of an elemental anarchy resolved by hierarchy or equality is found in the organization of the universe as well as the city, and again in therapeutic concepts of the human body. I claim it is a specifically Western metaphysics, for it supposes an opposition between nature and culture that is distinctive of our own folklore – and contrastive to the many peoples who consider that beasts are basically human rather than humans

basically beasts. These peoples could know no primordial "animal nature," let alone one that must be overcome. And they have a point, inasmuch as the modern human species, *Homo sapiens*, emerged relatively recently under the aegis of a much older human culture. By our own paleontological evidence, we too are animal creatures of culture, endowed with the biology of our symbology. The idea that we are involuntary servants of our animal dispositions is an illusion – also originating in the culture (Sahlins 2008: 1–2).

Animal Spirits (Akerlof and Shiller 2009), together with *Nudge* (Thaler and Sustein 2008), *Driven* (Lawrence and Nohria 2002) or even *The Map and the Territory* (Greenspan 2013), to name a few recent achievements, exemplify quite well the type of social-scientific streams that justifies the worries expressed by Sahlins in the above extract, as well as in earlier disquisitions (Sahlins 1976a; 1976b). The paragraph following the preceding quote also applies:

> I am going against the grain of the genetic determinism now so popular in America for its seeming ability to explain all manner of cultural forms by an innate disposition of competitive self-interest. In combination with an analogous Economic Science of autonomous individuals devoted singularly to their own satisfaction by the "rational choice" of everything, not to mention the common native wisdom of the same ilk, such fashionable disciplines as Evolutionary Psychology and Sociobiology are making an all-purpose social science of the "selfish gene." But as Oscar Wilde said of professors, their ignorance is the result of long study. Oblivious to history and cultural diversity, these enthusiasts of evolutionary egoism fail to recognize the classic bourgeois subject in their portrait of so-called human nature. Or else they celebrate their ethnocentrism by taking certain of our customary practices as proof of their universal theories of human behavior. In this kind of ethnoscience, *l'espèce, c'est moi* – I am the species (Sahlins 2008: 2).

The breadth of what may be called the 'behavioural shibboleth' is indeed observable in numerous quarters of the social sciences, but also in the conduct of policy and, more widely, in the worldviews that control mundane talk about what is meant when 'the social' is uttered. Why a 'shibboleth'? A shibboleth determines the extent to which one is a legitimate member of a community on the grounds of how authentic the use of a keyword sounds. The shibboleth shall here denote the belonging to an all-encompassing folklore in which the thing that is referred to as 'social' (e.g. 'social phenomena' or 'social dynamics', but also 'social problems' and their 'solutions') is haunted by the idea of units of behaviour that interact with each other (through whatever medium, including electronic mass telecommunication), and which partakes, in one form or another, of the ultimate social science, i.e. an extended 'Economic Science'. What follows is an attempt to contribute to the preoccupation signalled by Sahlins, but to do so in a rather condensed and purposeful manner. The point here is not to analyse, but to alert – and to provide, accordingly, a counter-shibboleth, a sort of an amulet. This might, arguably, be of some interest to those who already share Sahlins' sense of dismay, but it is addressed more emphatically to those who have found themselves carrying out research inside a medium of data excitement (electronic mass telecommunication, for example) or participating in creative disciplines (design, computing, architecture) in which the shibboleth often goes unremarked.[1]

BEHAVIOURAL FOLKLORE

The constant reference to the idea of 'human nature' seems to be, for Sahlins, one particularly salient cultural trait of the phenomenon under scrutiny here. Other manifestations, less vividly marked by the rule of naturalism, might however play a deeper role in the establishment of the behavioural shibboleth. Googling 'society' (vernacular for the quick harvesting of dominant expressions of the shibboleth) might of course precipitate the proverbial images of wolves, sheep and a few leviathans. But a far more telling render of the shibboleth might be observed, in scientific guise, if one looks more carefully: the drawings of little dots with arrows that one is likely to encounter in the course of this visual exercising (Fig. 8.1).[2] Epstein and Axtell (1996) provided a landmark with their pioneering 'agent-based' computational models of 'society' and their collections

of 51 x 51 cell grids in which agents look around for sugar. With the refine-
ment of the cybernetic imagination came the time of 'emergent behaviour' in
'complex systems', a time which duly blended into that of the 'social network'
(Watts 2003). The magic of 'network visualisation' augmented this time with
the spectacle of order springing from the disorder of information (Lima 2011).
One might very well just raise an eyebrow at all this and then pass on. But the
task here consists in furthering the characterisation of the shibboleth within
these visions in order to address its dangers at root level.

The behavioural shibboleth can be recognised through at least two important
structural traits. The first is indeed what might be called the 'little dotted agent'.
The unit of analysis takes the form of a schematic, delineated individual agent
whose conduct corresponds to the conjunction of contextual signals (be they
consumption offers, regulatory constraints, data impulses, monetary incentives,
or such like) and internal schedules (be they preferences, orientations, aversions,
beliefs, habits, desires, or such like), often considered in terms of more or less
neat or limited forms of computation. The analysis of the conduct of this little
dotted agent indeed requires the intervention of hypotheses on human nature
(because such agents are considered to be human) which usually go along the
line of selfishness (maximisation of utility, reputational gaming, opportunism,
survival, strategic solidarity) doubled with some kind of narrowness (bias,

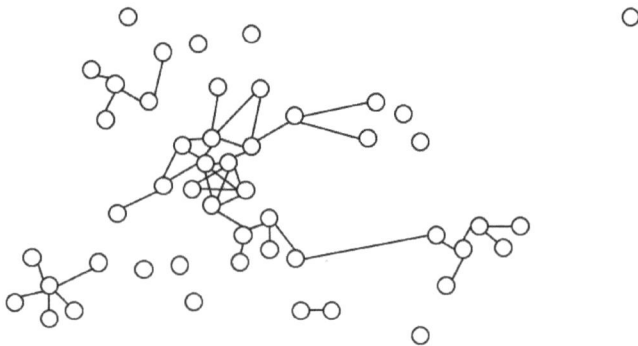

FIG. 8.1   A usual rendering of society (adapted by the author from a quick online
search)

opacity, knowledge deficit, bounded rationality).[3] The conduct of sets of these agents translates into the emergence of aggregate phenomena (also termed 'social') that are mapped and analysed in terms of influence, network dynamics, imitation, calculation, herd behaviour, contagion, socially-driven rationalities and irrationalities, and so forth. Critics have claimed extensively and intensively that this view is flawed – e.g. 'reductionist' – when not silly (e.g. Barnes 1995). But these terms, which may seem rather absurd if one tries to apply them seriously to one's own acts in one's own life, lose their absurdity and gain in relevance when applied to the little dotted agent (Fig. 8.2).

FIG. 8.2 The little dotted agent

The second important trait of the behavioural shibboleth is 'scientific estrangement'. Knowledge produced about the little dotted agent is in essence knowledge possessed by an actor – the scientist – who is qualitatively different from the little dotted agent. In short, otherness is crucial: I am not the little dotted agent. Although reflexivity and self-analysis are not excluded in principle, the idea of the behaviour of agents is in practice usually at odds with that of the behaviour of oneself as a scientist. Scientific estrangement is in part the cause of an interesting paradox in the behavioural sciences: the more the analysed situation gets closer to a process of ordinary life as experienced by oneself (e.g. shopping in the bazaar), the more it will appear as scientifically messy and meaningless (e.g. it cannot be modelled), and the more the scientist will feel alienated. Conversely, the more trivial and alienating for participants is the analysed situation (e.g. bidding in a blind auction), the more the scientist will find it meaningful and controllable (e.g. it can be modelled). This is what Jean-Pierre Dupuy once called 'Von Foerster's Conjecture', in reference to a conversation with Heinz Von Foerster (Dupuy 1982: 11–28; 1992: 255–62). The behaviour of agents is always a curious object for 'us' scientists, even if our scientific penchant is, naturally, for trivial machines (waiting lines, computer clicks, traffic jams). 'Our' behaviour, conversely, irrespective of how poorly trivial it might be (e.g. writing this, arguably), would not strike us as a curious object at all. Otherness, produced through the device of an overhead view, thus stands as a crucial element of the behavioural shibboleth (Fig. 8.3, Fig 8.4).

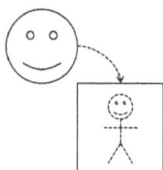

FIG. 8.3
Scientific estrangement

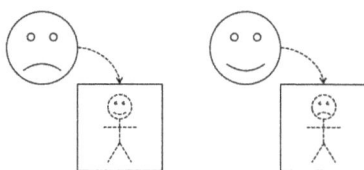

FIG. 8.4
Von Foerster's Conjecture

Both the little dotted agent and scientific estrangement are perfectly legitimate ingredients for particular kinds of scientific endeavour. They are also terribly enticing.[4] But they are also both artefacts of our behavioural folklore, and this piece is just a humble guideline to help us recognise where we are.[5] The academic areas where this can be noticed (once the incantatory effect has been dispelled) are abundant. For a rewarding catch, one has only to follow the track of the 'animal spirits' literature signalled above. It leads inevitably to the realm of behavioural economics and to one of its favourite fetishes, namely the stock market 'crowd', which it willingly shares with the sociological perspectives that see in financial markets, and in markets in general, yet another version of the Empire of Information and its cortege of 'dynamics' (see Preda 2009). Another, quite different variant of the syndrome under scrutiny here can be observed in the particular blend of 'people textures' or 'scalies' offered in competition renderings of architectural designs as a way of improving their behavioural plausibility (Houdart 2013). But what should be done about the shibboleth once spotted?

SCIENTIFIC CORRECTIVE

Once it has been correctly identified, the behavioural shibboleth invites a number of possible objections. It is, at this point, particularly crucial not to fall into the trap of what may be called 'chimeric scientism'. This refers to the all-too-often heard critique of the inhuman aspect of the scientific, positivistic logic governing behaviourism, that is, the implicit assumption that the trouble with the behavioural shibboleth is that it subjects the mystery of human experience to the cold rule of metric reason – the problem, it is said, is science itself, and its monstrous objectifying power. Why not indulge in this otherwise affable critique? Because this would be, precisely, the triumph of the behavioural shibboleth: that of equating its science with sound science, for better or worse. It is as if in effect the two main ingredients of the behavioural shibboleth (the little dotted agent and scientific estrangement) were in fact ingredients of the scientific viewpoint as such (Fig. 8.5). Its condemnation would then waver between impressionistic rejections of scientific 'objectification' in general (a basically hollow idea) and lateral disquisitions on the 'politics' behind the science (e.g. it comes from neoliberal cold warriors).[6] Chimeric scientism leaves the heart of the behavioural shibboleth untouched.

FIG. 8.5 Chimeric scientism

Let us position ourselves instead in the positive, propositional realm of sound science. It is necessary to point to the fact that the ingredients of the behavioural shibboleth, despite the noise they make, have been disqualified to a great extent by scientific investigation, and especially by the scientific specialty whose object is, precisely, scientific culture – namely, science studies.[7] One thing that has been shown and repeated ad nauseam in such quarters is that anyone with an interest in the behaviour of people should develop an interest in the behaviour of people studying the behaviour of people. And this is not a chimeric deviation from the subject matter (an elevation into intra-academic reflexivity) but a result of scientific evidence. I am referring here to the well-known fact that behaviour is an artefact of the behavioural apparatus.

Well known? Well, just think about one particularly pressing problem of behaviour today: that of energy consumption. The contemporary engineer-led turn towards the consumer in large utilities translates into a particularly powerful invocation of the behavioural shibboleth. We are talking about 'demand response' in the energy sector, for example, and the now pervasive use of social sciences to serve it. Two increasingly relevant and quite contrasting constraints seem to justify this invocation. The first is privatisation, and hence competition, with the idea that the disarticulation of public services follows a focus on the requirements of demand (the demanding little dotted agent). The second is the rise of the ecological preoccupation, with the idea that price signals would suffice if the objective shifted from obeying demand to taming it.

But what kind of behaviour is energy consumption? It is the behaviour of electrical equipment and of electricity grids linked to electricity sources.[8] It makes sense to say that people consume kilowatts, willingly or not, but it only makes sense insofar as we acknowledge that 'people' is here a euphemism that stands in reality for buildings, rooms, heating technologies, appliances and machines. Economists may not understand that quite straightforwardly, but engineers do. They do because their job consists precisely in engineering these electric apparatuses. Hence the counter-shibboleth: the study of behaviour shall be but, to begin with, that of engineers and their engineered and engineering creatures. Or, in other words, the right science of behaviour starts when one looks not at the little dotted agent but at the other end of scientific estrangement.

Examples abound in which sound social-scientific knowledge requires precisely abandoning the two ingredients of the behavioural shibboleth indicated above. The little dotted agent fades out in favour of what one can readily call the 'behavioural configuration': collective assemblages, socio-technical devices, institutional apparatuses. There is no shortage of names with which to refer to these units of analysis (Fig. 8.6). And scientific estrangement disappears to the benefit of both a reflexive sense of affinity (the behaviour of science is part of the problem to be dealt with, as scientists should know) and an honest methodological acceptance of the performative condition of social-scientific inquiry (Law 2004). We might want to call 'performative entanglement' the articulation of a scientific antidote to the behavioural shibboleth (Fig. 8.7).

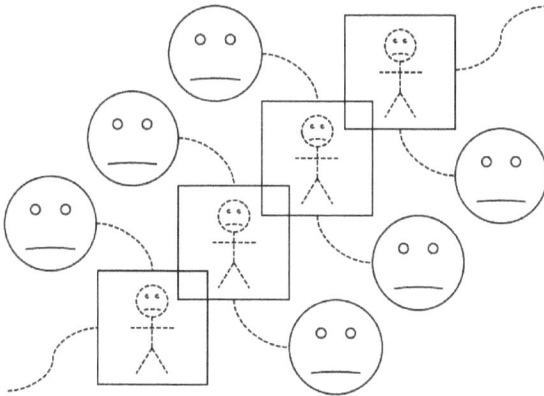

FIG. 8.6   The behavioural configuration

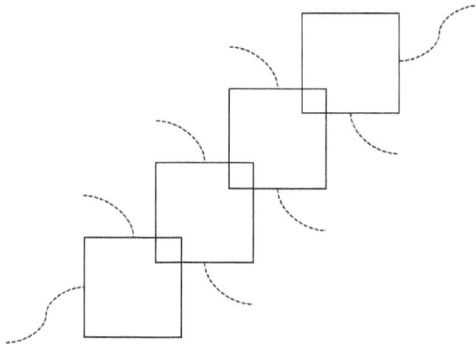

FIG. 8.7   Performative entanglement

INSTITUTIVE CAVEAT

But let us take a step aside. Not all is about science, and one has the right to enquire into other kinds of concerns. Drawing attention to the 'juristic damper' is here in order: the function of the killjoy has been eloquently assumed by a number of comparatist jurists, anthropologists and historians of law that are severely preoccupied with the growing role of the modern social sciences in general, and the behavioural in particular, in the institution of society (Fig. 8.8). Pierre Legendre has been quite explicit about that, in his usual reactionary way (Legendre 1995), and, in different style, Yan Thomas has also dealt with this quite clearly (Thomas 1999, 2005; see also Supiot 2005, 2015).[9] First, these critics claim, 'the social' is, if anything, a legal artifice. The law is the prime vehicle for the institution of society. It is through juristic craft, and more precisely through the performative technology of the juristic fiction, that parties are delineated, objects formulated, agencies attributed and properties ascribed. And it is through jurisprudence, widely understood, that human institutions can be shaped and made sense of. But, second, this does not mean that the law is about human facts, not at all. What the juristic damper tends to emphasise, especially through its interest in Roman Law and its Christian interpretations, is that juristic formulation is an artifice. It is through the articulation of a legal fiction that society can be formed. The 'operations of the law' – to use an expression that happens to be shared by both the French school of the historical anthropology of law and by the North American tradition of legal realism (Thomas 2011) – are performative in essence. They are not there to respect a supposedly positive, social-scientific appraisal of social behaviour, but to institute what society is

FIG. 8.8 The juristic damper

about. The conclusion is that any attempt by judges to ground their decisions on a sound scientific appraisal of social reality is silly at best, reckless at worst.

How does the juristic damper speak to the behavioural shibboleth? The shibboleth serves several purposes. One is to recognise fellow social scientists, people skilled in the arts of observing and comprehending social behaviour. But the second is political: to recognise fellow policy advisers and social engineers preoccupied with the improvement of society (e.g. Banerjee and Duflo 2011). It is through a sound – that is, economic – recognition of behavioural patterns and social mechanisms (their wording) that collective wealth and wellbeing can be augmented.[10] What is the trouble, then? It is not just that the proverbial 'Nudge Unit' (the expert political cabinet that you may enter as you pass the behavioural shibboleth) is fostering an undemocratic understanding of what the improvement of society means (how can the little dotted agent be considered as the locus of sovereign power, that is, as the people in 'We the people'?).[11] In the end, technocratic paternalism is not the worst thing that can happen. The problem is rather the anthropological menace of the collapse of the foundations of society – significantly more daunting. Reinventing society on the ground of the behavioural shibboleth (e.g. through a behavioural analysis of law) would only amount to destroying it, according to the juristic damper.

THE RIGHT BEHAVIOUR

But would society really be destroyed by such a reinvention? Perhaps not. The juristic concern is not raised here with the purpose of intimidating us or of hampering the arguably inescapable progress of the reconstitution of society by other means. What we need is just an antidote to cancel the full impact of the behavioural shibboleth, not another religion. A juristic approach is only fine to the extent that it lays open explicitly how society is constructed. But this reactionary statement is helpful for the articulation of what the antidote should consist of. As we have seen, both the little dotted agent and scientific estrangement can be easily countered in the domain of science, provided we equip science with the right kind of science studies. But, as we very well know, the fact of being scientifically right does not guarantee sanity in the business of constituting what the social should be about.

Social research today is marked by two imperatives that can, unfortunately, turn the researcher into easy meat for the behavioural shibboleth: these are data and design. 'Data' is the name that is given in our own culture of computer business to the traces behaviour (social or otherwise) leaves behind, and ultimately consists of. Abundant and complex, by the very same cultural standard of the behavioural shibboleth, data can orient the researcher towards archetypical problems of visualisation (Fig. 8.1), and modelling (Fig. 8.2), but also of epistemic perplexity and informational escalation (Fig. 8.3, Fig. 8.4). 'Design' is a new word for politics – especially when connected to other crucial notions of our economic cosmology, such as that of innovation – but with politics understood as the modern art of the informed fix. How appropriately informed a design solution is to anything social depends, quite naturally, on the intelligence felt by or conferred to the researcher-qua-designer (Fig. 8.4), but also on the eradication of a view that would downplay this intelligence hubris, or consider design to be itself part of the problem (Fig. 8.6, Fig. 8.7).

There is nothing wrong with data and design as such, but they can certainly encourage a form of scientific folklore that paves the way to the behavioural shibboleth. Who has not seen the little dotted agent lurking in the graphs of the internet sociologist, in the renders of the environmental architect, in the models of the crowd economist or in the indicators of the policy consultant? There is no such a thing as a latent behavioural menace in data and design practices. On the contrary, engagement with data and design opens tremendous opportunities for critical awareness and reflexive elucidation (Law and Ruppert 2013; Lury, Parisi, and Terranova 2012; Lury and Wakeford 2012; Ruppert, Law, and Savage 2013). But data and design constitute a medium in which the shibboleth can spread rapidly once it has made its way into it. What an anthropological interrogation can introduce at this point, better than a regressive rebuff (Fig. 8.5), is precisely a critical examination of the juristic complex on which the very political relevance of data and design is grounded (Fig. 8.8).[12] Where does the ownership, alienability and purpose of data reside? When does something qualify as such, under which jurisdiction and for what?

What is the mandate of design? Where does its authority come from? How are its liabilities formulated? Tackling these questions from the standpoint of a pragmatics of jurisprudence (which is what our amulet would consist of) can certainly contribute to an understanding of 'behaviour' as a compound of imputations, which is exactly what it is.

Should the researcher, then, behave as a lawyer when facing the behavioural shibboleth? Take at least enough time to examine all relevant clauses? Impose a moratorium? What kind of lawyer, though? An anthropologist in a corporate lawyer suit? Marshall Sahlins might agree: in the latest instalment of his take on the subject, Sahlins sees in 'the triumph of capitalism' the crux of our behavioural folklore:

> This libertarian political economy is believable because it is an average common experience of the participants in a full-blown capitalist society in which all happiness indeed depends on getting and spending, as virtually everything is for sale including of necessity one's own commodifiable attributes. The conditions of people's existence then depend on husbanding their monetary resources, always scarce relative to the possible benefits on offer, in order to acquire the good things in life – to maximise one's satisfactions, as economists say. And since, as they also say, there's no going behind people's tastes, and moreover what people desire is apparently a matter of personal choice, it seems to all concerned that the entire social and cultural order is laid down by economic behaviour (Sahlins 2015: 10).

NOTES

1   An earlier version of this piece was prepared for 'Inventing the Social', a symposium celebrating the tenth anniversary of CSISP at Goldsmiths, 29–30 May 2014. I thank the organisers and participants, and the CSISP (now CISP) at large, for the discussion. I am thankful in particular to Daniel Neyland for his splendid commentary, and to Noortje Marres for her continuing critique. The argument borrows heavily from an earlier exchange with Catherine Grandclément and Emilio Luque: I thank them for the concern and for half of the ideas. Acknowledgement is also due to the support of the European Research Council (ERC Starting Grant 263529).

2 Google Images, the image content search service provided by Google Inc., behaves in this regard with more clarity when one augments the usual wording (e.g. 'society', 'social', 'behaviour', 'conduct') with the keyword 'network'.

3 The notion of 'bounded rationality' works as a magic caveat that immediately dissipates the objections that a too narrow view of rational interest might raise. The notion of 'altruism' too, conveniently translates into utilitarian nature (i.e. solidarity is good for others and therefore also good for oneself, since oneself is other for others).

4 One particularly telling example of the behavioural shibboleth's power to defeat an intellectual mind can perhaps be found in the late Alain Resnais, who, after the unsettling profoundness of *Providence*, just bought into Henri Laborit and came up with *Mon Oncle d'Amérique*, a comforting interpretation of the life of characters in terms of their shallow struggle for reward (see Lemerle 2009).

5 It should be noted that this critique cannot claim to be an STS-informed critique, as STS (the amalgam of approaches that gathers under the rubric of 'science and technology studies') can very well and very easily display the traits that are emphasised here.

6 Is the behavioural movement in the social sciences just bad because of its entanglements with the Cold War (game theory, cybernetics, operations research and other instances of 'the mechanisation of the mind')? Or are these entanglements (which are interesting in and by themselves) of little help in preparing a critical reaction to its scientific claims? For a discussion, see Amadae (2003), Davies (2014), Dupuy (2000), Erickson et al. (2013), Hayles (1999), Mirowski (2002) and Turner (2006). Adam Curtis, in his 2011 BBC television documentary series *All Watched Over by Machines of Loving Grace*, provides both a vivid illustration of the span of this movement and a daunting examination of its political implications.

7 I am referring to the portions of STS that engage in an empirical examination of the conditions and productions of scientific activity. For a notable entry-point for the case of the social sciences, see Steinmetz (2005).

8 For indications on the EDF complex, for example, see Cihuelo, Jobert, and Grandclément (2015).

9 For an introduction to Legendre in English, see Goodrich (1997).

10 Among the best antidotes available are Will Davies' examination of the neoliberal critique of law (2014), immediately followed by his critique of behavioural policy (2015).

11 'Nudge Unit' is the nickname of the Behavioural Insights Team (BIT), a service originally set up as a team within the Cabinet Office of the government of the United Kingdom with the purpose of applying behavioural analysis to public policy. The word 'nudge' refers here to the central notion of the same-name bestseller (Thaler and Sustein 2008). On the rise of a nudge-inspired behavioural analysis of law, see Alemanno and Sibony (2015).

12 Engagement with data and design in the field of appropriation art provides, in some particularly remarkable instances, palpable demonstrations of the potentials of juristic experimentation for the circumvention of the behavioural shibboleth. A particularly relevant example would be *No Ghost Just a Shell*, a project by Pierre Huyghe and Philippe Parreno that can be read as a study of juristic artifice in the determination and critique of the behavioural medium (see McDonough 2004; Barikin 2012).

REFERENCES

Akerlof, G. A., and R. J. Shiller, *Animal Spirits: How Human Psychology Drives the Economy, and Why It Matters for Global Capitalism* (Princeton, NJ: Princeton University Press, 2009).

Alemanno, A., and A-L. Sibony, eds, *Nudge and the Law: A European Perspective* (Oxford: Hart Publishing, 2015).

Amadae, S. M., *Rationalizing Capitalist Democracy: The Cold War Origins of Rational Choice Liberalism* (Chicago, IL: University of Chicago Press, 2003).

Banerjee, A. V., and E. Duflo, *Poor Economics: A Radical Rethinking of the Way to Fight Global Poverty* (New York, NY: Public Affairs, 2011).

Barikin, A., *Parallel Presents: The Art of Pierre Huyghe* (Cambridge, MA: The MIT Press, 2012).

Barnes, B., *The Elements of Social Theory* (London: UCL Press, 1995).

Cihuelo, J., A. Jobert, and C. Grandclément, eds, *Énergie et transformations sociales: enquêtes sur les interfaces énergétiques* (Paris: Lavoisier, 2015).

Davies, W., *The Limits of Neoliberalism: Authority, Sovereignty and the Logic of Competition* (Thousand Oaks, CA: SAGE, 2014).

——*The Happiness Industry: How the Government and Big Business Sold us Well-Being* (London: Verso, 2015).

Dupuy, J.-P., *Ordres et désordres: enquête sur un nouveau paradigme* (Paris: Seuil, 1982).

——*Introduction aux sciences sociales: logique des phénomènes collectifs* (Paris: Ellipses, 1992).

——*The Mechanization of the Mind: On the Origins of Cognitive Science* (Princeton, NJ: Princeton University Press, 2000).

Epstein, J. M., and R. Axtell, *Growing Artificial Societies: Social Science from the Bottom Up* (Cambridge, MA: The MIT Press, 1996).

Erickson, P., et al., *How Reason Almost Lost its Mind: The Strange Career of Cold War Rationality* (Chicago, IL: University of Chicago Press, 2013).

Goodrich, P., ed., *Law and the Unconscious: A Legendre Reader* (New York, NY: Palgrave Macmillan, 1997).

Greenspan, A., *The Map and the Territory: Risk, Human Nature, and the Future of Forecasting* (New York, NY: The Penguin Press, 2013).

Hayles, N. K., *How We Became Posthuman: Virtual Bodies in Cybernetics, Literature, and Informatics* (Chicago, IL: University of Chicago Press, 1999).

Houdart, S., 'Peupler l'architecture: les catalogues d'êtres humains à l'usage des concepteurs d'espace', *Revue d'Anthropologie des Connaissances*, 7 (2013), 761–84.

Law, J., *After Method: Mess in Social Science Research* (Abingdon: Routledge, 2004).

Law, J., and E. Ruppert, 'The Social Life of Methods: Devices', *Journal of Cultural Economy*, 6 (2013), 229–40.

Lawrence, P. R., and N. Nohria, *Driven: How Human Nature Shapes Our Choices* (Hoboken, NJ: Jossey-Bass, 2002).

Legendre, P., 'Qui dit légiste, dit loi et pouvoir: entretien avec Pierre Legendre', *Politix*, 32 (1995), 23–44.

Lemerle, S., 'Les habits neufs du biologisme en France', *Actes de la Recherche en Sciences Sociales*, 176–7 (2009), 68–81.

Lima, M., *Visual Complexity: Mapping Patterns of Information* (New York: Princeton Architectural Press, 2011).

Lury, C., L. Parisi, and T. Terranova, 'Introduction: The Becoming Topological of Culture', *Theory, Culture and Society*, 29 (2012), 3–35.

Lury, C., and N. Wakeford, 'Introduction: A Perpetual Inventory', in C. Lury and N. Wakeford, eds, *Inventive Methods: The Happening of the Social* (London: Routledge, 2012), pp. 1–24.

McDonough, T., 'No Ghost', *October*, 110 (2004), 107–30.

Mirowski, P., *Machine Dreams: Economics Becomes a Cyborg Science* (Cambridge: Cambridge University Press, 2002).

Preda, A., *Information, Knowledge, and Economic Life: An Introduction to the Sociology of Markets* (Oxford: Oxford University Press, 2009).

Ruppert, E., J. Law, and M. Savage, 'Reassembling Social Science Methods: The Challenge of Digital Devices', *Theory, Culture and Society*, 30 (2013), 22–46.

Sahlins, M., *Culture and Practical Reason* (Chicago, IL: Chicago University Press, 1976a).

——*The Use and Abuse of Biology: An Anthropological Critique of Sociobiology* (London: Tavistock Publications, 1976b).

——*The Western Illusion of Human Nature: With Reflections on the Long History of Hierarchy, Equality and the Sublimation of Anarchy in the West, and on Other Conceptions of the Human Condition* (Chicago, IL: Prickly Paradigm Press, 2008).

——'An Anthropological Manifesto: Or the Origin of the State', *Anthropology Today*, 31 (2015), 8–11.

Steinmetz, G., ed., *The Politics of Method in the Human Sciences: Positivism and its Epistemological Others* (Durham, NC: Duke University Press, 2005).

Supiot, A., *Homo juridicus: essai sur la fonction anthropologique du droit* (Paris: Seuil, 2005).

——*La Gouvernance par les nombres: cours au Collège de France (2012–2014)* (Paris: Seuil, 2015).

Thaler, R. H., and C. R. Sustein, *Nudge: Improving Decisions About Health, Wealth, and Happiness* (New Haven, CT: Yale University Press, 2008).

Thomas, Y., *Los Artificios de las Instituciones: Estudios de Derecho Romano* (Buenos Aires: Universidad de Buenos Aires, 1999).

——'Les artifices de la vérité en droit commun médiéval', *L'Homme*, 175–176 (2005), 113–30.

——*Les opérations du droit* (Paris: Seuil, 2011).

Turner, F., *From Counterculture to Cyberculture: Stewart Brand, the Whole Earth Network, and the Rise of Digital Utopianism* (Chicago: The University of Chicago Press, 2006).

Watts, D. J., *Six Degrees: The Science of a Connected Age* (New York: W. W. Norton & Company, 2003).

9

THE SOCIAL AND ITS PROBLEMS: ON PROBLEMATIC SOCIOLOGY

Martin Savransky

Ce qui oblige à changer d'optique théorétique, ce sont des problèmes à résoudre

Judith Schlanger (1975)

INTRODUCTION: THE SOCIAL AND ITS SOLUTIONS

YET AGAIN, THE PERENNIAL QUESTION: WHAT IS 'THE SOCIAL?' IF THERE is one commonplace that seems to traverse the multiplicity of practices we have come to associate with the so-called 'social' sciences, it is the implicit sense that the nature of 'the social' constitutes a problem. Indeed, far from serving as an agreed first principle capable of articulating a scientific community, the definition of the social has become a problem which persists in the many attempted solutions that have been proposed as a response to it over and beyond the history of the social sciences. In this sense, as intellectual historians have attested, struggles with the problematic nature of the social by far predate their emergence. Keith Baker (1994: 95), for example, notes that already in 1775 the Comte de Mirabeu characterised the social as 'a dangerous word' whose senses were multiple, while some early attempts at solving the problem – in the sense at least of providing an authoritative definition for the term[1] – can already be found in the *Encyclopédie* of Diderot and D'Alambert (1779).

By the late nineteenth century the problem of the nature of the social may be said to have found scientific expression, thereby giving rise to more systematic endeavours to capture it through the emerging disciplines of sociology, anthropology, economics and psychology (Wagner 2000). It is evident, however, that this modern expression did not, by itself, make the problem disappear. Many of the so-called 'founding fathers' of such disciplines and the various traditions they gave birth to disagreed about the nature of the social, finding possible solutions to the problem in – to name but a few – the mode of solidarity and sociability that emerges from the constraints of a collective morality, as in Émile Durkheim's case; the orientation of human behaviour and meaning-making to the existence of others, as Max Weber would have it; or indeed, in a more Marxist vein, in the historical forms of production and exchange by which individuals become organised into classes (for a detailed study of such attempts, see Halewood 2014).

The nature of the social has been, and still is, widely recognised as a problem, but only to the extent that it poses a problem *for thought or knowledge*, and therefore for particular kinds of scientific inquiry concerned with it. And insofar as the nature of the social seemed to pose a problem for knowledge, the fate of the social *sciences* became inescapably tied to the discovery, or the fabrication, of solutions to it. Thus, in his *Sociology,* Georg Simmel (2009: 27) began his exploration of the study of social forms as a means of coming to terms with, and clarifying, 'the fundamental problem' that called for the development of sociology. Similarly, Max Weber (2011 [1949]: 68. Emphasis in original), who was convinced that 'it is not the "actual" interconnections of "things" but the *conceptual* interconnections of *problems* which define the scope of a science', and on this basis suggested that a new science emerges in the pursuit of 'new problems' by new methods, complained about the ambiguity and generality of the 'social'.[2]

The various functionalisms and social constructivisms that for a period of time in the second half of the twentieth century dominated much of the social sciences did attempt to break away from this problem. They did so, though, by equating 'the social' with reality *tout court*. In this way, if the very existence of 'nature' was to be conceived as a 'social construction', then surely to ask what the nature of the social may be was rather absurd, the mere product of a weakness of thought. As a result, a generation of social scientists was cultivated who, when confronted with the question of the meaning and purpose of the social sciences, were 'much more articulate [...] about the science half of this lexical couple' than about the social half, and became 'satisfied to let the "social" in social science take care of itself' (Sewell 2005: 319).

More than a solution to the problem of the social, then, theirs was arguably a *dissolution,* an active forgetting of the problem that only rendered the social tautological, the pervasive product of a circular play between nouns and adjectives. In this way, 'society' came to be defined in terms of 'social relations' and 'social constructions', and these, in turn, were defined in terms of 'society'. The social became *dissolved* into everything, and apart from it, there was nothing, bare nothingness.

Nevertheless, as problems do, the problem of the social has stubbornly persisted in its attempted dissolutions. Its persistence becomes apparent in more recent discussions by those who claim to have witnessed its demise under the auspices of advanced liberal forms of government (Rose 1996) and are now witnessing its reemergence under different media devices (Davies 2013); by those who have attempted to put it down themselves (Baudrillard 1983); and even by those whose aim has been to 'reassemble' it by restituting a tradition – that of Gabriel Tarde – that had itself fallen prey to the amnesiac solutions that often seem to characterise the so-called 'progress' of the social sciences (Latour 2005; Candea 2010).

In light of the persistence of this problem, the aim of this chapter is neither to simply add another case of solution – or of *dissolution* – nor to argue that 'we have never' really known what the social is. It is not here a matter of explaining the problem away by repeating what, *pace* social scientists' own embracing of his concept of the 'paradigm', Thomas Kuhn (2012 [1962]: 48, 159–60) had already observed. That is, that the social sciences remain pre-paradigmatic – hence pre-scientific – endeavours whose histories are 'regularly marked by frequent and deep debates over the legitimate methods, problems, and standards of solution' that 'serve rather to define schools than to produce agreement'. Instead, in what follows I will attempt to take the commonplace seriously, and to take the risk of thinking *from and with* it by opening it up to a different sense. A sense that perhaps might, in its turn, open up what it is that we do when we engage in inquiries into the social – or what, for want of a better word, I shall here *speculatively* dub 'sociology'.[3]

In other words, it is not so much that we have never known what the social is, but that perhaps we have known it all along – the social *is* a problem. Taking this commonplace seriously forces us to move carefully, but it also demands that we take a risk, which is to shift our mode of attention with regards to the *sense* of this assertion. In other words, it is no longer a matter of asking again what the nature of 'the social' is. As I will show, to suggest that the social *is* a problem has the paradoxical effect of launching us beyond the question of what may constitute the essence of the social, that is, beyond the question 'What is the social?'.

The task, rather, is to begin from the other half of the proposition. That is, to ask what a *problem* may be, once we resist the longstanding habit of assuming that problems are only of knowledge or thought, that they only have a subjective, epistemological, or methodological existence. In contrast, as I will suggest, problems have an existence of their own, a mode of existence that is never just immanent to thought, but to a historical – which is to say, unfinished – world; as such, they can never be reduced to a matter of human psychology, epistemology, or methodology. Problems, in other words, are not that which a certain mode of thinking or knowing encounters as an obstacle to be overcome, but that which sets thinking, knowing and feeling in motion.

Conceived thus, to say 'the social is a problem' may cease to be a euphemism for 'we are not sure what the social is' and become instead a provocation to develop a different kind of sociology. How might we envisage a manner of doing sociology that would take the social not as a rallying flag, not even as its central foundation or ontological ground, but as an open problem to be developed here and there, in the heterogeneous cultivation of a world in process? What kinds of knowledges might emerge from such adventures?

Would we still need to call them 'knowledge'? What might we mean by it if we did? My hope is to suggest that as soon as we come to terms with the mode of existence of problems, what was once a commonplace may become a novel source of perplexity, and a new lure for thinking, knowing, and feeling. For, at the same time, as soon as we affirm that the social *is* a problem, *being* becomes an entirely different thing.

In this way, what follows is animated by the hope that this coming to terms with the *problematic existence* of the social might contribute to opening up, simultaneously, the possibility of a different understanding of the nature of problems, a different orientation to the nature of the social as such, as well as some preliminary steps to imagining a mode of social inquiry that is fundamentally *problematic*. That is, an inquiry at once singularly sensitive to the heterogeneous events by which the problem of the social may and does come to matter in diverse ways, and experimentally oriented towards the creation of novel forms of sociality. It is this mode of inquiry that I will here tentatively call a 'problematic sociology'.

OPEN THE SOCIAL:
ON THE MODE OF EXISTENCE OF PROBLEMS

Perhaps the first step required for the task of imagining a problematic sociology is to attempt to come to terms with what Gilles Deleuze (1994: 165) once referred to as 'the coloured thickness of the problem'. Indeed, as intimated above, my sense is that one of the reasons why the commonplace has never succeeded in becoming a different kind of lure might be related to the fact that we insist on treating problems negatively, as diaphanous, subjective conditions that testify to the limits of our knowledge, our certainty, and to the imperfections of our methods. Problems, it would seem, are what we are confronted with at those unhappy moments when we do not yet 'know'.

Moreover, this requirement to come to terms with the thickness of problems seems particularly pressing for some fields of study that, in the process of trying to dissolve the problem posed by the coming into being of the social, in the 1970s and 1980s proclaimed a certain expertise in what were then termed 'social problems' (e.g. Blumer 1971; Spector and Kitsuse 2009 [1987]). Following the strategy of dissolution referred to above, the turn from the question of the problem of the social to the study of 'social problems' had the effect of melting the thickness of problems themselves, turning problems into nothing but definitional activities, into the *products* of subjective and intersubjective human acts of claim-making.[4] Indeed, one consequence of the then 'new' study of social problems was to undermine the objective nature of problems as such, confusing the actual, progressive determination of problems with the various manifestations and practices by means of which they acquire public expression.

In contrast to this habit of understanding problems in terms of non-being or lack, in terms of subjective or intersubjective (confused) states of mind, 'as though problems were only provisional and contingent movements destined to disappear in the formation of knowledge' (Deleuze 1994: 159) or by the moral resolution of 'putative' – hence not quite real – conditions (Spector and Kitsuse 2009), coming to terms with the thickness of problems requires that we endow them with 'a minimum being' of their own (Deleuze 2004: 67). It requires that we affirm that they do not simply exist in our heads but are 'a state of the world, a dimension of the system and even its horizon or its home' (Deleuze 1994: 280).

But does this invitation to think of the social as a problem and to assign a positive ontology to problems, to endow them with their own thickness, not throw us back into that paralysing habit of trying to determine the ultimate nature of the social as such, of seeking a final word on what constitutes the social? Does this not promote a form of essentialism that rejects that the social could be, in any non-trivial way, *invented*? Is this not, at the end of the day, an invitation to stick with the perennial question 'What is the social?' as if the nature of the social could finally be captured in a single clenching of a mental fist? The answer, as I have already anticipated above, is a resolute 'no' – because to affirm that problems exist does not imply that their existence is essential, nor that a problem comes ready-made and is simply awaiting its one true solution.

Rather than existing as fixed essences, problems 'occur here and there in the production of an actual historical world' (Deleuze 1994: 190). Thus, it is not just that problems *are*, but that they become: problems are posed by events. Rather than emerging from ignorance or from so many other negative mental or epistemological states, in this alternative sense, problems are *the noise the future makes as it is folded into the present*. Problems are, literally, 'com-pli-cations'[5] – relational foldings of tension and transition, of entangled incompossibles that events introduce into the world as they demand to be implicated in it. Thus, the mode of existence of problems belongs to the call, and the process, of inheriting an event; they exist as a reality-to-be-done. This has happened, or is about to happen; it cannot be taken away: how to inherit it? For this reason, Deleuze (1994: 64) argues that, 'the mode of the event is the problematic. One must not say that there are problematic events, but that events bear exclusively upon problems and define their conditions [...]. The event by itself is problematic and problematizing'.

In other words, insofar as problems are brought into existence by the differences that emerge from, and subsist in, those happenings that mark the pulse of reality; if they are the result of time being thrown out of joint, marking a difference between a 'before' and an 'after' (Savransky 2016); then problems are real, but they are not for that reason finished, complete or closed.[6] For if the force of an event is the production of an irreversible call for a future – and an equally irreversible past – then this future comes always undetermined, posed in the form, not of a prescription, but of a noisy, complicated question. In other words, events happen whether we want them to or not, but they are not the bearers of their own signification (Stengers 2000). They demand to be inherited, but they do not dictate the terms in which their heirs might inherit them. Events pose problems, but they never determine how those who are faced with the problems they pose will come to develop them.

Thus problems and questions go hand in hand, the former emerging in fact 'from imperatives of adventure or from events which appear in the form of questions' (Deleuze 1994: 197). Therefore, like James Joyce's *Finnegan's Wake* (2012 [1939]), which begins and ends in the middle of the same sentence; or like Julio Cortázar's *Hopscotch* (1966), which '[i]n its own way [...] consists of many books, but two books above all', and where the reader, by confronting the possibility of reading the chapters of the book in many different orders, is invited to create her own *sense* of the development of the story; like these works, the mode of existence of problems is fundamentally 'open'. Open, that is, in the way that a good debate might be said to be open. Not because it is made of indefinite suggestions and propositions, or because it is thoroughly transparent, but because while the problem demands solutions, these must be produced by the collective practices of those who partake in the task of determining its sense (on the open work, see Eco 1989).

Thus, because problems exist yet do so as the open, incorporeal, troubling effects of events that make up our historical, natural-cultural worlds, to come to terms with the thickness of problems is not, cannot be, a matter of defining their true 'essence'. Rather, the being of problems is *difference* itself. In this way,

> [o]nce it is a question of determining the problem [...] as such, once it is a question of setting the dialectic in motion, the question "What is X?" gives way to other questions, otherwise powerful and efficacious, otherwise imperative: "How much, how and in what cases?" [...] These questions are those of the accident, the event, the multiplicity – of difference – as opposed to that of essence, or that of the One, or those of the contrary and the contradictory (Deleuze 1994: 188).

By the same token, then, once it is a question of determining the problematic existence of the social, the logic of contradiction and closure involved in the perennial question 'What is the social?' ceases to take hold, and we are instead called upon to explore – not in the abstract, but as a matter of practical inquiry – the degrees, manners and scopes in which the social comes to matter as an open problem that demands to be developed. In other words, to say that the social is a problem is not simply to reiterate that it poses a problem to thought, or to particular kinds of knowledge. It is to assert that the social is the name for a problem that the world poses to itself, that certain events pose in the futures they create. Thus, rather than taking a general, unitary abstraction such as 'society' to be the ground upon which a special form of inquiry, a 'sociology', may be founded, we may think of *societies*, in the plural, as the historically contingent, partial, and always provisional *solutions* to heterogeneous events that have here and there posed the social as an open problem to be developed.

To be sure, to refer to the plural genesis of societies as cases of solution for the problem of the social is not meant to imply that we need to speak of many different societies in the anthropological sense of the term. For such an invitation already assumes society to be a bounded entity, and as Marilyn Strathern (1996: 51) has rightly argued, this additive operation cannot free itself from 'our mathematics of whole numbers, the tendency to count in ones'. Indeed, the mathematics of whole numbers that is presupposed by the concept of society as a bounded entity already betrays the open problem of the social as such. By counting in ones, such an understanding of the plurality of societies still rests on an opposition of abstractions – 'society' versus 'individual' – that closes down the problem of the social by conceiving of it merely as the shadow of a particular case of solution. For what is an individual if not itself a solution to a problem that sets a process of individuation into motion?[7] When we begin from the opposition between society and individuals, we are left with the false problem, or the 'unreal question', as John Dewey dubbed it, of how individuals come to be organised in societies and groups:

> *the* individual and *the* social are now opposed to each other, and there is the problem of "reconciling" them. Meanwhile, the genuine problem is that of adjusting groups and individuals to one another (1954 [1927]: 191. Emphasis in original).

Indeed, Strathern (1996: 51) already noted the mistake we make in projecting the problem of the social backwards from such abstractions, 'in that we cannot really count them [societies] up'. As she put it elsewhere,

> anthropologists [and many other social scientists too] by and large have been encouraged to think of number [in such a way] that the alternative to one is many. Consequently, we either deal with ones, namely single societies or attributes, or else with a multiplicity of ones brought together for

some purpose. [...] A world obsessed with ones and the multiplication and divisions of ones creates problems for the conceptualization of relationships (Strathern 2004: 52–53).

Therefore, if we must begin somewhere,[8] rather than doing so from the opposition that would allow us – or not – to add up and count Societies and Individuals as bounded entities, to speak of societies and individuals as plural, lower-case solutions to events that pose the social as a problem is to begin, like James Joyce, from the middle, that is, from the fact of togetherness (Whitehead 1978: 21) of the entities that compose every 'here' and 'there' in the becoming of an actual historical world. To begin in the middle, in the midst of togetherness, moves us away from the opposition between the 'one' and the 'many' and towards their reciprocal presupposition, such that

[t]he term 'many' presupposes the term 'one', and the term 'one' presupposes the term 'many' [...]. The novel entity is at once the togetherness of the 'many' which it finds, and also it is one among the disjunctive 'many' which it leaves; it is a novel entity, disjunctively among the many entities which it synthesizes. The many become one, and are increased by one (Whitehead 1978: 21).

In this way, the problem of the social is not projected backwards from one of its possible solutions – namely, the upper-case, abstract concept of 'Society' – and it cannot be a matter of explaining the relation of individuals to Society. Instead, it forces us to inquire into the modes of togetherness, or the actual and possible forms of sociality, that ensue as solutions or ways of folding the events that pose the social as a problem. Coming to terms with the thickness of problems, with their own modes of existence, enables us to entertain the proposition that *the mode of existence of the social is the problematic.* That it is the open adventure of togetherness by means of which and in response to which, contingent, novel modes of sociality come into existence while giving the problem new means of expression.

In so doing we may understand, for example, the introduction of the terms 'social' and 'civil society' in the *Encyclopédie* – and obviously, beyond it – as a historically contingent and provisional, but also conceptual and secular, enlightened solution to the problematic modes of human togetherness brought about by the reformist resurgence of Augustinianism in the religious sensibilities of the seventeenth century. Thus, as Keith Baker (1994: 119) reads it,

> [i]n religious terms, then, it seems that *société* emerged, in response to the problem of Augustinianism, as a bearable middle-ground between grace and despair. [...] A world from which God was hidden was a world in which authority was deligitimized and political order dissolved. It was a world condemned to civil strife and religious wars. [...] But the Enlightenment evaded that choice. And it did so by recourse to the notion of society as an autonomous ground of human existence, a domain whose stability did not require the imposition of order from above, and whose free action did not necessarily degenerate into anarchy and disorder below.

Moreover, as I have suggested above, like all problems the social insists and persists in the solutions or modes of sociality that are contingently created as a response to it. And it is renewed as solutions give way to possible futures that in turn problematise existing modes of togetherness, inducing novel expressions, differences and challenges. Think, for instance, of the 'national' socialites that emerged, according to Wagner (2000), as a result of the French Revolution, and in relation to which the problem would also later find seminal scientific expressions in the early discipline of sociology. Also, more recently, think of the heterogeneous modes of togetherness involving viruses, medical specialisms, novel modes of gay activist socialities, antiretroviral drugs, and new forms of treatment and intervention that became together as provisional, evolving cases of solution to the problem posed by the event of HIV/AIDS (Epstein 1997). These solutions have never ceased to mutate as they have become exposed to, and been forced to inherit, the problems posed by the events of novel subjectivities, practices of knowledge, technologies of communication, and forms of treatment and prevention to which they themselves gave rise (Rosengarten 2009).

In this sense, it seems to me that an advantage of approaching the thickness of the problem of the social from the middle of togetherness is that it prevents us from presupposing ready-made Societies or Individuals, and that it does not force us to assimilate 'the social' to 'the human'. Indeed, in one sense, both human and other-than-human beings are individuals, such that 'for some purposes, for some results, the tree is the individual, for others the cell, and for a third, the forest or the landscape' (Dewey 1954: 187). But in another sense, what are particular human and nonhuman individuals if not themselves contingent *solutions* to the problems posed by the togetherness of their internal and external, and natural and cultural, milieus (Simondon 2005)? What are they if not *societies* themselves, as Alfred North Whitehead (1967; 1978) would call all enduring organisms?[9]

Undoubtedly, to think of the social as an open problem, and of modes of sociality as historically contingent cases of solution, presupposes the ubiquity and multifariousness of associations. Neither problems nor solutions, however, can be *reduced* to these associations. To begin from the middle of a togetherness of things is to affirm that there is nothing as such which is alone in the world, developing an isolated existence in separation from others. But to affirm that the social exists in the form of a problem is not the same as claiming, as some versions of Science and Technology Studies (STS) and Actor-Network Theory (ANT) would seem to suggest, that it is synonymous with the associations between humans and nonhumans (e.g. Latour 2005). For as Dewey (1994 [1927]: 188) argued, 'while associated behavior is [...] a universal law, the fact of association does not itself make a society'.[10] Rather, societies of diverse shapes and manners, with diverse capacities and interdependencies, emerge here and there as contingent solutions whenever the social is posed as an open problem by the events that make up our historical world.

This last point begs the question of what this attention to the social as an open problem entails for those practices of inquiry that we have come to relate to 'the social'. In other words, it raises the possibility, but also the challenge, of wondering about the ethical constraints that might situate the adventures I have here associated with the notion of a 'problematic sociology'. This, then, will be the aim of the following and final section of this chapter.

FOR AN ART OF TOGETHERNESS:
STEPS TO A PROBLEMATIC SOCIOLOGY

The relationship between problems and methods is far from straightforward. Just as solutions are not given in advance but emerge at the same time, or better, at the same pace, as the sense of a problem becomes determined and is articulated in one or other mode of historical expression, so must methods in practice adjust themselves to the thickness of problems, learning to pose questions at the same time that answers become amenable to development.[11] Problems, I have suggested, are open, and they do not say how they should be developed. Thus, in a chapter titled 'Method, problem, faith', political theorist William Connolly (2004: 332) challenges the view that a mode of inquiry could be simply determined either by its methods or by the problems it attends to, and instead argues that an 'intervening variable' needs to be brought into play – namely, that of the different *existential faiths* that animate the tones and affective dispositions of any form of inquiry:

> [a]n existential faith is a hot, committed view of the world layered into affective dispositions, habits and institutional priorities of its confessors. The intensity of commitment to it typically exceeds the power of the arguments and evidence advanced [which does not mean that] existential faith is immune to new argument and evidence [...] rather, it is seldom exhausted by them (Connolly 2004: 333).

Elsewhere I have also called this faith an *ethics* (Savransky 2016),[12] in the sense neither of the discernment of good and evil, nor of the production of a code of conduct for research, but of an *ethos* of inquiry – an existential orientation to a mode of knowing, thinking and feeling that makes inquiry not just a practice directed towards 'knowledge', but a matter and manner of cultivating a whole way of inhabiting the world. At the beginning of his chapter, Connolly (2004) suggests that it is through an examination of these existential commitments that we may understand the relationships between problems and methods in the conduct of inquiry. I fully agree with him that the ethical dimension of inquiry, that which makes rationality more of a sentiment than a faculty, is in need of attention, as it often gets lost or suppressed in the rationalising hubris of debates around methods and methodology. On this occasion, however, I am less interested in the issue of the *priority* of the ethical than in the reciprocal entanglements through which ethics, methods, and problems become articulated in the practice of inquiry. In other words, I am interested here in the question of whether an attention to the open thickness of problems and the problematic existence of the social might become, not a foundation, but a lure for cultivating a different mode of social inquiry.

Admittedly, the open nature of problems generates difficulties for outlining strict prescriptions for inquiry. The reason for these difficulties lies in the fact that, when this insight is taken to its limit, the openness of problems makes them different in kind from the solutions that may be provided as a response to them.[13] While a solution is always already a manner of determining the sense of a problem, problems as such transcend any single field of solvability (Deleuze 1994: 179).[14] This is why they persist and insist in their solutions, rather than being dissolved in them. And it is also for this reason that Deleuze claims rather enigmatically that we should not apply the test of truth and falsehood to solutions, but to problems themselves. For a 'solution always has the truth it deserves according to the problem to which it is a response, and the problem always has the solution it deserves according to *its own* truth or falsity – in other words, in proportion to its sense' (1994: 159; emphasis in original).

Solutions are always dependent on problems, just as answers are always dependent on questions. Not the other way around. Thus, as Mariam Motamedi Fraser (2009: 76) has rightly argued, '[t]he best that a solution can do therefore is to develop a problem'. At the same time, however, problems become *actualised* by means of the determination of their sense, that is, by way of solutions. Thus, a problem is simultaneously transcendent and immanent with regards to its solutions. It is incarnated in the latter in such way that it 'does not exist, apart from its solutions'. (Deleuze 1994: 163).

The above situates any mode of inquiry in something of a bind with regards to problems. On the one hand, it must be said that no form of inquiry – no matter how methodologically sophisticated, how politically radical, or how 'practically' grounded (read policy/impact/etc.) it may claim to be – can 'solve' problems, if by that we mean making problems disappear. We live, it seems, in a world populated through and through by questions and problems. Indeed, as Dewey (2004 [1920]: 80) was always at pains to stress: 'a life of ease, a life of success without effort, would be a thoughtless life, and so would be a life of ready omnipotence'.

'*And so would be a life of ready omnipotence*': In my view, cultivating an ethics of problems belongs less to the question of which methods to deploy, than to the development of humbler sensibilities with regards to the question of what a 'method' may be capable of. This, it seems to me, is a point that deserves to be stressed. Following a long period in which almost every reference to 'method' was associated with a reactionary and narrow-minded, positivist past, the last ten to fifteen years have witnessed a renewed interest in social and cultural research methods (e.g. Back and Puwar 2012, Law 2004, Lury and Wakeford 2012, Vannini 2015, among others). A considerable part of this renaissance of methods research has been animated by a particular interpretation of John Austin's theory of the illocutionary force of performative utterances, according to which the claims that the social sciences make about the worlds they study – and therefore the means through which those claims are achieved – are said to bring those worlds into being, instead of merely representing them. As John Law and John Urry (2004: 392–393) succinctly put it in a programmatic text with the telling title 'Enacting the Social': 'The argument, then, is that social science is performative. It *produces* realities'.

There is much that I find unconvincing – and on occasion, misleading – about such propositions, but not all of my disagreements with these arguments are directly pertinent here.[15] For our current purposes, suffice it to say that, in such performative accounts, the social appears to be seen as a *product of*, rather than as a problem for (and beyond), social inquiry. Accordingly, the renewed fascination with methods in social research is concerned less with the representational validity of the knowledge claims to which certain methods give rise, than with their inventive capacities for 'enacting the social' or for 'problem-making' (e.g. Michael 2012).

As I hope the discussion above makes clear, however, it is the becoming of problems that sets inquiries into motion, rather than the reverse. Thus, to the extent that inquiry emerges *in response* to the problems posed in the indeterminate futures opened up by events, it cannot but remain on the side of propositions, of solutions, determining the senses of problems, failing and succeeding here and there in accomplishing its ends and effecting consequences. Thus, if we are overstepping the mark whenever we claim to have solved, or to be able to solve, problems, I fear we do so too when we assign to methods of inquiry the capacity to 'enact' the social, to 'frame' or 'make' problems, as if problems were yet another product of our omnipotent performativities. For the question is not whether methods 'solve' or 'make' problems, but whether or not the solutions that they articulate can enable problems to develop in alternative and valuable ways.

To suggest, then, that there are no ultimate solutions to problems, that our inquiries are incapable of making problems disappear, is not to say that everything is lost, that inquiry is the result of an error, or indeed, of a false problem that takes problems themselves to be confused states of mind susceptible to dissolution. The openness of problems is not the negation of inquiry, concerned as it inevitably is with the production of solutions. Solutions there must be, no matter how partial, provisional, and contingent these inevitably are. Deleuze expresses this paradox in the following way:

> It would be naive to think that the problems of life and death, of love and the differences between the sexes [as well as the problem of the social] are amenable to their scientific solutions and positings, even though such positings and solutions *necessarily* arise without warning, even though they *must* necessarily emerge at a certain moment in the unfolding process of the development of these problems (1994: 107. Emphasis added).

The question, rather, is 'what can solutions do?' The short answer is 'we never know'. But rather than inviting the *laissez-faire* and rather omnipotent attitude cultivated in claims that methods produce realities, this 'we never know' is instead an invitation to remain vigilant about the ways in which solutions – and methods – are proposed. Thus, I think that if this coming to terms with the open thickness of problems has any ethical implications – in the sense of ethics defined above – then perhaps these involve an invitation to conduct a form of inquiry neither oriented toward producing solutions that could put an end to problems, nor toward the hubris of making its own problems. As I have argued elsewhere (Savransky 2016), an event constitutes a break in the order of causality, an effect that is irreducible to its cause. Thus, just as an event cannot be explained away by historical reasons,[16] a science, a theory, or a method may will an event and work with a view towards its possible actualisation; but no one, no method or solution, can claim to *produce* events at will, nor to become the 'condition of possibility' for their becoming. An event is, after all, *the transformation of the possible.*

Rather than lend itself to methodological prescriptions, therefore, an ethics of problems invites us to cultivate a singular sensitivity to the manners and occasions where the social insists and persists in the form of a problem with its own thickness, its own folds and snags, consistencies and determinations, tensions and potentialities, as well as to the many different modes of sociality that emerge historically as contingent cases of solution. To engage the social as an open problem is therefore also to imagine a form of inquiry whose task is that of a permanent experimentation with problems themselves. An experimentation that trusts the possibility of developing problems otherwise, so that their solutions, always partial, provisional, and contingent, may themselves engender new differences that transform the sense of a problem. These novel differences may certainly be deemed events of *invention*, but it is to the event that such an inventiveness belongs. As Celia Lury and Nina Wakeford (2012: 7; emphasis added) acknowledge in their *Inventive Methods*, what they refer to as the 'inventiveness' of methods, that is, 'their capacity to address a problem and change that problem as it performs *itself* – cannot be secured in advance'.

Perhaps, then, the challenge for a problematic sociology is neither to dissolve nor to make problems but to cultivate an *art of togetherness*. An art concerned with producing, in the course of its own creative activity, intellectual, material and felt tools that emerge in the unfolding process of the development of problems. Tools that are necessarily insufficient with respect to any final capture of problems themselves, but that nevertheless may, sometimes, provide certain determinations and pathways for problems to find new means of expression.

Acknowledging this necessary insufficiency of any mode of inquiry with regards to the mode of existence of problems does not, however, entail viewing such inquiries as fundamentally lacking or flawed. Rather, it is a provocation to think of and engage in inquiry as an ongoing practice of experimentation with open problems. It is what makes sociology, like the development of problems themselves, an infinite task.

NOTES

1 As they defined it, the 'social' – which was classified as an adjective rather than a noun – was 'a word recently introduced in language to define the qualities that render a man useful within society' (Diderot and D'Alambert 1779: 216).

2 While Weber (2011 [1949]: 68; emphasis in original) suggested that 'new problems' were generative of new inquires because they were capable of opening up new and 'significant points of view', he complained that the 'social', 'when taken in its "general" meaning', was too ambiguous and multifarious a reality to provide a 'specific' point of view. He thus rejected both the assumptions of the Marxist traditions that would reduce the social to the economic, and the very possibility of an 'absolutely "objective" scientific analysis of […] "social phenomena" independent of special and one-sided viewpoints according to which – expressly or tacitly, consciously or unconsciously – they are selected, analyzed and organized for expository purposes.' (2011: 72).

3 Speculatively, that is, because rather than serve as a reference to an actual, disciplinary state of affairs that could be contrasted with that of anthropology, psychology, economics, geography, or other social sciences, the term 'sociology' here is addressed to what could be, that is, to the creation of a possible (Savransky 2016). This is a possible whose seeds are perhaps contained in the challenge posed by the very composition of the term itself – the challenge, that is, of a *logos* of the *socius*, of a *com*panion-talk, of addressing those we are *with*, those with whom we exist *together*.

4 For a more recent approach that, although not in direct conversation with this literature, reverses this sociologising tendency in order to think about how publics are *made by*, instead of making, problems, see Marres (2005, 2012).

5 It is perhaps no coincidence that terms like 'complication', 'implication', and 'explication', all crucially retain the presence of the morpheme '*pli*', which is the French word for 'fold'.

6 Instead, closed or overdetermined problems would be a case of 'false' problems, as in the conventional pedagogic scenario when a teacher poses a problem the solution to which is known in advance, and the student is assigned the task of solving it. Despite the notable

efforts of John Dewey (see e.g. 2009 [1909]), this conception not only pervades much research in education on – tellingly – 'problem-solving' but, more disquietingly, it still pervades pedagogical practices at all levels, as it incarnates itself in the situation of exam questions. This is the scene that constitutes 'the problem as obstacle and the respondent as Hercules' (Deleuze 1994: 158). Deleuze calls this an 'infantile prejudice' but I wonder whether this would not be better called an 'adult' prejudice, pivotal as it is in the jealous demarcations of 'expertise' and in the entire economy of seriousness that sustains them.

7   Thus, the philosopher of individuation Gilbert Simondon (2005), who was a source of inspiration for Deleuze, would describe the various phases of individuation (physical, vital, psychic, collective) as cases of solution to problems posed by relations of tension at a previous phase. For example, the becoming of a living individual is thought as a solution to the tension emerging in the relations between a physical individual and its milieu, while this solution would subsequently pose its own problems by introducing a new tensed relation between perception and affectivity, thereby giving rise to a new solution that involved a process of 'psychic' individuation, and so on.

8   My sense is that, from the point of view of practical, empirical inquiry, it is not clear that we must *begin* at all. Rather, as I will argue in the next section, inquiries always 'begin' *after* events that have posed a problem, and their challenge is always how to inherit the event and how to develop the problem (Savransky 2016). The question of beginnings is thus entirely speculative, in the best sense of the term.

9   On Whitehead's concept of 'society' see also Savransky (2016) and Halewood (2014).

10   As far as STS is concerned, the problem of the social may arguably make itself felt more keenly in what Bruno Latour (2004) has called 'matters of concern'. From this perspective, moreover, the insistence and persistence of problems is what makes Maria Puig de la Bellacasa's (2010) concept of 'matters of care' vital for the development of a problematic STS.

11   Or else they may give rise to false problems, to imposed problems that emerge not out of real historical situations but out of an excessively rigid, dogmatic ethics of method.

12   As indeed has Connolly (1995) himself.

13   This difference in kind is, of course, the ontological difference stressed by Bergson and Deleuze between the actual and the virtual. Problems are ultimately always virtual with regards to their 'actual' solutions and thus can neither be contained by, dissolved into, or reconstructed from the latter. Although the virtual dimension of problems in Deleuze is philosophically important and intellectually stimulating, it introduces a transcendental dimension that, I fear, risks situating problems well beyond the remit of whatever we might take 'sociology' to be, or indeed, beyond that of any other science (a risk also noted by Fraser [2009: 76]; for an account of the transcendental in Deleuze's thinking see Bryant [2008]). Worse still, overemphasising the virtual, elusive character of problems in approaching the social bears the enormous danger of opening the door to familiar social theory rhetorics of ineffability, excess and unknowability, whose consequences are, to my mind, counterproductive for practical, ethically committed forms of inquiry. Surely,

there are things that are 'unknowable,' in the sense that they have nothing to do with knowledge as such. But to acknowledge this is quite different, I think, from celebrating 'unknowability' in relation to a 'knowledge-practice.' When it is a matter of the latter, I stand with Whitehead (1978: 4): 'the unknowable is unknown.' Moreover, as I will show below, placing problems entirely in the realm of the virtual is indeed a betrayal of the problem itself, for problems are also crucially *immanent* to their solutions, insisting only in the latter, and being developed as solutions are produced (Deleuze 1994: 163).

14 This is why a problematic sociology should not concern itself simply with something called 'social problems', as if some problems were 'social' to begin with. As I have suggested above, it is the social that is a problem, and not the problem that is social.

15 For a more in-depth, critical exploration of contemporary social science debates about the 'performativity' of knowledge see Savransky (2016. Especially the chapter titled 'Modes of Connection').

16 Which does not mean that it does not tolerate that stories about it be told.

REFERENCES

Back, L., and N. Puwar, *Live Methods* (Oxford: Wiley-Blackwell, 2013).

Baker, K. M., 'Enlightenment and The Institution of Society: Notes for a Conceptual History', in W. Melching and W. Velema, eds, *Main Trends in Cultural History: Ten Essays* (Amsterdam and Atlanta: Editions Rodopi, 1994), pp. 95–120.

Baudrillard, J., *In the Shadow of the Silent Majorities, or 'The Death of the Social'* (New York: Semiotext(e), 1983).

Blumer, H., 'Social Problems as Collective Behavior'. *Social Problems*, 18 (1971), 298–306.

Bryant, L., *Difference and Givenness: Deleuze's Transcendental Empiricism and the Ontology of Immanence* (Evanston: Northwestern University Press, 2008).

Candea, M., ed., *The Social after Gabriel Tarde: Debates and Assessments* (London: Routledge, 2010).

Connolly, W., *The Ethos of Pluralization* (Minneapolis: University of Minnesota Press, 1995).

——'Method, Problem, Faith', in I. Shapiro, R. M. Smith and T. E. Masoud, eds, *Problems and Methods in the Study of Politics* (Cambridge: Cambridge University Press, 2004), pp. 332–49.

Cortázar, J., *Hopscotch* (New York: Pantheon Books, 1996).

Diderot, D., and J. D'Alambert, *Encyclopédie, ou Dictionnaire Raisonné des Sciences, des Arts et des Mètiers*, vol 31 (Geneva: Chez Pellet, 1779).

Davies, W. 'Neoliberalism and the Revenge of the Social', <https://www.opendemocracy.net/william-davies/neoliberalism-and-revenge-of-'social'> [Accessed 5 April 2015].

Deleuze, G., *Difference and Repetition* (New York: Columbia University Press, 1994).

——*The Logic of Sense* (London: Continuum, 2004 [1969]).

Dewey, J. *How We Think* (Mineola: Dover Publications, 1997 [1909]).

——*The Public and Its Problems* (Athens, OH: Swallow Press, 1927/1954).

——*Logic: The Theory of Inquiry* (New York: Irvington Publishers, 1938/1982).

Eco, U., *The Open Work* (Cambridge, MA: Harvard University Press, 1989).

Epstein, S., *Impure Science: AIDS, Activism, and the Politics of Knowledge* (Berkeley and Los Angeles: University of California Press, 1996).

Fraser, M., 'Experiencing Sociology', *European Journal of Social Theory*, 12 (2012), 63–81.

Halewood, M., *Rethinking the Social through Durkheim, Marx, Weber and Whitehead* (London & New York: Anthem Press, 2014).

Joyce, J., *Finnegan's Wake* (Ware: Classics, 2012 [1939]).

Kuhn, T., *The Structure of Scientific Revolutions* (Chicago: The University of Chicago Press, 2012 [1962]).

Latour, B., 'Why Has Critique Run Out of Steam? From Matters of Fact to Matters of Concern', *Critical Inquiry*, 30 (2004), 225–248.

——*Reassembling the Social: An Introduction to Actor-Network Theory* (Oxford: Oxford University Press, 2005).

Law, J., *After Method* (London: Routledge, 2004).

Law, J., and J. Urry, 'Enacting the Social', *Economy & Society*, 33 (2004), 390–410.

Lury, C., and N. Wakeford, eds, *Inventive Methods: The Happening of the Social* (London: Routledge, 2012).

——'Issues Spark Publics into Being. A Key But Often Forgotten Point of the Lippmann-Dewey Debate', in B. Latour., and P. Weibel, eds, *Making Things Public: Atmospheres of Democracy* (Cambridge, MA: The MIT Press, 2005), pp. 208–17.

——*Material Participation: Technology, the Environment and Everyday Publics* (London: Palgrave Macmillan, 2012).

Michael, M., 'De-signing the Object of Sociology: Toward an 'Idiotic' Methodology', *The Sociological Review*, 60 (2012), 166–183.

Rose, N., 'The Death of the Social? Re-figuring the Territory of Government', *Economy & Society*, 25 (1996), 327–56.

Rosengarten, M., *HIV Interventions: Biomedicine and the Traffic between Information and Flesh* (Washington: University of Washington Press, 2009).

Puig de la Bellacasa, M., 'Matters of Care in Technoscience: Assembling Neglected Things', *Social Studies of Science*, 41 (2011), 85–106.

Savransky, M., *The Adventure of Relevance: An Ethics of Social Inquiry* (London & New York: Palgrave Macmillan, 2016).

——'Modes of Mattering: Barad, Whitehead, and Societies', *Rhizomes: Cultural Studies in Emerging Knowledge* (2016).

Schlanger, J., *Penser la bouche pleine* (Paris: Mouton, 1975).

Sewell, W., *Logics of History: Social Theory and Social Transformation* (Chicago: The University of Chicago Press, 2005).

Simmel, G., *Sociology: Inquiry into the Construction of Social Forms* (Leiden & Boston: Brill, 2009 [1908]).

Simondon, G., *L'individuation à la lumiere des notions de forme et d'information* (Grenoble: Éditions Jérôme Millon, 2005).

Spector, M., and J. Kitsuse, *Constructing Social Problems* (New Brunswick, NJ: Transaction Publishers, 1987/2009).

Stengers, I., *The Invention of Modern Science* (Minneapolis: University of Minnesota Press, 2000).

Strathern, M., 'The Concept of Society is Theoretically Obsolete', In T. Ingold, ed., *Key Debates in Anthropology* (London & New York: Routledge, 1996 [1989]), pp. 50–5.

——*Partial Connections* (Walnut Creek: Altamira Press, 2004 [1991]).

Vannini, P., ed., *Non-Representational Methodologies: Re-envisioning research.* (London: Routledge, 2015).

Wagner, P., '"An Entirely New Object of Consciousness, of Volition, of Thought": The Coming into Being and (Almost) Passing Away of "Society" as a Scientific Object', In L. Daston, ed., *Biographies of Scientific Objects* (Chicago: The University of Chicago Press, 2000), pp. 132–57.

Weber, M., *Methodology of the Social Sciences* (New Brunswick, NJ: Transaction Publishers, 2011 [1949]).

Whitehead, A. N., *Adventures of Ideas* (New York: Free Press, 1967).

——*Process and Reality: An Essay in Cosmology* (New York: Free Press, 1978).

10

THE SOCIALITY OF INFECTIOUS DISEASES

Marsha Rosengarten

IN HIS PREFACE TO JORGE LUIS BORGES' *LABYRINTHS*, ANDRE MAUROIS BRINGS the reader's attention to the significance of problem-making. We are offered a glimpse of what we might expect from Borges' text through reference to the idea for a 'frightening story' by the renowned writer and poet Paul Valéry: 'it is discovered that the only remedy for cancer is living human flesh. Consequences' (Maurois 2000:11). This eerie and, as I read it, paradoxical remedy that requires what it also aims to succour, serves as a provocation to reflect on the manner by which a problem is posed (Fraser 2010; Michael and Rosengarten 2013; Savranksy, this volume).[1] I offer it here as a foretaste of a problem-making arguably no less labyrinth-like than Borges' tales. In what follows I ask in what manner might it be said that the biomedical endeavor of dealing with infectious disease conceives the social as a resource? But, also, what might infection suggest otherwise?

Throughout the chapter, my primary focus will be HIV, with mention also of the newly emergent Zika virus as well as Ebola and Tuberculosis (TB). Of these latter three, TB will be discussed in more detail as a co-infective agent with HIV in the concluding sections. As I hope will become evident, the biomedical notion of the social, as it is posed in response to each of these life-threatening events, is not simply for sustaining. Indeed, by way of a small number of textual examples, I want to expose the manner by which the biomedical depends on constituting the social as its purpose but, in doing so, treats it as little more than a passive or disruptive obstacle to the challenge of dealing with such infections. I argue that this bears conceptual but, more crucially, questionable cost to human life, despite science's not infrequent achievements.

CONSEQUENCES

When I first began working as a social scientist in the HIV field my late friend Alan Brotherton, connoisseur of many things that no doubt contributed to the brilliance of his activism and policy making, said to me 'we got antiretroviral drugs which are by no means ideal but their presence has interceded in the possibility of something better'.[2] I've often contemplated this statement, or a version of it, in relation to the manner in which pharmaceuticals have acquired a claim on approaches to the epidemic with the consequence that other dimensions of HIV, commonly perceived as the social dimensions of the epidemic, have become marginal for inquiry. Arguably, one of the most notable of these has been the inventive engagement of those now targeted and, without argument, aided by pharmaceutical interventions. Long before HIV antiretroviral drugs showed efficacy in suppressing the virus, safe sexual practices were enabled by gay sexual communities instituting condom use. Yet despite this potentially telling feature of what has contributed to preventing transmission, alongside medical advancement, other novel and inventive modes of risk negotiation that have emerged with the drugs are often reduced within biomedical narratives to simply risky or not (Kippax and Race 2003; Rosengarten 2009; Stengers 1997). Brotherton's observation was made at a time when the drugs were considerably less sophisticated, not only reducing viral presence but also, for many, inducing damaging life disruptive drug effects (Rosengarten, 2009). Although it was these drugs' unanticipated unwanted effects — the iatrogenics of HIV biomedicine — that initially provoked me to contemplate the work of biomedical intervention, here I wonder how this connects with a conception of the social in the continuing problem-making of HIV as well as other infectious diseases such as Zika, Ebola and TB.

During the 2014–2015 Ebola epidemic in Guinea, Liberia and Sierra Leone, biomedical approaches involved drastic measures such as placing those infected (or thought to be infected) in isolation wards, without their families or others close to them knowing whether they were still alive, and unable to provide them with any form of care. Another drastic intervention was to isolate villages suspected of harbouring the infection, leaving entire communities without access to vital necessities. A third intervention involved heavy-handed security threats of jail terms for those caught hiding someone with the virus (Mullen 2014:e550 Marí Sáez, Kelly and Brown 2014). Because underdosing with antibiotic TB drugs can result in drug resistance (CDC 2016), TB treatment is prescribed through directly observed therapy (DOT) in countries with high prevalence and poor infrastructure. The treatment involves an onerous daily dosing regimen (usually for six months) that may incur feeling dizzy, sick, flu-like symptoms and jaundice, while the strategy of DOT demands repeated, often lengthy and costly travel to a clinic (Harper 2010; Noyes and Popay 2006).

When I was preparing to write this chapter, the Zika virus dominated the headlines of major news outlets because of its capacity to be transmitted by a strain of mosquito bite, with life-damaging consequences to the foetus carried by a pregnant woman (Baud et al. 2017). One of the most prominent newspapers in the United Kingdom, the *Guardian*, reported on 3 February 2016 that a race was on to produce a vaccine to protect 'the unborn' (Milman 2016). Noting that this aim was made difficult by the need to test drugs on pregnant women, a group 'normally shielded from experimental trials,' Mike Turner, head of immuno-biology at the Wellcome Trust, was quoted as stating, '[t]esting a vaccine on pregnant women is a "practical and ethical nightmare".'[3] Nonetheless, amidst acknowledgement that it would be difficult to produce a vaccine for the current epidemic, Anthony Fauci, Director of the US National Institute of Allergy and Infectious Diseases, was reported to state that a vaccine to prevent future infections might be available by 2017. Leaving aside the complexities of vaccine development, a year later, the means for preventing the damage of Zika infection to a foetus continues to reside with vulnerable women.[4] The website of the US Centre for Communicable Diseases (CDCa no date) includes the following advice to women of child-bearing age: 'If you live in or must travel to one of these areas, talk to your doctor or other healthcare provider first and strictly follow steps to prevent mosquito bites and practice safe sex'. Needless to say, it is not always possible for women to control safe sex, as is well-known from the experience of HIV prevention. Compounding what is constituted as a highly gendered biomedical problematic of Zika prevention, termination of a pregnancy is illegal in many of the affected countries (Aiken et al. 2016).

My hunch is that the above style of media reporting does well to highlight the crucial need for intervention and then, with the suggestion of a biomedical solution, provides reassurance to those of us at some distance from the identified site and source of infection that its problem will, eventually, be solved. But as the risk of Zika infection for pregnant women and the foetus shows, the promise of a biomedical solution is able to take centre stage while glossing the demands on those affected by the agent of infection. Although a medically inscribed public health approach to Zika, Ebola and TB may be thought a necessary protective measure for the greater good of more lives saved, others argue, with differing modes of emphasis, for a more patient or community oriented approach (Hanson, Zembe and Ekstro 2015; Harper 2010; UNICEF 2016).[5] In HIV, the challenges of preventing transmission continue despite the advent of treatments and, although as I have noted above, drugs have radically improved there is no cure in sight (Sankoh et al. 2015).

However, it is the different but not unconnected effects arising from the biomedical response to HIV, Zika, Ebola and TB that lead me to propose a related, yet somewhat differently oriented focus to that addressed to individual and community needs. Leaving aside the no doubt important focus on health economics and poor infrastructure raised by others and predominantly in the field of anthropology (Harper 2010; Farrar & Piot 2014; Ghazanfar et al. 2015), I would like to bring into question the logics and indifferences that, as Isabelle Stengers (1997; 2011) has shown, succeed in constituting a situation of concrete difficulties. But because in this chapter I am unable to do justice to Stengers' complex undertaking for a different science, I shall attempt the beginning of a response to a more modest set of questions: How does biomedicine remain cocooned from accountability, despite evidence of a vastly complex array of dynamic relations that cut across a conventional science/social divide to effect what becomes biomedical intervention? What labyrinth-like process are we – scientists, social scientists, policy makers and those directly affected, including health professionals – caught within? And, not least, by what mode of attention might this process be opened to the possibility of consequences different to those analogous, in some manner, to feeding human flesh to attenuate cancer?

NAVIGATING THE LABYRINTH

For the reader who may be thinking that I have ventured too far into the phantasmagorical by drawing an analogy between Valéry's tale and that of modern medical science, I want to say that, in truth, I have my own reservations. I am most certainly hesitant about my decision to pursue the analogy if it should be mistaken as a damning of medical science. I am taken with the analogy precisely because it enables me to dramatise the boundary that constitutes the social as external to biomedical science and, arguably, as it does so, forecloses the possibilities for a more responsive or, as Maria Puig de la Bellacasa (2017) proposes, 'caring' science. That is, a science attentive to its own selective, yet highly infective modes of knowing, and the consequences that may follow in the endeavour of bringing about a finite solution (Rosengarten 2009; Race 2012; Edelstein, Angelides and Heymann 2015).

Of the three infections discussed in this chapter, HIV has acquired considerably more resources and its networks are vast, involving specific public and philanthropic funding, multiple disciplines, numerous national and global civil society organisations, and ring-fenced social research in contrast to what may be observed in response to the much longer event of TB and, perhaps less surprising, to the more recent events of Zika and Ebola. Indeed, the field of HIV can be viewed as exemplary for the labyrinth-like manner that those of us working across the field of infectious diseases – if not health and medicine more broadly – may be caught within. While on the one hand, it is evident that health resources but also continued debate and reflection are crucial for responding to the dynamics of health and disease, it can also be said that what attracts resources is the field's legitimation by science as an object worthy of inquiry.[6] In short, and based on my direct involvement in the HIV field, I am inclined to deduce that resources come hand-in-hand with entrenched logics and modes of practice and that, as I show below, once such logics are established, they serve to inoculate against other modes of engagement.

The first international conference on HIV took place in 1985. Since its fledgling beginnings, it has now grown under the auspices of the International AIDS Society to attract delegates in the thousands (the Washington DC 2012 conference had close to 20,000 delegates), including scientists of multiple persuasions as well as members of numerous activist civil society organisations, national public health authorities from all over the globe plus major public, philanthropic and commercial research funders.[7] Not surprisingly, conference proceedings are watched over by invited local and international media outlets and, since the introduction of antiretroviral drugs in 1996, there is invariably much ado about what suffices as the latest scientific findings. Shoring up the reputation of such conference events as worthy of national and global media attention, high-ranking politicians such as Bill Clinton and the late Nelsen Mandela are now an expected feature of the opening and closing addresses, along with prominent biomedical scientists and activists.

To be sure, such forums with their public advocacy for HIV has import for maintaining funding support for research and intervention. Nonetheless, it is important to bear in mind that what is active in their possibility of public advocacy is an assemblage inclusive of a veracious virus and the paraphernalia that has come with this, for example: diagnostics, drugs, prevention education, social marketing, chairmanships, grant applications, changes in sexual practice and the more nuanced work of a diverse array of civil society organisations. And, as is acknowledged amidst such forums, also included are the millions who have died and those who are now infected or at risk of infection. As this collective and highly complex dynamic is presided over, and massively overshadowed, by the weighty orchestration of a biomedical conference agenda, an attentiveness to what has come to matter and the complex manner in which it bears on the costs of this to life, is peculiarly subsumed within the thinking constraints of modern science and the world it expresses. Within such forums, presentations – whether scientific, social scientific, policy or activist – are required to comply with one of two formats for first stage abstract review: option 1 must contain a background and hypothesis tested, methods, results and conclusions with future implications; option 2 must contain a background and objectives of a programme, project or policy, a description of the project, lessons learned, conclusions/next steps. In short, there is no place for exploratory conceptual work that attempts to experiment with different modes of engagement, modes that might, for example, pursue an appreciation of the designated 'social' as more than composed of distinct agentive human actors warranting aid and/ or correction.

This blatant exclusion of what else might come to matter beyond or contrary to a modern scientific schema came home to me during the opening speeches of the 2012 IAS Conference in Washington DC when Fauci, cited above in reference to Zika, and whose research and advocacy have no doubt contributed to gains in the HIV epidemic, took the stage to announce 'the end of AIDS' was now on the horizon, thanks entirely to the singular achievements of biomedical antiretroviral drugs and other biomedical developments. If the consequences of Fauci's seeming indifference to the deemed 'non-scientific' for what will change the epidemic were not so apparent in his claim, the statement might have been laughable – suggesting that the rest of us 'non-biomedical scientists' could go home to wait for the cure. Fauci's statement was mediated just a little in its backing by Hillary Clinton, at the time Secretary of State for the United States of America. As a major American international political figure, Clinton's opening speech underscored the acclaimed role of biomedicine, but did so with a somewhat different claim of the coming of an 'AIDS Free Generation'. Perhaps her speech writers had the foresight to recognise that none of the biomedical interventions currently available offer the likelihood that existing HIV infection is soon to be cured, and the experience of HIV ended. That said, Clinton's promise ventured no further than Fauci's in its premise that a generation free of HIV infection would be achieved through the prioritising of a finite biomedical solution.[8]

Leaving aside the conflation of HIV and AIDS in both Fauci and Clinton's pronouncements — with AIDS no longer a near inevitable consequence of HIV due to antiretroviral drugs to prevent HIV infectivity, their having already been established as preventative of AIDS — the world audience might have been tempted to believe we are on the cusp of an extraordinary biomedical achievement, an achievement premised on an inert social in wait or, at best, as we see below, to be held against its deficit tendencies that might prevent the singularity of biomedicine.

Since the Washington (2012) and also Melbourne IAS (2014) conferences – the latter turning on the announcement that consistent dosing with antiretroviral drugs can function as a form of pre-exposure prophylaxis (PrEP) for HIV negative people, a claim that informed Clinton's speech – Kane Race (2015: 7) has challenged the HIV field to attend to what he terms its compartmentalised/ non-relational thinking and, specifically, a 'presumptive negativity of sex' in dealing with the virus. By paraphrasing the research questions cited in biomedical presentations at the IAS and other international HIV conferences, namely: 'Had trial participants adhered to the dosing requirements? How do we know? Are they telling the truth? How should we measure this?' Race (2015: 9) underscores how medical science logics are fixed to their own project as if above and beyond what has called for intervention. By illuminating how the demand for dosing not only excludes what makes for its happening, but succeeds in doing so by reducing the social that we might otherwise expect to be paramount for its complex possibilities, Race proposes a different perspective. Acutely attuned to the worlds of gay cultures and their togetherness with other entities in the event of HIV prevention *and* pleasure, his challenge to the field goes to the heart of what might be more responsively considered at stake:

> [C]omparatively little thought or attention has been given to the processes through which HIV-negative and untested individuals might (or might not) become subjects of HIV prevention. [...] How might we think about and begin to exercise responsibility at a scene whose appeal consists, to some extent, for its participants, in the way it promises to suspend or momentarily interrupt any grip on the sovereign or rational subject that is taken to be the foundation of responsibility in modern culture? Or, put differently, how might we attend responsibly and effectively to pleasure, where this pleasure

consists in some form of ecstasy or de-subjectification? I'm talking about
sex and drugs (Race 2013).

By pointing to the coming together of sex and non-medical drugs in the pursuit
of sexual pleasure – precisely where, as he sees it, a mode of 'de-subjectification'
or 'de-rationalising' may be the experienced effect – Race not only contests the
exclusionary and somewhat contradictory assumptions by the HIV biomedical
field that come with the causal framing of the problem of dosing adherence.
Going beyond this, he highlights the situated process by which HIV transmission may or may not take place. This is a process that well exceeds simple
presuppositions that the social is merely the doing of human actors, thus
extending the research terrain and resisting the foreclosure of biomedicine
on what could be claimed as its concern for a sustained achievement of HIV
prevention.

DEEP WITHIN THE LABYRINTH

Race's pithy account of the social for biomedicine and the import of the notion
of 'togetherness' in his proposal raises, in turn, the question of what drives the
knowledge-making that mobilises his concern. Exemplary, I suggest, in exposing Stengers' (2011) claims of the indifference of modern science to what it
regards as the 'non-scientific', is the RCT. Without detailing the method and
the many critical accounts that it has elicited (see for example, Michael and
Rosengarten 2013; Timmermans and Berg 2003; Will and Moreira 2010), I cite
one particular article that suggests the method has come to matter more than
those whose health it claims to act for. Lead authored by Nancy Padian with a
long list of prominent co-author HIV trialists, the article, entitled 'Weighing
the Gold in the Gold Standard: Challenges in HIV Prevention Research', was
published in the esteemed journal, *AIDS* (Padian et al. 2010), thus not only
earning endorsement, but also, arguably, assisting in the cultivation of what has
become of decided importance to clinical research and, hence, evidence-based
research, namely, methodological success.

Beginning with an explicit expression of concern about the failure of the majority of RCTs to produce statistically significant findings, over the length of the HIV epidemic, for assessing the efficacy of biomedical prevention technologies, Padian et al. (2010: 621) explain that only six out of a total of 37 at the time of their writing had achieved 'demonstrated definitive effects on HIV incidence'.[9] 'Demonstrated definitive effects' are statistical differences between the product and control arms, irrespective of what the effects suggest about the product or, indeed, the methodological design of the RCT. This exclusive interest in a statistical difference is made explicit in the authors' mention of the trial of nonoxynol-9 gel for vaginal use. The trial is positively noted as one of the few to have achieved a demonstrated effect. But it is also well known – if not infamous – for the manner in which it did so. As the article notes, without additional commentary or reflection, a 50% *increase* in HIV incidence was able to be demonstrated because the intervention, nonoxynol-9, *increased* vulnerability to the virus (Padian et al. 2010: 624). Insofar as the article is explicit in its aim to examine 'the design, implementation, and contextual considerations that may limit detection of a positive or adverse effect in HIV prevention trials', some might argue that the question of harm or benefit – that is, the type of effect – was not relevant to its discussion. But, if so, it is not difficult to draw the conclusion that a demonstrated difference in numbers is what matters, and not the experience of the effect.

It is, however, the authors' complaint about ethical requirements that concerns me particularly, as it underscores the strange nature of what I am suggesting has come to matter in the logic of biomedical of science. The following quote from the authors poses the question of what is ethical when carrying out an RCT in low-and middle-income countries, while making clear that the pursuit of a biomedical solution supersedes other considerations:

> The ethical issues of offering enhanced HIV prevention services in the comparison arm must be weighed against the ethical issues of lengthy and expensive prevention trials that provide the control group with an unsustainable level of prevention services that does not reflect community standards. Further, such trials may jeopardize our ability to identify and

offer participants and at-risk individuals around the world additional effective HIV prevention options […] in most [RCTs], risk-taking behavior was
reduced in both [intervention and control arms]. Some of this change may
be attributable to enhanced prevention services offered in the trial (Padian
2010: 631).

In short, it is evident that caring for trial participants is seen to be at a cost to
research findings. To put this more bluntly, the non-biomedical or relevant designated social – here, research participants – is a resource only for achieving a
demonstrated effect. And a risky resource at that. Despite what we might assume
to be the intended beneficiaries of medical science, in the above weighing of the
difficulties faced by RCTs, research participants are responsibilised for potentially
undermining the method either by: (i) those in the control or placebo arm *not*
contracting HIV during the research, thereby failing to provide a comparison
with the trial product; or (ii) by not complying with the requirements of the
protocol which might well generate evidence achieved in a manner qualitatively
indifferent to their HIV vulnerability.

THE AWFUL AND WONDROUS CREATIVITY OF INFECTION

Having shown how the endeavour of dealing with infectious disease holds to a
narrow conception of the social and how this provides a resource for science, I
now want to consider whether the very notion of infection might lend itself to
a rethinking of biomedical problem-making. To pursue this question, I propose
to hold in suspension the desire to deem 'infection' a purely deductive force.
To do so, I need to offer one final empirical example, an explanatory statement
by the World Health Organisation (WHO 2014) on HIV/TB co-infection:

People infected with TB bacteria have a lifetime risk of falling ill with TB
of 10%. However persons with compromised immune systems, such as
people living with HIV […] have a much higher risk of falling ill. People

who are co-infected with HIV and TB are 21 to 34 times more likely to become sick with TB.

Although at first reading, the extract may appear to speak only of the destructiveness of the association of HIV and TB, I propose that we pause on how this concern follows from the manner in which these infections jointly achieve their destructiveness. The two different infections are said to affect each other within the milieu of a body that is necessary to their complex dynamic. Moreover, their respective differences within this milieu create conditions conducive to the other. To backtrack a little, their modes of entering into the milieu are distinctly different: TB by breath, HIV by bodily fluids. But nonetheless, the two achieve an advantage for each other as they *become together* as multi-morbidity, and with a multiplying of effects. Indeed, it is precisely the conception that the body-with-infection – bacterial (TB) or viral (HIV) – can be further differentially transformed while retaining or holding an enduring distinctiveness of the other that contributes to the current patterning of drugs (their molecular composition) and the sequential ordering of their usage: treating first TB then HIV co-infection (McShane 2005).

Without discounting the complexities and problems that might be raised in relation to treating HIV/TB co-infection, and perhaps along the lines of Brotherton's earlier comment on HIV antiretroviral drugs, we could say that the above description of infection effects is not so out of character with Race's effort to provoke thought on the 'togetherness' of sex, drugs and HIV prevention. To put this another way, it seems that the above description by the WHO of infection as a mode of 'togetherness' speaks, in part, to a relational conception of infection. Indeed, the description is not entirely at odds with Alfred North Whitehead's notion of infection as integral to relationality and endurance:

That which endures is limited, obstructive, intolerant, infecting its environment with its own aspects. But it is not self-sufficient. The aspect of all things enter into its very nature. It is only itself as drawing together into its own limitation the larger whole in which it finds itself (Whitehead cited in Stengers 2011: 156–57).

Infection is, as Stengers elaborates in relation to the above quote, a 'holding-together' (2011: 158) and, as such, a determinate shaping of a dynamic existence. It pertains, as Whitehead proposes, to all modes of endurance, including viruses, bacteria, dosing and bodies, as well as those we might regard as non-animate such as rocks but also, and no less, to human thought. All 'prehend' or, in less technical terms can be said to feel or grasp. Prehending the world is integral to the processes by which, for Whitehead (1978), the creativity of transformations and endurances happen. The success of this process is, as Stengers (2011: 158) states, 'a co-production between this being and "its" environment'. Taking up this notion of infection, Martin Savransky (2016: 141) describes the process as requiring a speculative response: 'the milieu *feels* [sic] the invention and the invention the milieu, [such] that a transformation of *both* [sic] might take hold in a way that *cannot be fully anticipated* [my emphasis]'. With hindsight, this resonates well with the unanticipated events of all four infections, and also with biomedical intervention: new modes of HIV transmission in the co-production of a milieu that involves sex, antiretroviral drugs and viruses (Auerbach and Hoppe 2015), emergent TB drug resistance (Zignol et al. 2012), and also the continuing toll on human life as a consequence of the Ebola epidemic (Clark et al. 2015).[10]

Certainly, the want of a technoscience solution of drugs, vaccines, containment and so on that presumes an infection may be brought to a finite end may be difficult to resist. But without disregarding what are known as biomedical achievements, a solution is a static affair whose closure is only possible to the extent to which the focus follows the threads of a labyrinth-like prevailing biomedical thinking. This focus may misguide us away from a productive sociality to the narrowly prescribed social for biomedical intervention that I have criticised in this chapter.

But there is another dimension to the notion of infection made available by Whitehead that both Stengers and Savransky illuminate above. And this dimension is the crux of what I want to raise in reference to the pervasive work of scientific knowledge and practice. That is the prevalence of modes of knowing and practice that are in themselves an achievement of infection, yet whose possibilities for a more attentive, nuanced thinking are subsumed in the orchestration of a problem-making that all too readily becomes a problem of the narrowly prescribed social. To put this another way, if we accept the proposition that infection is the work of a co-adaption achieved through the situated or 'grounded' prehendings of the entities involved (and these may extend beyond what may be observed), then the dull, detracting social of biomedicine may well be attributed to the lure of biomedical promise and assurances. This is a lure that vectorises a mode of sense-making that falls well short of a sociality in which all entities are active in the creativity of the future (Whitehead 1967; 1968; 1978). Moreover, it does so by a logic that understands itself apart from the work of infectivity, which it claims as merely its object and not in connection with its process. Feeling or prehending are not merely concepts for expanding the logic of modern science, but for reflecting on its drawing together a sociality cultivated in the scientific endeavour.

CONCLUSION: REPOSING THE PROBLEM

Insofar as the achievements of biomedical science are generated in the varying endurances and transformation of objects, the latter cannot be held distinct and deficient or lacking unless only contingently. If we recall the examples of the nonoxyl 9 trial where the unwanted and unexpected novelty of infection emerged in the form of a vulnerability to HIV; or where dosing compliance may be superseded by events of an entirely different order than those held to matter by biomedicine, as observed by Race (2013), the problem is not foremost deficiency or lack. Rather it is the contribution of other elements that have come into existence with a differential degree of co-adaption or togetherness. Such events are not absences; on the contrary, they are creative and demand a response that remains attentive to what they bring forth.

In sum, it is not the infectiousness of viruses and bacteria alone that make for a social conceived as necessarily subject to biomedical intervention. Rather, we might say, it is also the infectiousness of scientific thought orchestrated through a host of uncontested events, all too briefly sketched here: authoritative media reporting; conference circuitry whose triumphal accounts of biomedicine mesh well with the want of spurious promises about the future; high-ranking scientific journal publications; and, not least, lauded methods of inquiry indifferent to the 'non-scientific'. While viruses and bacteria are doing well to achieve a 'hold' or 'co-adaptation', so too, it can be said, has biomedicine achieved, through an infection of ideas (and, therefore, analogous to its viral and bacterial objects), a hold that constitutes a social made insubstantial as the site and source of no more than a given or potential deficit.

This hold of biomedicine remains delimited in its grasp or feeling for other modes of 'holding together', modes that might otherwise be considered for the possibility of more preferable consequences of health and medical intervention. In contrast to the current mode of biomedical problem-making, if the aim is to intervene in the consequent killer effects of infectious disease and, as I suggest, resist analogy with the feeding of human flesh as the solution to cancer, the notion of infectivity may have something to teach us. By not posing it as a given problem of a social or, indeed, a biological/biomedical object, distinguished as these are along disciplinary lines within health and medicine approaches, it might be that new territory for thinking about infectious disease may be availed.

ACKNOWLEDGEMENTS

I want to express my gratitude to the editors of this collection, to two generous reviewers, and especially to Martin Savransky, Kane Race, Rosalyn Diprose and Cath Le Couteur for pushing my thinking during the genesis of this work. Of course, none should be held responsible for what I have made from this.

NOTES

1 Although living flesh could be said to refer to the use of stem cells, my reading is based on a more commonplace understanding of flesh as human life.
2 For an account of the contributions of Alan Brotherton, see Race and Stephenson (2016).

3 Elaboration on this claim is provided in a Wellcome Trust report (see Wellcome, 2017).

4 For details of this damage, see CDC Report on Microcephaly & Other Birth Defects (no date).

5 Since the Ebola epidemic in Guinea, Liberia and Sierra Leone, the World Health Organisation (WHO) has reviewed its response process and the need to consider better humanitarian approaches. The WHO Secretariat's response to the Report of the Ebola Interim Assessment Panel August 2015 (WHO 2015) serves as one example, although considerably more is offered by the anthropologists who raised key concerns about the Ebola response during the epidemic (for detailed commentaries during and postDESCRIB the epidemic see Somatosphere <http://somatosphere.net/tag/ebola> [accessed 3 May 2018].

6 See Epstein's account of how difficult it was to raise the spectre of an unusual disease that came to be known as HIV until it had been laboratory evidenced.

7 See McGoey (2015) for a complex study on the influence of philanthropic funding and the scientific bias of the Bill and Melinda Gates Foundation.

8 See Johnson (2012) for an account of Clinton's speech.

9 A detailed discussion of this method can be found in Michael and Rosengarten (2013) and Savransky and Rosengarten (2016).

10 Reports of a host of effects are now being reported. These include, for example, painful and mobility limiting arthritis, vision-threatening eye inflammation (uveitis) and mental health difficulties, all transmitted through the fluids of semen and breast milk (Beeching, Fenech, and Houlihan 2014; Vetter et al., 2016: e8s).

REFERENCES

Aiken, A., et al., 'Requests for Abortion in Latin America Related to Concern about Zika Virus Exposure', *New England Journal of Medicine* 375, 4 (2016), 396–398.

Auerbach, J. D., and T. A. Hoppe, 'Beyond "Getting Drugs into Bodies": Social Science Perspectives on Pre-Exposure Prophylaxis for HIV', *Journal of the International AIDS Society*, 18.4 (Suppl 3) (2015) <http://dx.doi.org/10.7448/IAS.18.4.19983> [accessed December 2015].

Baud, D., et al., 'An Update on Zika Virus Infection', *The Lancet* (June 21 2017) <http://dx.doi.org/10.1016/ S0140-6736(17)31450-2> [accessed September 2017].

Beeching, N. J., M. Fenech, and C. F. Houlihan 'Ebola Virus Disease' *BMJ* 349.g7348 (2014).

CDC 'Report on Microcephaly & Other Birth Defects' (no date) <https://www.cdc.gov/zika/healtheffects/birth_defects.html> [accessed January 2017].

——'Drug-Resistant TB' <http://www.cdc.gov/tb/topic/drtb/> (no date) [accessed February 2016].

Clark, D. V., et al., 'Long-Term Sequelae after Ebola Virus Disease in Bundibugyo, Uganda: A Retrospective Cohort Study', *The Lancet Infectious Diseases* 15.8 (2015), 905–12.

Edelstein, M., P. Angelides, and D. L. Heymann, 'Ebola: the Challenging Road to Recovery' *The Lancet* 385 (2015) http://www.thelancet.com/pdfs/journals/lancet/PIIS0140-6736(15)60203-3.pdf [accessed January 2016].

Farrar, J.J. and P. Piot 'The Ebola Emergency – Immediate Action, Ongoing Strategy', *The New England Journal of Medicine* 371 (2014): 1545–1546.

Fraser, M., 'Facts, Ethics and Event' in C. Bruun Jensen and K. Rødje, eds, *Deleuzian Intersections in Science, Technology and Anthropology* (New York, NY: Berghahn Press 2010) pp. 57–82.

Ghazanfar, H., et al., 'Ebola, the Killer Virus', *Infectious Diseases of Poverty* 4. 15 (2015) <https://www.ncbi.nlm.nih.gov/pubmed/25866626> [accessed October 2017].

Hanson, S., Y. Zembe and A. Ekstro, 'Vital need to engage the community in HIV control in South Africa', *Global Health Action* 8 (2015), 10.3402/gha.v8.27450.

Harper, I., 'Extreme Condition, Extreme Measures? Compliance, Drug Resistance, and the Control of Tuberculosis', *Anthropology & Medicine,* 17. 2 (2010), 210–14.

Johnson, C., 'AIDS 2012: Clinton announces "blueprint" for "AIDS free generation"',*Washington Blade* (July 2012) <http://www.washingtonblade.com/2012/07/23/aids-2012-clinton-announces-blueprint-for-aids-free-generation/#sthash.VzN7O2g9.dpuf> [accessed March 2016].

Kippax, S., and K. Race, 'Sustaining Safe Practice: Twenty Years On', *Social Science & Medicine* 57 (2003), 1–12.

McGoey, L., *No Such Thing as a Free Gift: The Gates Foundation and the Price of Philanthropy* (London and New York: Verso 2015).

McShane, H., 'Co-infection with HIV and TB: Double Trouble' *Int J. STD AIDS* 16.2 (2005), 95–100.

Marí Sáez, A., A. Kelly, and H. Brown, 'Investigating the Zoonotic Origin of the West African Ebola epidemic, EMBO Molecular Medicine', *Somatosphere* (2014) <http://somatosphere.net/2014/09/notes-from-case-zero-anthropology-in-the-time-of-ebola.html> [accessed October 2017].

Maurois, A., Preface to Jorge Luis Borges' *Labyrinths: Selected Stories and Other Writings* (London and New York: Penguin Books 2000), pp. 9–14.

Michael, M., and M. Rosengarten, *Innovation and Biomedicine: Ethics, Evidence and Expectation in HIV* (England: Palgrave MacMillan, 2013).

Milman. O., 'Race is On to Develop Zika Vaccine but Tests on Pregnant Women Raise Concern' *The Guardian.* (3 February 2016) <https://www.theguardian.com/world/2016/feb/03/zika-virus-vaccine-research-tests-pregnant-women-raise-concern> [accessed October 2017].

Mullen, Z., 'Ebola: The Missing Link', *The Lancet* 2.10 (2014), e550.

Noyes, J., and J. Popay, 'Directly Observed Therapy and Tuberculosis: How Can a

Systematic Review of Qualitative Research Contribute to Improving Services? A Qualitative Meta-synthesis', *Journal of Advanced Nursing*, 57. 3 (2006), 227–43.

Padian, N. S., et al., 'Weighing the Gold in the Gold Standard: Challenges in HIV Prevention Research Editorial Review', *AIDS*, 24 (2010), 621–35.

Puig de la Bellacasa, M., *Matters of Care* (Minneapolis: University of Minnesota Press 2017).

Race, K., and N. Stephenson, 'Introduction to Alan Brotherton's "The Circumstances in Which They Come": Refiguring the Boundaries of HIV in Australia' *Australian Humanities Review*, 60 (2016), 39–43.

Race, K., 'Framing Responsibility', *Journal of Bioethical Inquiry*, 9.3 (2012), 327–38.

——'Reluctant Objects', *GLQ A Journal of Gay and Lesbian Studies*, 22 (2015), 1–31.

——'Reluctant Objects', paper presented at the *Canadian Annual HIV Conference* (Vancouver 2013).

Rosengarten, M., *HIV Interventions: Biomedicine and the Traffic between Information and Flesh* (Seattle and London: University of Washington Press 2009).

Sankoh,O., et al., 'Prevention, treatment and future challenges of HIV/AIDS: A decade of INDEPTH research', *HIV & AIDS Review* 14. 1 (2015), 1–8.

Savransky, M., *The Adventure of Relevance: An Ethics of Social Inquiry* (London: Palgrave MacMillan, 2016).

Savransky, M. and M. Rosengarten, 'What Is Nature Capable Of? Ontology, Evidence, and Speculative Medical Humanities', *Medical Humanities,* 42 (2016), 166–72.

Somatosphere, 'Tag Archives: Ebola' (no date) <http://somatosphere.net/tag/ebola> [accessed October 2017].

Stengers, I., 'Drugs: Ethical Choice or Moral Consensus', *Power and Invention: Situating Science* (Minneapolis, MN and London: University of Minnesota Press, 1997).

——*Thinking with Whitehead: A Free and Wild Creation of Concepts,* trans. M. Chase (Cambridge, Mass: Harvard University Press 2011).

Timmermans, S., and M. Berg, *The Gold Standard: The Challenge of Evidence-based Medicine and Standardisation in Health Care* (Philadelphia: Temple University Press, 2003).

UNICEF, Zika virus outbreak in Latin America and the Caribbean: Regional Response Plan: UNICEF, 2016. <http://www.unicef.org/about/annualreport/files/Honduras_2016_COAR.pdf> [accessed June 2018].

Vetter, P. V., et al., 'Sequelae of Ebola Virus Disease: The Emergency within the Emergency', *Lancet Infectious Diseases,* 16 (2016), e82–91.

Wellcome, 'Zika vaccine research: guidance for including pregnant women' (2017) <https://wellcome.ac.uk/news/zika-vaccine-research-guidance-including-pregnant-women> [accessed October 2017].

Whitehead, A. N., *Science and the Modern World* (New York: Free Press, 1967).

——*Modes of Thought* (New York: Free Press, 1968).

——*Process and Reality* (New York: Free Press, 1978).

Will, C., and T. Moreira, *Medical Proofs, Social Experiments: Clinical Trials in Shifting Contexts* (England: Ashgate, 2010).

WHO (World Health Organisation), Secretariat Response to the Report of the Ebola Interim Assessment Panel (August 2015) <http://www.who.int/csr/resources/publications/ebola/who-response-to-ebola-report.pdf?ua=1> [accessed October 2017].

——'Tuberculosis' <http://www.who.int/mediacentre/factsheets/fs104/en/index.html> [accessed 4 January 2014].

Zignol, M., et al., 'Surveillance of Anti-Tuberculosis Drug Resistance in the World: An Updated Analysis, 2007–2010', *Bulletin of the World Health Organization*, 90.2 (2012), 111–19.

I I

SOCIAL MEDIA AS EXPERIMENTS IN SOCIALITY

Noortje Marres, Carolin Gerlitz

INTRODUCTION

What does the 'social' in social media refer to? This question has been much debated in recent years, and the range of answers provided is impressively wide (Coleman 2013; Van Dijck 2013; Davies 2015). Some argue that today's social media are not that special, as media technologies have always been social: older incarnations like the telephone and the radio equally depended on their uptake in social life for their functioning and success, and earlier internet applications like email and online discussion forums facilitated many of the forms of social connection and exchange that are today associated with popular online platforms dubbed 'social media' (Coleman 2013; Papacharissi 2015). Others have countered that we shouldn't just go along with the designation of online platforms as 'social media', as this is to confer legitimacy, or 'street cred', onto them: we should in fact criticise this very label. Thus, Couldry and Van Dijck (2015) argue that the 'social' in social media lacks a referent: in their view, and contrary to popular opinion, online platforms are *not* social but anti-social, as their mode of operation goes against many long-held norms and values regulating social life, such as the ideal that sociality should serve no other end than itself. In sharp contrast to this, many platforms frame sociality as an instrumental activity that serves other objectives such as gaining influence or attention, or of generating metrics and data. Finally, according to yet others, we should not so readily dismiss the possibility that a special relationship exists between the digital technologies known as social media and sociality. For one, popular platforms such as Facebook and Twitter are remarkably well-aligned with sociological understandings of social life, such as the idea that people form 'social networks' or 'perform' the self in everyday life (Thielmann 2011; Hogan 2010; Healy 2015).

In this chapter, we seek to contribute to this debate about social media technologies by offering a fourth, different answer to the question of what makes social media social. On online platforms, we propose, sociality becomes the subject of experimentation. An outstanding feature of social media is that they not only facilitate existing social activities, practices, and relations, but also encourage the creation of new ones, allowing for what some have called the 'enhancement', 'augmentation' or 'elaboration' of sociality (Healy 2015; Bucher 2013). In this article, we want to make the case that this has important consequences for our wider understanding of the relations between media technologies and sociality in our age. Specifically, it follows from the above that we should *not* treat mediated sociality as a given attribute of existing media technological infrastructures, arrangements, and practices. Instead, we must treat the sociality of social media as an *experimental* accomplishment: whether or not sociality is successfully realised with these technologies depends on how digital infrastructures, devices, and practices are *configured,* more or less deliberately so. We should, then, not only be debating whether social media are social or not – whether in and of themselves these technologies support social connections, expression, exchange, reproduction, and so on. We should equally examine how the accomplishment of different forms of sociality depends – in a non-straightforward way – on how digital infrastructures, devices, and practices are assembled in practice, and the contributions that social researchers themselves can make to this.

In this chapter, we explore such an experimental take on the sociality of social media platforms in two ways: first, we situate the debate about digital sociality in the context of recent debates in social theory about the status of 'the social' in contemporary societies. We propose that the online platforms popularly known as 'social media' re-open a debate that many thought was closed, namely that

SOCIAL MEDIA AS EXPERIMENTS IN SOCIALITY

about the relations between the social and the technical. Second, we discuss a collaborative project in social media analysis which we developed together with Esther Weltevrede and others during the Digital Methods Summer School in Amsterdam in 2013, and in which we sought to develop an experimental understanding of sociality with social media technologies. This project found its starting point in a remark by the British sociologist Emma Uprichard, who during a pointed exchange in the summer of 2012 insisted, 'Just because it is called social, doesn't make it social!' (see also Marres 2017). Adopting this dictum, our project took up the tools of Twitter analysis to develop a range of experimental answers to the question 'what is social about social media?' Finally, we draw on this pilot study to argue that digital platforms enable a distinct type of of 'arte-factual' sociality, one that invites or even requires the development of new, experimental research strategies for understanding social life with social media.

WHAT SOCIAL MEDIA CAN TELL US ABOUT 'THE SOCIAL': IT'S BACK BUT IT HASN'T RETURNED

Arguably, social media can be considered part of a bigger family of what social theorists have come to refer to 'the new socials'. Mike Savage (2009: 171)[1] has noted that digital arrangements affect the everyday organisation of society as an object of knowledge, as 'ordinary transactions, from websites, Tesco loyalty cards, CCTV cameras in your local shopping centre etc., are the stuff of the new social'. Will Davies (2015) has commented on the proliferation in the last decade of neologisms such as social enterprise, social technology, social design, social marketing, social innovation, social analytics, social bonds, social jour-nalism, and so on. These 'socials' can be called 'new' insofar as these arrange-ments and labels can be contrasted with 'old socials' associated with an earlier era of progressive investment in the planned society, such as social policy, social housing, and perhaps indeed, social research. Thus, while many of the 'old socials' are connected with the welfare state, the new socials signal efforts to bring economy, culture, and politics together under a regime of innovation that no longer depends on centralist planning. The advancement of new socials, furthermore, often involves efforts to bring technology and society into closer relation, where the former is no longer considered antithetical to the human bond, but somehow generative of community, togetherness, and related values – a capacity especially ascribed to digital technologies. It has for instance been argued that what makes the digital economy different from other economies is its relation to 'the social': Will Hutton opposed the social entrepreneurship of Palo Alto to the 'anti-social' economy of austerity Britain (Marres 2017).[2] We can even observe a recent tendency to claim that the digital has the capacities to make *any* sector, arrangement or practice 'more social': social media technologies allegedly enable companies to be more engaged, responsive, in touch, aware, and so on. However, this introduction of digital devices into social practices remains a largely instrumental operation, mainly serving the aim of understanding audiences (through monitoring), cultivating markets (social branding), and/or extracting data and value. As such, the new 'socials' mostly do *not* refer to anything that sociologists call by that name, but rather invoke conceptions of sociality that have been prevalent in marketing, audience research, and strategy where informal exchange and mundane interaction have long been recognised as a valuable conduit for the cultivation of brands and markets (Moor and Lury 2011).

However, this is not all there is to recent invocations of the social. To begin with, it is *not* the case that labelling online platforms as 'social' operates on the level of 'sloganeering' or 'labelling' only. Many online platforms also implement versions of sociological theory and methods (Bucher 2013; Healy 2015). Take 'People You May Know', the algorithm developed by the professional networking site LinkedIn and subsequently implemented by Facebook, where it is used to suggest users to connect with (to 'friend'). As LinkedIn itself proclaims on the company blog, this algorithm implements a concept developed by the sociologist Georg Simmel, namely his principle of triadic closure, the phenomenon that if one person knows two people, these people are likely to know each other.[3] As such, it could be argued that social media enable the 'materialisation' of sociological methods and concepts across organisations and social life, as their uptake across settings results in the partial reformatting – and perhaps to an extent also the re-organisation – of social life as analysable phenomena: as social networks, social trends, and so on. Partly for this reason, we think it would be a mistake to assume too strict an opposition between 'the new socials' advanced with the aid of digital technologies and 'the social' as conceived in social theory and social research.

Furthermore, the uptake of social concepts in contemporary technological, creative and organisational contexts can be understood as posing a wider challenge to debates in social theory about the fate of 'the social' in technological and knowledge-intensive societies. From the 1980s onwards, social theorists announced 'the end of the social': in this period, Bruno Latour (1993), Nikolas Rose (1996), Karin-Knorr Cetina (1994) and Jean Baudrillard (1988) developed different versions of the claim that we were moving beyond 'society' and entering a post-social epoch. While their interpretations of this general idea differ, each of them argued that the ideal conception of society as a homogeneous whole directed from a position outside it was losing plausibility in our time, either because of the demise of the ideal of a socially engineered society and the welfare state (Rose 1996), or more positively, because of the emergence of a different ethical and political proposition for the organisation of society, such as that of heterogeneous collectives (Latour 2005), in which not just humans but also non-humans participate. This latter approach presented society and post-society – or rather non-society – as mutually exclusive: either we continue to adhere to classic understandings of human society, or we affirm the existence of heterogeneous collectives, and being for society meant being against the recognition of non-humans as participants in social life.

Seen against this backdrop, digital media present social theory with a usefully heretical proposition: they combine both positions – society and heterogeneity – in remarkably successful and unsettling ways. In the case of online platforms, it is perfectly possible to specify a given formation as both heterogeneous in composition and social in form and orientation. These platforms present us with a Janus face: they constitute a socio-technically heterogeneous phenomenon made up of technical and social entities *and* they enable the organisation and analysis of classic social formations such as community and society (Marres 2017). How to account for these Janus-faced, heterogeneous socials?[4] It is important to recognise that the approximation between sociological methods and concepts and technological infrastructures that is so clearly observable in the case of social media technology, is not 'new' as such. Sociologists have long drawn attention to this very phenomenon in discussions of historical devices, infrastructures, and practices of social organisation and knowledge: in particular, social research instruments such as the survey, the opinion poll, and the focus group have been characterised in terms of their double function as serving both as a tool for the *analysis* of societies and as an instrument for *intervention* in public, economic, and social life (Didier 2009; Osborne and Rose 1999; Lezaun 2007; Law and Ruppert 2013). As such, social media reactivate sociological debates about the necessarily reflexive quality of social life and social research, as theorised for example by Anthony Giddens (1987) in his work on the double hermeneutics that make ideas circulate between sociology and social life, and by Aaron Cicourel (1964), who famously argued that social methods are only applicable to social life by virtue of the uptake of the categories built into these methods across social life. Social media platforms invite us to explore these ideas anew, but we propose that they also *disrupt* some assumptions associated with concepts of the 'reflexivity' of social life and social analysis.

To see this, there is a further point that requires attention: social media technologies highlight the 'arte-factual' quality of digitally mediated sociality. The social activities, practices, and relations enabled and made visible by social media are not necessarily representative of society at large, partly because they are informed by media technologies themselves. Both expert and popular debates increasingly recognise that social media are biased towards certain forms and types of sociality (Gerlitz and Helmond 2013). One way in which this bias became clear is when we visualised students' Facebook networks in a classroom setting: these networks often told us much more about how Facebook works ('the platform encourages the accumulation of friends') and about Facebook-specific behaviours ('he is a very active Facebooker') than about people's social relations. Social media platforms are designed for 'social enhancement', and the sociality they enable and make visible often does not exist before or outside the platform. Sociality enabled by social media, then, resists naturalization: it is demonstrably an arte-factual accomplishment. We find this is among the most interesting and important provocations of social media to our understandings of sociality, one that has the potential to translate into a wider 'experimentalisation' of the social, which would mean that the forms of sociality enabled by these and related socio-technical infrastructures are not given but 'curatable' and potentially open to reinvention.

To better understand this potential (re-)qualification of the social in digital media environments, we need to take a step back and consider whether and how this idea of 'experimental' sociality relates to another, better-known concept, that of the 'performance' of social life, which has been used by social theorists to demonstrate that social life is not a natural or given phenomenon but staged, produced, and realised deliberatively and effortfully (see the introduction to this volume). A performative account of society suggests that there is no such thing as an 'independently existing' social order, and sociality must instead be understood as – to use Harold Garfinkel's terminology – an ongoing accomplishment. Social media have granted empirical plausibility to this understanding of performed sociality, as they are designed to enable both distinct (and often economically valuable) performances of the 'self' through profile pictures, tag lines, walls, and so on, as well as the performative demonstration of social formations such as social networks and collective dynamics, with the aid of network maps and trend lists (Ruppert, Law and Savage 2013). Drawing on Harold Garfinkel's ethnomethodolgy, the German media scholar Tristan Thielmann (2011) has pointed out that online platforms enable everyday actors to produce 'accounts of social life as part of social life'. Platforms from Facebook to Instagram prompt users to generate reports of mundane occurrences (Where did you have dinner? With whom?). As such, social media appear to realise Garfinkel's ethnomethodological idea that social life 'accounts for itself': they enable the proliferation of accounting devices that render mundane moments and informal interaction recordable, analysable, and curatable for practical purposes – and this by way of data formats defined and made available by the media themselves, such as like shares, status updates, friend requests, and so on.

However, in other ways, today's social media platforms also precisely go against this kind of sociological understanding of social life as an object of knowledge. For Garfinkel, highlighting the performative quality of social life was a way of dismantling the status of sociology as an independent discipline. If social life can account for itself, this would make the development of distinct methods for sociological inquiry obsolete. But today the intensification of the accountability of social life is accompanied by loud reassertions of 'the social' as a distinctive form of organisation, and of the need for a new 'science of society'. The head of the Facebook data science team not so long ago referred to himself as a 'digital sociologist' (Simonite 2012). Social media, then, present sociology with a paradox: the infrastructures, devices, and practices that are associated with 'the new socials' equally exhibit features that sociologists associate with the 'end' of the social. Another way of putting this is to say that, from a sociological perspective, social media platforms appear to be methodologically and conceptually promiscuous: they exemplify insights from performative sociology but equally support a realist science of society. Indeed, is it not partly *because* social media platforms come with various in-built 'performative' devices that elicit the 'accounting for social life as part of social life', that they enable the proliferation of rather 'conventional' sociological measures and methods?

The easiest, most feasible way of conducting social research with social media is to take up popular free online data tools which facilitate things such as the analysis of personal (human-to-human) networks, or the measurement of reputation and influence – all forms of sociological analysis that have been part of the sociological repertoire since at least the post-war period. In some ways, social media radicalise these forms of analysis. One could say that ethnomethodologists held on to a certain idea of social life as given, insofar as that 'performative' quality of social life was for them an un-changing attribute, an ontological truth. Also, while the performative sociology of the 1960s had assumed that the formats for accounting 'for everyday life as part of everyday life' were mostly readily available in and as social life, today these formats have become the object of rather intense efforts to design, innovate, and domesticate 'new' devices of social accounting.

The work of information theorist Philip Agre (1994) is relevant here: in his studies of employee management, Agre proposed the notion of 'grammars of action'. This notion recognises that the production of 'accounts for social life as part of social life' involves instruments and the configuration of infrastructures, whilst also attending to the design efforts involved. Employers devise these grammars as predefined sets of actions – such as conversation scripts in call centres or step-by-step guidelines for dealing with customer complaints – that immediately enable their own datafication, rendering them recordable and analysable. The distinction between actions and their capture collapses in the process of grammatisation, and both are subject to intensive design, standardi-sation and formatting. In the context of social media platforms, pre-structured platform activities such as liking, tweeting or replying can be considered as examples of such grammars, which are offered by platforms and realised by users. However, these grammars can only standardise the form of action and data, not its interpretation by users and other stakeholders, who, to a certain degree, can inscribe their own practices and meaning into the grammars pro-vided, taking advantage of interpretative flexibility (Pinch and Bijker 1984; Paßmann and Gerlitz 2014).

As such, social media, and possibly other new socials too, do not quite comply with a performative understanding of social life. They present us with a further 'experimentalisation' of the social: it is today *not* self-evident what forms of sociality, what theory of society or of social life, will be realised as a consequence of the proliferation of devices for 'accounting for social life as part of social life'. There are myriads of possibilities: for example, will the paradigm of incentivising and nudging by way of social media buttons trans-late into the invention of a behavioural society, one constituted of more or less atomistic individuals defined by their actions? Or will organic forms of society be reinvented in the sense of a return to the imagination of a collective body that transcends the individuals that make it up? While theorists of the 'end of the social' in the 1980s and 90s considered this debate more or less closed (in favour of the former), we consider it reopened: 'the social is back' as an issue to be grappled with. And this return does not necessarily present a return to the familiar: today's situation signals a possible experimentalisation of the social. We face a paradoxical situation, one in which sociality figures as an intense object of design, engineering, and analysis, while the theories of sociality that are deployed towards this end tend to conceptualise society in terms of a human population or community. The rise to prominence of 'social media' correlates with increased levels of 'artifice' involved in the making of sociality, but at the same time the claim that social data enable an 'unfiltered' understanding of a given society is widely endorsed. It is in order to hold on to these paradoxes that we insist that today we are facing a 'not quite' return of the social. And it is this 'not quite' that we seek to specify, by approaching social media as a site for the '(re)invention of sociality'.

METHODOLOGY: HOW TO STUDY NEW SOCIALS WITH SOCIAL MEDIA

We are struck, then, by the odd confluence of ideas, devices, and imaginaries of sociality in social media, at least some of which seem mutually incompatible or in tension with one another. This situation can be investigated by different means: it can be engaged theoretically, for example by tracing genealogies of the concept of the social (Halewood 2014), or it can be analysed empirically, through case studies of particular social media technologies, such as buttons or flags, to specify their role in the performance of mediated sociality (Helmond and Gerlitz 2013; Crawford and Gillespie 2014). But in what follows we adopt not so much an empirical but an experimental approach: we do not just ask what definitions of sociality are being advanced through social media, which would be a way of delegating the definition of sociality to our empirical object. We also do not attempt to locate sociality in the technical features of social media platforms and the possibilities they offer for interaction and connectivity (Boyd and Ellison 2007), in the content created by users (which invites spreading) (Langlois 2014), in the context of use (Slater 2002) or in the data they render available, such as social network connections (Gerlitz and Rieder 2017). Instead we would like to engage with social ontology as something that is collectively accomplished in social media environments, and approach this accomplishment as something in which we – as social media researchers and theorists – actively participate.

We thus approach the social as a 'happening', to take up the concept offered by Nina Wakeford and Celia Lury (2012): a distributed accomplishment of users, technicity, data, practices, methods, measures, and other yet to be determined elements, of which the collective effect is fundamentally uncertain. We then approach the question of 'what's social in social media?' in an open-ended way: rather than conceptualise the productive capacities of methods and devices in terms of enactment, we think of them in terms of participation. In doing so, we also take our cue from Michel Callon (2006), who insists that empirical sociology must be willing to derive its classifications from the case at hand. In his discussion of how to analyse large numbers, Callon suggests that '[o]ne way of testing the relevance and robustness of a proposed categorization is to allow the entities studied to participate in the enterprise of classification' (2006: 8). In our view, such attention to actor-defined categories is significantly complicated in digital research, as it is not just the actors (that is, the users, the platforms, or associated developers), but also contexts of interpretation, tools for data analysis and their settings, the issue at hand, visualisation strategies, and so on, that play a role in establishing the (ir)relevance of particular classifications and assumptions over others. The task of experimental social inquiry is to formulate research strategies that render such participation methodologically viable.

To give some concrete examples of this experimental strategy in social inquiry, we will discuss a group project that we initiated during the Digital Methods Summer School 2013 to address the question of 'what makes social media social?'[5]. The Digital Methods Summer School is an annual postgraduate event, initiated by Richard Rogers and hosted by the University of Amsterdam, which introduces students and scholars to digital media research through participation in collaborative research projects. Small-scale projects are designed, realised and presented within a week. The aim of our project was to use digital methods for practice-based social research (Rogers 2013). For this particular edition of the summer school, we collaborated with Esther Weltevrede to pitch a project called 'Detecting the Social', and developed it together with around twenty scholars, designers, programmers, and activists, bringing together expertise in media studies, sociology, computing, design, and science and technology studies (STS). In what follows we will narrate selected findings of this project in order to illustrate the range of 'socials' that we found to be 'in play' in social media, and to discuss what an experimental approach to new socials might look like.

Starting with the idea of the 'happening' of the social (Lury and Wakeford 2012), we abstained from preconceived accounts of sociality and explicitly recognised the heterogeneity of social concepts, methods, and forms that are designed and practised in digital media environments, and the participation of our methodological apparatus in them. To structure the project, we divided our group into three sub-groups, each of which was tasked to explore a different 'way into' the social: interaction (Gerlitz), the non-human (bots) (Weltevrede), and content (Marres). Our aim was to produce an overview or 'mapping' of different happenings of sociality that are 'detectable with social media' (see for a similar approach, Kelty et al. 2012). In line with the prevalent approach adopted by the Digital Methods Summer School (Rogers 2013), we limited ourselves to using methods of online data analysis and visualisation, and focused on one platform only, namely Twitter. It is important to note that relying on platform data in this way offers a highly partial view, one which does not account for user interpretations and practices, or socio-material and organisational features of social media infrastructures. However, this narrow focus seemed to us well attuned to our wider methodological project of studying the 'happening' of the social: we could account for the sociality enacted in and with Twitter 'from the inside', and examine a range of forms of sociality with the same data set: user interactions, content dynamics, and the composition of collectives (humans and non-humans).

Twitter was chosen as a site of experimentation as the platform is known for the relative ease of data access, the diverse character of at least some of its content, and its explicit yet limited grammars of action and interaction (tweets, @mentions, retweets, user accounts, hashtags, and so forth). To account for media and content dynamics, we settled on a topical dataset containing tweets relating to the topic of 'privacy', as captured with the Digital Methods Twitter Analysis and Capture Tool (TCAT) (Borra and Rieder 2014). These tweets were posted between 23 May 2013 and 15 June 2013.[6] During this period, the news of Edward Snowden's data leak broke, an event which operated across a variety of registers, including journalistic, activist, tongue-in-cheek, and geo-political. This broad scope of the event seemed helpful for our project of capturing different modalities of interaction and collective expression on Twitter.

Each of the three groups examined the sociality of Twitter from a distinct angle, namely interaction, non-human activity, and content or hashtag dynamics, and issue composition. We were aware that by choosing this approach we aligned ourselves in various ways with dominant measures built into Twitter and Twitter analysis. The platform is famously biased towards particular forms of sociality, such as popularity (trends), celebrity (star users) or viral dynamics (memes). However, our own preoccupations – with interaction, non-humans and issue formation – in this project have a clear sociological signature, as each is associated with more or less established sociological approaches such as interactionism, Actor-Network Theory (which has introduced the concept of the non-human), and issue mapping (Marres and Rogers 2005). Our commitment to 'detect' sociality certainly does not imply that we adopted a 'blank' attitude (Mackenzie 2012): we did not only invite the medium to tell us what makes it social, but rather attempted to deploy social research methodology in order to detect happenings of sociality that do *not* derive from platform features.

SOCIAL 1: USER INTERACTIONS

To get at forms of sociality enacted with Twitter, the first group focused on features or grammars that Twitter makes available for users to interact with other users, namely tweets, @replies, retweets, and interaction chains. In doing so, this group sought to attune its method to the medium by exploring how Twitter features are instantiated in Twitter use, with a focus on detecting interactional patterns in the data. Aware of Twitter's own focus on the most popular or frequently occurring (top trends, popular users), we started by identifying peaks of activity and interactivity. Starting from the pragmatic assumption that the more active a user is, the more likely the disclosure of interactive patterns, we identified the twenty most active and interactive users. The group manually categorised these top users, generating a range of user categories (journalists, celebrities, and so on) in the process: Figure 11.1 shows the resulting categories, with number of tweets on the left and received mentions on the right.

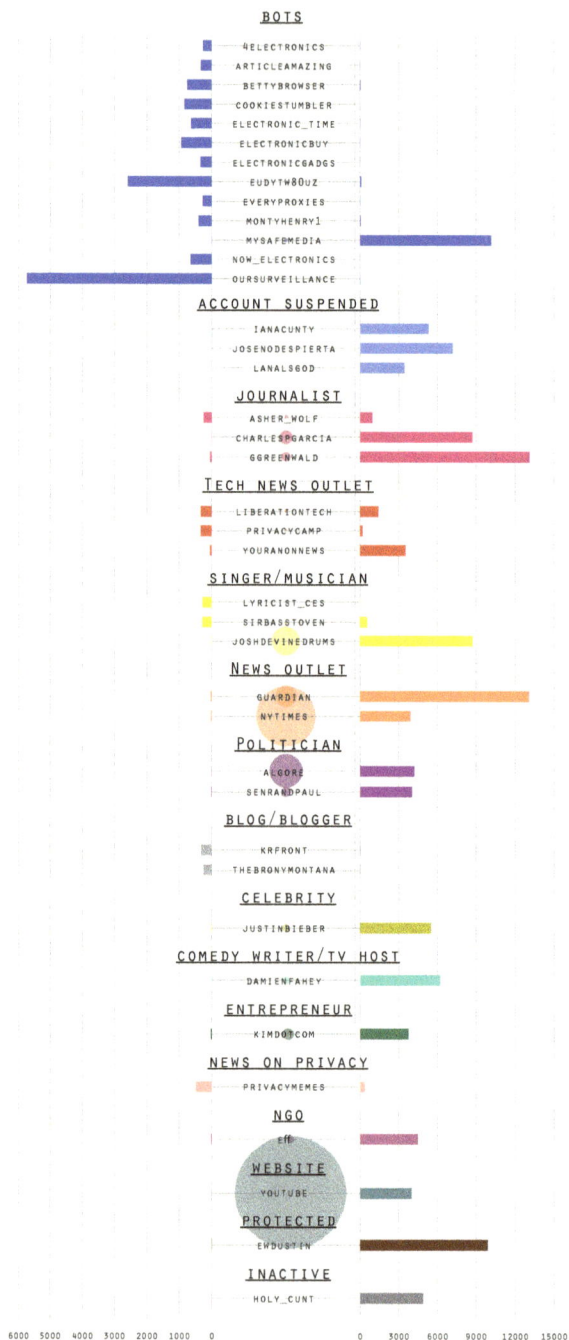

TWEETS   USERS (&FOLLOWERS)   MENTIONS

BOTS
- 4ELECTRONICS
- ARTICLEAMAZING
- BETTYBROWSER
- COOKIESTUMBLER
- ELECTRONIC_TIME
- ELECTRONICBUY
- ELECTRONICGADGS
- EUDYTW80UZ
- EVERYPROXIES
- MONTYHENRY1
- MYSAFEMEDIA
- NOW_ELECTRONICS
- OURSURVEILLANCE

ACCOUNT SUSPENDED
- IANACUNTY
- JOSENODESPIERTA
- LANALSGOD

JOURNALIST
- ASHER_WOLF
- CHARLESPGARCIA
- GGREENWALD

TECH NEWS OUTLET
- LIBERATIONTECH
- PRIVACYCAMP
- YOURANONNEWS

SINGER/MUSICIAN
- LYRICIST_CES
- SIRBASSTOVEN
- JOSHDEVINEDRUMS

NEWS OUTLET
- GUARDIAN
- NYTIMES

POLITICIAN
- ALGORE
- SENRANDPAUL

BLOG/BLOGGER
- KRFRONT
- THEBRONYMONTANA

CELEBRITY
- JUSTINBIEBER

COMEDY WRITER/TV HOST
- DAMIENFAHEY

ENTREPRENEUR
- KIMDOTCOM

NEWS ON PRIVACY
- PRIVACYMEMES

NGO
- eff

WEBSITE
- YOUTUBE

PROTECTED
- EHBUSTIN

INACTIVE
- HOLY_CUNT

TWEETS axis: 6000 5000 4000 3000 2000 1000 0
MENTIONS axis: 0 3000 6000 9000 12000 15000

FIG. 11.1 Top twenty most active users based on tweets and mentions (created by Stefania Guerra)

As a first pattern, we noted the wide gap between those users who are most active and those who are referred to most. Accounts with many mentions mainly included journalists, media and news outlets, celebrities, politicians, and (unavoidably) pop singers – that is, accounts that thrive on existing media exposure and popularity beyond Twitter. Among the most active users on the other hand, we mainly found automated accounts – which we categorised as bots, although we later came to problematise this category. Bot activity includes software-supported automated tweet production, or cross-syndication of content from other media sources. These bots receive few mentions, but output comparably high volumes of tweets. We speculated that the category of the individual user may not necessarily map well onto that of a social media account, as many of these accounts cannot be linked to a single agentive individual, but rather express potentially distributed professional activities (news outlets or celebrities may employ social media agents) and varying degrees of software-supported tweeting. These findings further elicited discussions about the usefulness of frequency-based measures for detecting the social, as those who speak most loudly on Twitter are not spoken back to, and vice versa. It appeared that focusing on the top frequency layer of social media data, at least in this case, means to value currency and liveness more than interaction, leading to a highly partial view.

Our initial exploration of the data produced, then, in Callon's (2006) expression, a moment of objection, in which our findings confronted us with the limits of our own measures and assumptions. We therefore decided to change our focus to users that are both active *and* mentioned, most of which can be found in a mid-level frequency tier of users who tweeted between 100 and 300 times, and who achieved at least twenty mentions. Focusing on the 120 *most inter/active* users, we again manually categorised their accounts and compared their tweets and mentions (Fig. 11.2). The majority of these inter-active users, we found, were activists and issue-focused journalists, engaging in mutual interactions. The exercise showed us that whilst it is tempting to focus on top-tier frequencies to 'sum up' a data set, its highly partial perspective exemplifies the importance of adjusting our measures to our data, in light of our question.

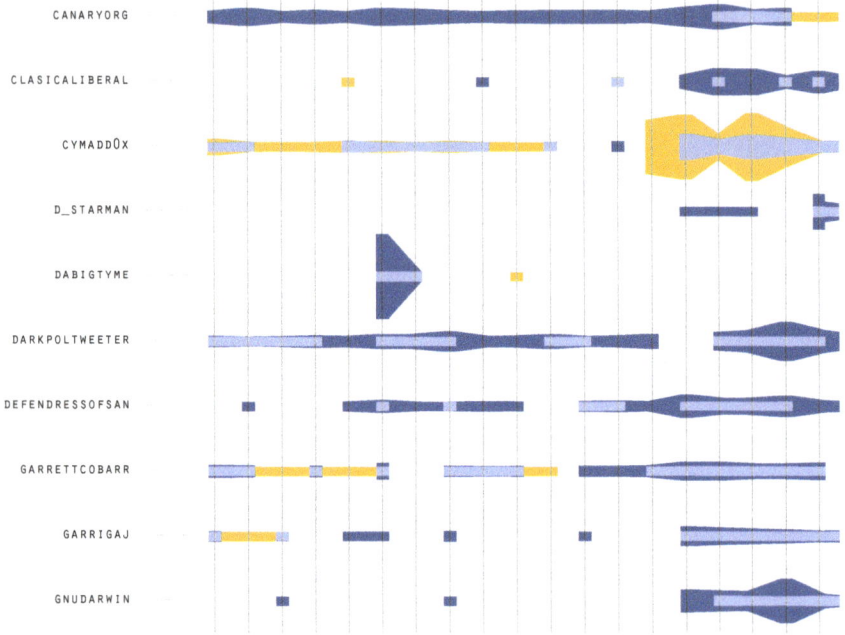

FIG. 11.2 Interactive users (fragment of a visualisation created by Gabriele Colombo)

In the last leg of Group 1's work, we moved from users to patterns of inter/activity. We traced reply-chains, that is tweets followed by at least one or more replies (Fig. 11.3), and found that the majority of chains only consist of two elements – that is, a tweet by user A and a response by user B (not followed by another response by user A), rather than taking the more lively form of mutual tweets and replies. This finding seems in line with the discrepancy between active and mentioned users noted above, as the majority of users that are being replied to do not reply back. Overall, we found three types of interaction prevalent in our dataset: (1) the chain, in which one tweet is followed by a number of mutual replies, (2) the star, in which a user receives multiple replies to their tweet but does not respond back (the most prominent formation in our data set), and (3) other forms that mix star and chain elements, in which some replies are answered. Chain-like conversations can mainly be found among users who have similar follower numbers. Within star constellations, the respondents mostly have significantly fewer followers than the originator. This indicated to us that mention activity does not necessarily point to interactivity.

To sum up, the work of Group 1 demonstrated to us the well-known methodological point that methods and measures participate in the specification of the phenomenon under study: by taking up tools of social media analysis, attention is initially drawn to dynamics favoured by the device (Twitter), such as celebrity and popularity, at the expense of interaction. However, in engaging proactively with this point during data exploration, we also moved beyond this observation: we adjusted our focus in order to bring into view dynamics that are less prominent but no less relevant. The notion of the performativity of social methods is rather asymmetrical, as it attributes the capacity to structure the phenomenon it is supposed to render observable *to the device*. By contrast, the procedure of the mutual adjustment of data, methods, and concepts we followed in our experiment allowed for a more symmetrical form of 'participation': our methodological operations allowed Twitter data to participate in the production of accounts of social interaction online, rather than focus solely on the demonstration of 'device effects' (Gerlitz and Lury 2014). Indeed, we actively sought to reduce specific reactive effects[7] that contribute to the enactment of some forms of sociality over others on Twitter.

SOCIAL 2: 'AUTOMATED' SOCIALITY

Our exploration of Twitter interaction above has already highlighted that humans can only account for part of this activity. In the context of social media, other-than-human activity is often labelled 'bot activity', as it involves the use of predefined, automated scripts of different sorts (Wilkie et al. 2014; Niederer and van Dijck 2010). Bots tend to be associated with spammy, promotional, and malicious behaviour, and as such they have been understood as threats to online sociality, undermining the general quality of online interaction and the quality of data (Hargittai and Sandvig 2015). However, Group 2 was not so much interested in taking a normative position towards the role of bots, but rather wanted to see whether and how 'bot activity' online was analysable in social terms (Jones 2015). After all, there is a significant legacy of non-social methods for identifying bots, of which the mentalist method of the Turing Test is the best known. This group, then, was interested in taking the term 'social bot' literally, to develop an account of the role of technological agents in social media environments that did not so much rely on mentalistic conceptions of what a bot is ('artificial intelligence'), or normative assumptions about whether it is good or bad, but rather considered the habits and practices of automated accounts. To do this, Group 2 began by dropping the term bot and taking up the idea that online sociality is automated to varying degrees. We favour the term automatisation over the discrete notion of bots, as the former allows for a more nuanced and inclusive conception of more-than-human activities online.

Research by Gerlitz and Rieder (2017) has noted the growing and varying degrees of software-assisted tweeting. Analysing a random Twitter sample, the authors identified the range of sources from which users tweet, each of which support different degrees of automatisation, such as button-supported tweets, cross-syndication of content from other platforms, in-app or in-game tweets, scheduled tweets, automated retweets based on keywords, hashtag or user mentions, fully automated accounts, account networks and retweet cartels. Mobile devices and clients are found to be taking over the Twitter web client as the main access point to Twitter, and this proliferation of sources and their features asks for a more fine-grained notion of automatisation. Rather than viewing the couple 'human and non-human' as a binary, then, we approach it as a continuum or spectrum based on activity patterns.

As a first step, Group 2 identified the sources from which users tweet.[8] In our dataset, tweets were sent from 4267 different devices and sources; Figure 11.3 shows the top fifteen. Twitter for Web, iPhone, and Android are among the most used, followed by a set of sources which support different degrees of automatisation. Tweet Buttons make it possible to send web content directly to Twitter. Twitterfeed, Tweetdeck, and Hootsuite are clients that allow users to access, organise, and post to Twitter, offering extended analytics on reach, engagement, interaction, and scheduled tweets.[9] Importantly, the majority of tweets are produced outside the interfaces provided by Twitter itself, which suggests that the 'degree of automation' is subject to a multi-faceted information ecology, of which Twitter is likely to form only one part.

The question is whether and how we can characterise this spectrum of differently automated accounts in social terms. To address this question, we explored the possibility of categorising automated accounts in terms of activity patterns. This proved relatively straightforward, as many automated accounts were remarkably mono-manic in their social media habits – they tend to send a disproportionately high number of tweets featuring specific selections of contents or hashtags. We reached this conclusion by tracing which hashtags are being used in tweets sent by specific sources. In the context of our privacy dataset, we discovered at least two orchestrated high-frequency promotional efforts. First, tweets sent from 'U tweet deals' mainly appear with the hashtags #home and #surveillance, and send users to ebay.com. Second, tweets using a combination of hashtags (#free, #blog, #photos, #websites, #videos, #mp3, #videochat and #emailblas) were linked to Mysavemedia.com. Interestingly, these tweets were not sent by a tweet automator, but via the Twitter web

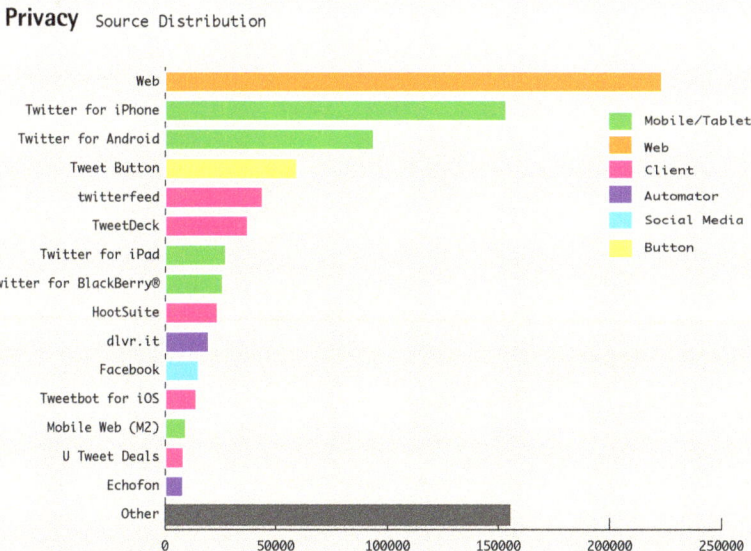

FIG. 11.3 Devices used to send tweets (created by Allessandro Brunetti)

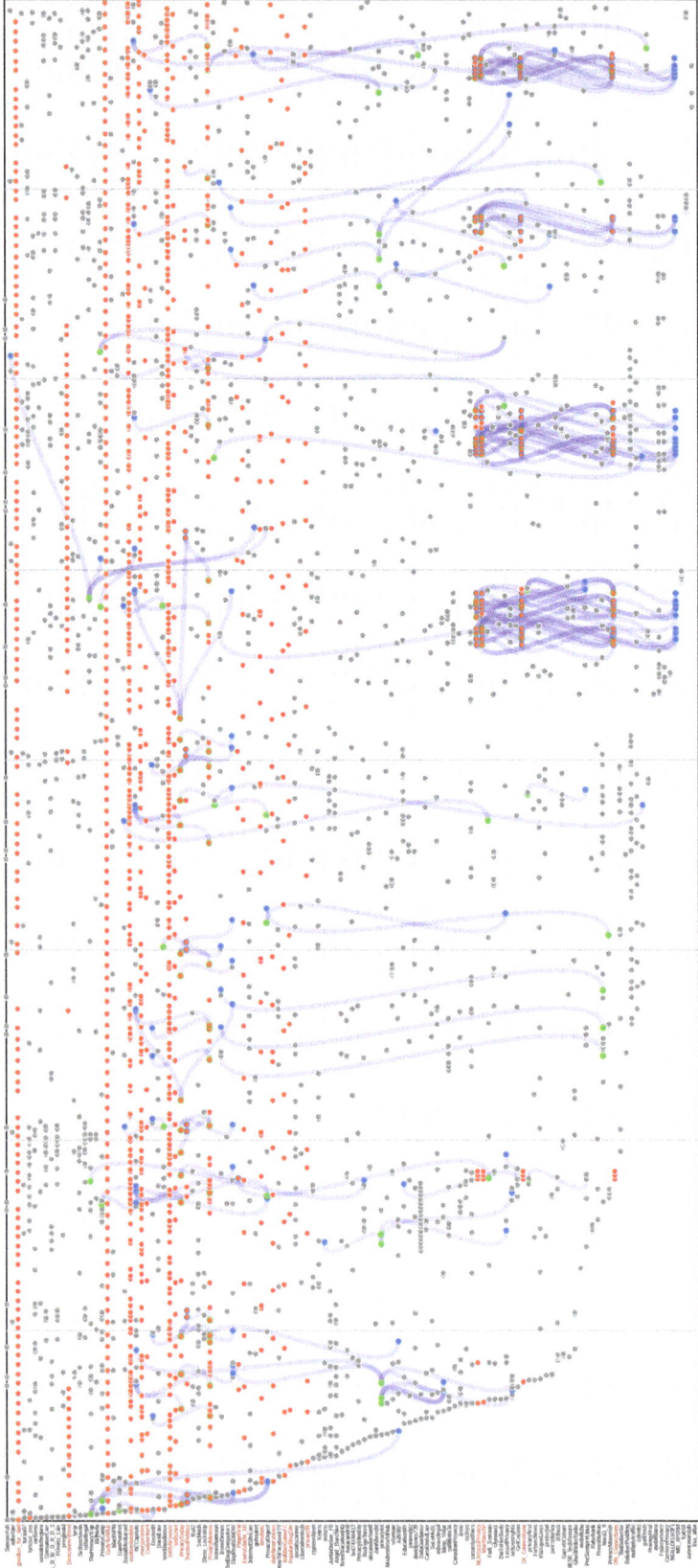

FIG. 11.4 Automated activity pattern (created by Carlo De Gaetano (unfinished))

interface. Digging deeper, we found that most Twitter widgets, including Twitter buttons, are routed via the Twitter web interface and thus also appear in the dataset as sent from Twitter web. So even sources that seemingly point to manual practices have to be treated with care and can be the result of automatisation. In both instances, automated activity takes advantage of the relative popularity of the topic (privacy) to create and broadcast to an audience as a promotional effort. Faced with this, we sought to discover whether we could plot automated Twitter activity along a spectrum that goes from broadcasting to more interactive forms of publicity. Are some bots more social than others?

To explore this, we produced a cascade visualisation (Fig. 11.4), which lists users on the y axis and plots their activity along the x axis, where each tweet marks a dot (grey: tweet, green: mention, blue: retweet). As tweets are depicted chronologically, the x axis also marks a timeline. Taking up the user categories proposed by Group 1, we coloured red those accounts that we identified as automated in some form. Our initial assumption that automated tweeting follows a fairly stable, high-paced pattern was confirmed, but the Figure also helps to further specify this claim: among the automated accounts we found clusters of retweeting – the purple s-shaped dongles going up and down – which suggests that automated accounts do attempt to generate interactive behaviour. Automated activity, we suggest, can also blend into and mimic popular social media dynamics, and perhaps, indeed, it is exemplary of the reactive dynamics we noted above, reinforcing what is considered valuable sociality on Twitter.

SOCIAL 3: HOW SOCIAL IS A HASHTAG?

While Groups 1 and 2 investigated the interactivity and activity associated with different kinds of Twitter accounts, Group 3 focused on the dynamics of content in our dataset of tweets on 'privacy'. This group asked to what extent we can ascribe sociality not only to actors that are active on Twitter, but to the objects (content) with which they engage? This question draws on object-oriented approaches to social life developed in social studies of technology and related fields (Latour 2005; Lash and Lury 2007), in order to investigate the capacity of social media objects to organise sociality on Twitter. This group's work was complicated by the fact that the definition of object-oriented sociality is itself called in question by social media analysis: should we define a Twitter object as 'social' when it facilitates *enduring* relations between actors and entities? Or is the cultivation of *happening* relations a sufficient mark of sociality? To investigate this, the group pragmatically decided to focus on a Twitter-specific objectual format, that of hashtags. Twitter studies have taken a special interest in the capacity of hashtags to organise social relations around and with objects, as in Burgess and colleagues' (2015) work on the hashtag as a hybrid forum that facilitates the formation of ad hoc publics. Focusing on hashtags also makes it much easier to investigate content dynamics in a large data set, but it also means adopting a partial perspective on the data, as only 25% of the tweets in our datasets use hashtags. Accordingly, we approach hashtags, not as representatives of Twitter content, but rather as specific devices that enable the creation of relations between tweets, issues, and users.

Sociality, however, cannot be considered a given capacity of hashtags, and much hashtag activity is marked by efforts to achieve popularity, which Group 3 deemed not to qualify as 'sociality', since popularity is about gaining attention, not making relations. Following this intuition, Group 3 sought to move beyond the recurring popularity dynamics of Twitter by taking up co-occurrence analysis, a fairly common method in Twitter studies that applies measures of network analysis to words, and is used to detect the emergence of new relations between words or hashtags (for a discussion see Marres and Gerlitz 2015). Group 3 analysed patterns of co-occurrence between hashtags in the Twitter data set in order to see which hashtags were connected and how these connections changed over time. We divided our data set into four intervals, two before and two after the initial Snowden leak,[10] and found a large number of promotional hashtags among the most connected terms.[11] The group speculated about the 'prize of success'. Where there is a broad uptake of a given term (such as 'privacy' after the Snowden leak) and accordingly a great potential for new relations, the consequence on Twitter is that the overall space of relationality degrades: generic, uneventful terms or promotional efforts take over, and these possess little apparent capacity to produce either enduring or happening relations.

A second answer to the question 'how is a hashtag social?' suggests itself in the form of hashtags containing phrases and jokes (e.g. #overlyhonestmethods; #igetannoyedwhenpeople, #markmywords). These hashtags indicate non-official uses of Twitter, and as such may be taken as an index of social activity, treating user invention as a marker of the social. To produce an overview of inventive hashtags, we considered the top fifty hashtags on each day of our selected period, retaining only those hashtags containing such invented language or neologisms.

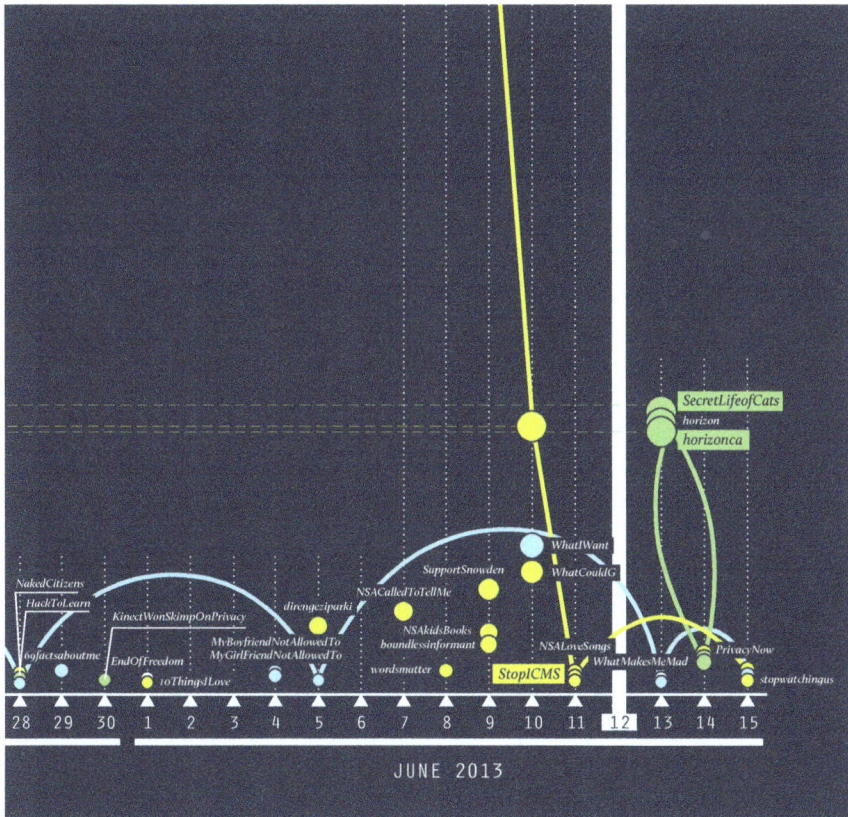

FIG. 11.5 Neologisms associated with #privacy (fragment of a visualisation created by Carlo De Gaetano)

Figure 11.5 plots the occurrence of such invented hashtags over time, with the colours indicating four categories produced by Group 3 through a close reading of the relevant Twitter data: entertainment (white), politics (yellow), pointless babble (blue), and news (green). To be sure, these categories are not neutral: the category 'pointless babble' implies a devaluation of off- or random-topic commentary.[12] And insofar as such off-topic commentary is common in social media, the use of neologisms points to medium-specific practices. However, at the same time, 'pointless babble' offers a useful contrast to political terms (I stand with Snowden), with the latter type becoming more prominent after the breaking of the scandal. It also usefully complicates our initial observation that newsworthiness and the widening of the topic space may translate into a reduction in the capacity to relate.

In a final step, Group 3 explored which hashtag relations in our data sets endured and/or varied over time, by mapping hashtag co-occurences in our data set. We speculated that hashtags more closely related to the news would be more ephemeral, appearing and disappearing in relatively quick bursts in accordance with news cycles. We thus selected a number of hashtags that were prominent in our data set across all the intervals and were not directly connected with the Snowden affair (that is, not 'NSA' or 'Prism', but 'privacy', 'Google', 'security', 'surveillance', 'Facebook', 'tech', etc.). For each of these hashtags, we produced an 'associational profile', a bar chart figure that shows with what other hashtags a hashtag co-occurs across intervals (e.g. Fig. 11.6, Fig. 11.7). We found that several hashtags' associations remain relatively stable over time (coloured lines), with new associations coming in but not displacing these enduring associations in the third interval, when the Snowden revelations first broke (in grey).[13] Exploring the distribution of enduring and emerging co-hashtag relations then led Group 3 to formulate two partly opposed indicators of sociality: firstly, the proliferation of neologisms, that is the re-appropriation of issues into everyday discourse, and secondly, enduring content relations which are not affected too much by news events and thus signal stable, institutionalised associations.

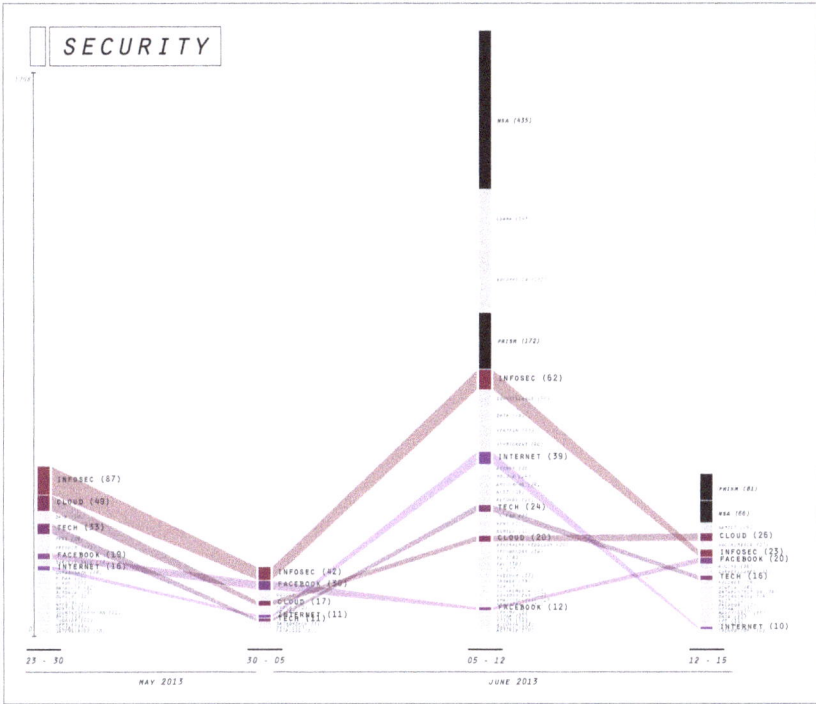

FIG. 11.6 Associational profile of #security (created by Carlo De Gaetano)

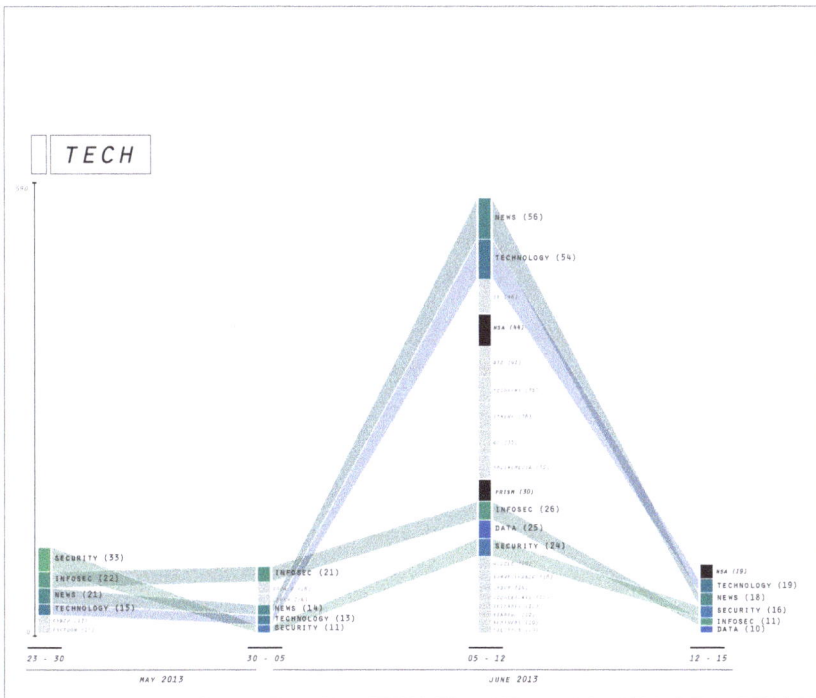

FIG. 11.7 Associational profile of #tech (created by Carlo De Gaetano)

CONCLUSION

Our summer school project moved from the definition of digital platforms as 'social' media to the experimental description of the forms of sociality one such platform, Twitter, enables. Our inquiries took as their starting point a sociological idea, namely the understanding of sociality as a distributed accomplishment, as something that happens among a variety of entities, and cannot be reduced to any singular entity, be it a collective of users, the platform or the content, or a singular conception of the social. This approach led us to produce what some may regard as rather artificial, counter-intuitive accounts of what is social about social media, as we produced the following list of potential indicators of sociality in social media: interaction, activity, creativity, and endurance. We do not claim that anything we detected on Twitter qualifies as *the* social, as we observed a series of competing, overlapping, and complementing socials. Our methods did not merely render them visible, but participated in their enactment.

However, our exploration of these proliferating socials did allow us to advance on the 'problem' with the 'social' of social media in two ways: first, it allowed us to elaborate a claim we presented at the beginning of this chapter, namely that social media are in line with the performative understanding of social life in some respects, but in other respects clearly go against it. In documenting patterns of interactivity, plotting automated accounts along a spectrum from human to non-human, and by tracing the happening of 'content', we produced what might be called 'methodological stories', that demonstrate how specifically social forms of life may be enacted in and with heterogeneous settings. We also formulated a problem with the sociality of social media of our own: one of the recurrent findings of our experimental exercise was what might be termed 'frequentism': we constantly faced the question of how to evaluate – and possibly adjust for – effects of volume. What to do with the 'power users' whose 'size' – in terms of followers, tweets, or mentions – crowds out and overshadows others? And what to do with the widely used hashtags that surface in our content analysis as a consequence of 'bursts' in retweet activity, not infrequently associated with automated accounts? Our heterogeneous group voiced different responses to such frequentism. According to some, 'volume effects' like the above obstructed our ability to detect sociality with social media. For others, however, 'frequent-ism' points to the heart of sociality in social media. It is what social media is all about: a new way of reaching and interacting with wider audiences without needing to pass via established gatekeepers ('the media'). Automated tweeting raised similar tensions. Some proposed that automatisation could *add* to the accomplishment of sociality, enabling the creation of more diverse human-non-human relations, whilst others argued that automatisation undermines the possibility for social interaction and exchange in social media, as for instance in the case of promotional hijacking of popular hashtags.

Insofar as many of these empirical effects cannot be affirmed, but must be actively – and creatively – countered in digital social research, this form of analysis invites us to move beyond 'empiricisation' towards an 'experimentalisation' of the social. Such an approach makes the participation of social research meth-ods in the making of sociality explicit: its task is to formulate methodological strategies that enable us to affirm the role of social research in the generation of its object of inquiry (Brown 2012). Instead of adopting a purely prescriptive position, that allows us to pass conclusive judgement on social media ('this is not the social'), we see it as our job to participate in advancing alternative configurations of social media, and to specify alternative modes of digital sociality, ones that we deem more productive, caring, demanding, desirable, and so on. Social media ask us to move beyond prescriptive and descriptive forms of knowledge and to test alternative, more experimental forms of inquiry. Different forms of sociality cannot be held separate as easily here as in other contexts. As a consequence, social media lure us into asking questions we haven't been trained to ask, questions that refuse a strict opposition between social realism and performativity, between independently existing societies and enacted heterogeneity (Mutzel 2009). How do bots participate in the society? Is automation – of all things – undoing the Thatcherite 'there is no such thing as society'? Could social networks really help to organise heterogeneous collec-tives? Critical and creative approaches to social research and social theory, we argue, should do more with the 'experimental' capacities of the online platforms dubbed 'social' by looking for ways in which their methods could participate in the reinvention of the social.

ACKNOWLEDGEMENTS

We would like to thank the participants of the Detecting the Socials DMI Summer School 2012 project group. Our team consisted of: team users & interactivity: Rasha Abdulla, Davide Beraldo, Augusto Valeriani, Navid Hassan, Tao Hong, Johanne Kuebler, Carolin Gerlitz; team bots: Evelien D'heer, Bev Skeggs, Wifak Gueddana, Esther Weltevrede; team hashtag and issue profiles: Diego Ceccobelli, Catharina Koerts, Francesco Ragazzi, Andreas Birkbak, Simeona Petkova, Noortje Marres; design team: Gabriele Colombo, Stefania Guerra, Carlo de Gaetano; and the tech team: Erik Borra & Bernhard Rieder.

NOTES

1 Savage (2009: 171) notes: 'the social sciences, where mundane descriptions, evoking ordinary transactions, from websites, Tesco loyalty cards, CCTV cameras in your local shopping centre, etc., are the stuff of the new social. In these environments, the issue (to again evoke Walter Benjamin) is the mechanical reproduction of social figures, what might be seen as 'the diagrammization of society' which is the terrain on which sociology should now operate. The task of sociology might not be that of generating exceptionally whizzy visuals, using the most powerful computers or an unprecedented comprehensive database, so much as subjecting those which are routinely reproduced to critique and analysis. This involves making the deployment of these devices a subject of social science inquiry.' Building on this performative analysis, we here argue for the need to engage, not just in empirical description, but also in experimental re-specification of sociality with digital technologies.

2 Successful entrepreneurship, Hutton claims, is about using frontier technologies to address human need and ambition.

3 Ryu, Janet (2010) 'People You May Know: Helping you discover those important professional relationships', <https://blog.linkedin.com/2010/05/12/linkedin-pymk> (accessed May 27, 2016).

4 Here we respectfully disagree with William Davies, who affirms the return of the social, but does not seriously consider its heterogeneity.

5 For a full description of the project, see https://wiki.digitalmethods.net/Dmi/ DetectingTheSocials

6 This dataset comprises 919.234 tweets produced by 482.195 unique users. TCAT allows the creation of collections of tweets, and offers various of means of querying

and analysing these datasets. It is available as open source tool on https://github.com/digitalmethodsinitiative/dmi-tcat

7 Reactivity is the term that economic sociologists Espeland and Sauder (2007) use to refer to the self-fulfilling prophecies that devices may produce when assessed entities reflexively adapt to their criteria of evaluation.

8 This information is provided via the Twitter Streaming API, and captures the software from which a tweet was send as named by the source or app creator.

9 In social media settings, the boundary between manual and 'automatic' is a fluent one. Services such as dlvr.it or U Tweet Deals allow for a broad array of automated actions, from automatic detection of trending hashtags, automatic replies or retweets based on keywords or hashtags, to automated account generation and more.

10 Interval 1: 23/05-30/05; interval 2: 31/05–05/06; interval 3: 06/06–12/06; interval 4: 13/06–15/06

11 Namely, the hashtags identified by Group 2 as stemming from automated behavior.

12 The entertainment category contains media entertainment and celebrity news (example: 'it's so sad that justin can't even have privacy at his home #givejustinhisprivacy'). Politics comprises political topics and concerns (example: '#IStandWithEdwardSnowden because I believe in the fundamental right to personal privacy.'). The pointless babble category summarises all tweets that are not connected to news, issues or events but refer to vaguely connected private concerns (example: '#WhatIWant - Privacy. - a lot of money. - someone who will love me. - my parents to be proud of me. - high speed internet connection.'). Tweets labelled 'news story' refer to news-related hashtags (example: 'I am disgusted at the BBC's invasion of privacy. There must be a judge-led inquiry! #horizon #SecretLifeOfCats #horizoncats').

13 Both hashtags #security and #tech are dominated by Snowden-related topics from the third interval onwards; other associations endure, as #security remains connected to #infosec, #cloud, #tech, #internet and various social media platforms. #tech continuous to share co-occurrences with #security, #infosec, #technology, #news, and #data, whilst #Facebook co-occurs with #Google, #security and #socialmedia.

REFERENCES

Agre, P. E., 'Surveillance and Capture: Two Models of Privacy', *The Information Society*, 10.2 (1994), 101–27.

Baudrillard, J., *Simulacra and Simulations* (Ann Arbor: University of Michigan Press, 1994 [1981]).

Borra, E., and B. Rieder., 'Programmed Method: Developing a Toolset for Capturing and Analyzing Tweets', in A. Bruns and K. Weller, eds, *Aslib Journal of Information Management*, 66.3 (2014), 262–78.

Boyd, D.M., and N.B. Ellison, 'Social Network Sites: Definition, History, and Scholarship', *Journal of Computer-Mediated Communication*, 13.1 (2007), 210–30.

Bucher, T., 'The Friendship Assemblage Investigating Programmed Sociality on Facebook', *Television & New Media*, 14.6 (2013), 479–93.

Burgess, J., A. Galloway, and T. Sauter, 'Hashtag as Hybrid Forum: The Case of# agchatoz', in: N. Rambukkana, ed., *Hashtag Publics. The Power and Politics of Discursive Networks* (New York: Peter Lang, 2015), pp. 61–76.

Callon, M., 'Can Methods for Analysing Large Numbers Organize a Productive Dialogue with the Actors they Study?', *European Management Review*, 3.1 (2006), 7–16.

Cetina, K. Knorr, 'Sociality with Objects: Social Relations in Postsocial Knowledge Societies', *Theory, Culture & Society*, 14.4 (1997), 1–30.

Cicourel, A., *Method and Measurement in Sociology* (NewYork: Free Press, 1964).

Coleman, G., *Coding Freedom: The ethics and Aesthetics of Hacking* (Princeton: Princeton University Press, 2013).

Couldry, N., and J. van Dijck, 'Researching Social Media as if the Social Mattered', *Social Media+ Society*, 1. 2 (2015), 1–7.

Crawford, K., and T. Gillespie, 'What is a Flag for? Social Media Reporting Tools and the Vocabulary of Complaint', *New Media & Society*, 18.3 (2016), 410–28.

Davies, W., 'The Return of Social Government: From "Socialist Calculation" to "Social Analytics"', *European Journal of Social Theory*, 18.4 (2015), 431–50.

Dijck, J. van, *The Culture of Connectivity: A Critical History of Social Media* (Oxford and New York: Oxford University Press, 2013).

Didier, E., *En quoi consiste l'Amérique: les statistiques, le New Deal et la démocratie* (Paris: La Decouverte, 2009).

Espeland, W. N., and M. Sauder, 'Rankings and Reactivity: How Public Measures Recreate Social Worlds', *American Journal of Sociology*, 113(1) (2007), 1–40.

Gerlitz, C., and A. Helmond, 'The Like Economy: Social Buttons and the Data-Intensive Web', *New Media & Society*, 15(8) (2013), 1348–65.

Gerlitz, C., and B. Rieder, 'Tweets are not created equal. Investigating Twitter's Client Ecosystem', *International Journal of Communication*, 11 (2017), 528–47.

Giddens, A., *Social Theory and Modern Sociology* (Cambridge: Polity, 1987).

Halewood, M., *Rethinking the Social through Durkheim, Marx, Weber and Whitehead* (London: Anthem Press, 2014).

Hargittai, E., and C. Sandvig, eds, *Digital Research Confidential: The Secrets of Studying Behavior Online* (Cambridge, MA: MIT Press, 2015).

Healy, K., 'The Performativity of Networks', *European Journal of Sociology/Archives Européennes de Sociologie*, 56.2 (2015), 175–205.

Hogan, B., 'The Presentation of Self in the Age of Social Media: Distinguishing Performances and Exhibitions Online', *Bulletin of Science, Technology & Society* (2010), 377–86.

Jones, S., 'How I Learned to Stop Worrying and Love the Bots', *Social Media + Society*, 1.1 (2015), 1–2.

Langlois, G., *Meaning in the Age of Social Media* (Basingstoke: Palgrave Macmillan, 2014).

Lash, S., and C. Lury, *Global Culture Industry: The Mediation of Things* (Cambridge: Polity, 2007).

Latour, B., *We Have Never Been Modern* (Cambridge, MA: Harvard University Press, 1994).

——*Reassembling the Social* (Oxford, Oxford University Press, 2005).

Lezaun, J., 'A Market of Opinions: The Political Epistemology of Focus Groups', *The Sociological Review*, 55.s2 (2007), 130–51.

Lury, C., and N. Wakeford, *Inventive Methods: The Happening of the Social* (London and New York: Routledge, 2012).

Mackenzie, A., 'Set', in C. Lury & N. Wakeford, eds, *Inventive Methods: The Happening of the Social* (New York and London: Routledge, 2012), pp. 219–31.

Marres, N., and C. Gerlitz, 'Interface Methods : Renegotiating Relations between Digital Research, STS and Sociology', *The Sociological Review*, 64.1 (2015), 21–46.

Marres, N., *Digital Sociology: The Re-invention of Social Research* (Cambridge: Polity, 2017).

Moor, L., and C. Lury, 'Making and Measuring Value: Comparison, Singularity and Agency in Brand Valuation Practice', *Journal of Cultural Economy*, 4.4 (2011), 439–54.

Niederer, S., and J. van Dijck, 'Wisdom of the Crowd or Technicity of Content? Wikipedia as a Sociotechnical System', *New Media & Society*, 12.8 (2010), 1368–87.

Osborne, T., and N. Rose, 'Do the Social Sciences Create Phenomena?: The Example of Public Opinion Research', *The British Journal of Sociology*, 50.3 (1999), 367–96.

Paßmann, J., and C. Gerlitz, '"Good" Platform-Political Reasons for "Bad" Platform-Data. Zur sozio-technischen Geschichte der Plattformaktivitäten Fav, Retweet und Like', *Mediale Kontrolle unter Beobachtung*, 3.1 (2014), 1–40.

Papacharissi, Z., 'We Have Always Been Social', *Social Media + Society*, 1.1 (2015), 1–2.

Pinch, T. J., and W. E. Bijker, 'The Social Construction of Facts and Artefacts: Or How the Sociology of Science and the Sociology of Technology might Benefit Each Other', *Social Studies of Science*, 14.3 (1984), 399–441.

Rogers, R., *Digital Methods* (Cambridge and London: MIT Press, 2013).

Rose, N., 'The Death of the Social? Re-figuring the Territory of Government', *International Journal of Human Resource Management*, 25.3 (1996), 327–56.

Ruppert, E., J. Law, and M. Savage, 'Reassembling Social Science Methods: The Challenge of Digital Devices', *Theory, Culture & Society*, 30.4 (2013), 22–46.

Savage, M. 'Contemporary Sociology and the Challenge of Descriptive Assemblage', *European Journal of Social Theory*, 12.1 (2009), 155–74.

Slater, D., 'Social Relationships and Identity Online and Offline', in L. Lievrouw and S. Livingstone, eds, *Handbook of New Media: Social Shaping and Consequences of ICT* (London and New York: Sage), pp. 533–46.

Thielmann, T., 'Taking into Account. Harold Garfinkels Beitrag für eine Theorie sozialer Medien', *ZfM*, 1 (2012), 85–102.

Wilkie, A., M. Michael, and M. Plummer-Fernandez, 'Speculative Method and Twitter: Bots, Energy and Three Conceptual Characters', *Sociological Review* 63(2014), 79–101.

COMMENTARIES

1 2

HACKING THE SOCIAL?

Christopher M. Kelty

'INVENTING THE SOCIAL' REVISITS A DEBATE THAT IN SOME TIMES AND PLACES seems to have been settled, only to reappear once more. The vexed question of 'the social' (does it exist? is it invented? has it come to an end?) remains as vital to social theorists as it is irrelevant to every ordinary 'member of society'. There are few concepts so obviously central to everyday thinking and yet so resistant to compelling and convincing theorisation.

Why 'invent the social' then (again)? For *Inventing the Social*, inventing the social is a way of working around the problem of *critique*. To claim that 'the social is invented' or that it is historical, or that it is contingent, or that it is over, has historically been proffered in opposition to some other claim that society is some simple natural entity, whether that be a self-evident experience of relationality or a Durkheimian metaphysical commitment. Most often, critique is carried out in order to contest a claim of naturalness as a basis for political decisions. Those who claim that the social is *not invented* usually have something to sell, and most often what they are selling is a way to (re)invent the social: to solve social problems, to create a great society, to nudge us, control us, secure us or to socialise us. So it needs to be said, every so often, that the social is invented, and to hope that this *caveat emptor* will serve as sufficient warning. But the funny thing about critique – which has been said to have run out of steam, though new reserves of critique are discovered in the shale sands of PhD programmes every day – is that its capacity to *compel* people to see the problem is *also* not a given, not natural, not obvious. Such a hope relies too much on the faith that lifting the veil, revealing the hidden, pointing out the contradiction, or demonstrating the absurdity flips a corresponding switch in readers' brains, and perhaps by virtue of that, in their emotions and commitments as well. So no matter how sophisticated the arguments, how detailed the historical or empirical work, or how rigorously erudite the philosophical acrobatics, the social, like a relentless multi-season zombie-themed TV series, keeps coming back. We might have become a little addicted to critiquing the social; we might, today, have such a high tolerance for critique that it wears off a bit too easily.

So I suspect that here, in this volume, it is the *critical* account of the social that is under arrest, as it were, and not the social as such. One reason to invent the social is to propose an alternative strategy to the conventional forms of critique: the tired act of raising once again, in writing and in increasingly marginalised academic publications, a warning about the social. It would be to stop for once the relentless interrogation of the social, the torturing of this incorrigible creature, in favour of putting critique instead on a kind of watch-list. Let us secure the future by inventing the social today – this will be our new approach.

But what figure, we must ask, of 'inventing the social' is at work here? What figure makes sense of the idea that the social has been or can be invented? For many scholars, the social is 'invented' in only the most anonymous and quasi-evolutionary way: some mixture of kings, bureaucrats, politicians, scholars, elites, markets and organisations encounter the social as a problem in the world, and 'invent' around it systems for controlling it, responding to it, occasionally enhancing it, but always being frustrated or surprised by this unruly, eternal thing that contains an inscrutable power to upend the desires of humans to control it (on the nature of the social as a problem, see Martin Savransky's piece in this volume).

However, a more likely figure of invention is the engineer. As the consummate Enlightenment figure, the engineer represents most clearly the desire to stand outside society, to calculate and plan it, to theorise and then straighten it into predictable lines, and to govern through it. When engineers invent the social they often do so from scratch – or what amounts to as much – by levelling whatever is in the way and replacing it with the ideal vision of a society (see e.g. Mitchell 1991; Rabinow 1989). The engineer (which might also include the statistician, the public health expert, and sometimes the revolutionary) is at the heart of the entity we call 'society' because he calls it into being, he invents it through both observation and practice (Hacking 1990; Donzelot 2015; Rose and Miller 2008; Tresch 2012).

Whether it is an anonymous force or the result of an engineering dream, the invented social we live with today is the layered landscape of yesterday's attempts to invent, and to engineer, the social. We don't live in the next epoch of the social (post-social or some neologism-yet-to-come) but in the lively ruins (or decimated landscapes) of past inventions of the social: some abandoned completely, others partially maintained here and there, retro-fitted with differing levels of enthusiasm, and yet others besides. There are reinventions as well, often as conscious attempts to fix past failures of invention, and sometimes to simply forget them. The forms of society diagnosed by Baron Hausmann, Max Weber, Talcott Parsons, or Ulrich Beck, become the materiel and ordnance of another invention. But there is another figure for invention at play today: the hacker.

Consider the cases of invention presented in *Inventing the Social*. Many, such as the work by Christian Nold, Alex Wilkie and Mike Michael, or Nerea Calvillo, mean by invention something close to participatory design (in its current meaning) – design which not only invites social relations into the process of design, but even takes social relations as the subject or perhaps medium of design. In these cases, what is designed is also intended to do two things: activate or 'invent' the social relations in question, and provide a materialised critique of those relations by and through this attempt to activate or invent them. So Nold's clever experiments in and around Heathrow and its sonic environment both bring people into relations with each other and the designer, and through the resulting designs, attempt to somehow change those relations. The residents are stuck in an old model of the social, whereas Nold sees an alternative: 'I suggest that the airport opponents' lack of success in challenging the metric [of acceptable noise levels] may be due to the fact that they have been unable to politicise the lack of care involved in the way community annoyance has been measured' (this volume, p. 102). In a provocative way, Nold suggests that the social itself (labelled here 'the issue') is his *client* – and not the council, the airport or the residents around

Heathrow. Others, such as the contributions by Noortje Marres and Carolin Gerlitz, or by Michael Guggenheim, Bernd Kräftner and Judith Kröll, mean by inventing the social an attention to how the social is being invented by others all the time – by social media users and designers, doctors and patients and anthropologists. As Guggenheim et al. suggest, invention here can be understood as 'a systematic transport of the breaching experiment (Garfinkel 1967) into practices of the self. It is a form of creating the social by lay people through the means of effecting systematic breaches and changes in their own conditions of living' (this volume, p. 69). There is also here an exquisite attention to how the social and technical intertwine, and how what counts as sociality worth having is never simply found but painstakingly made. As Marres and Gerlitz put it here, 'the accomplishment of different forms of sociality depends – in a non-straightforward way – on how digital infrastructures, devices, and practices are assembled in practice' (this volume, p. 254). To see that assembly from the inside is to see its vulnerabilities and its possibilities.

Still others (see, for example, Savransky, Clark or Muniesa) remain stubborn, returning again to the theorisation of the social, or the meta-theorisation of the social, or perhaps the theorisation of the meta-social, but all with an avowedly inventive attitude. They participate less in an old engineering mythos of inventing the social from scratch – those monstrous Parsonian (or Luhmannian) edifices of yore – and more in the style of the provocateur, the imp, the trickster, for whom all attempts at naive invention demand to be poked at, teased, trolled.

In all these cases I perceive a certain desire: to invent the social here means to intervene in it, to invert or to trouble it, and most importantly, to *be there* with and among others, as agent, tinkerer, designer, or even simply as theorist-agitators. For things do look different when one looks at the social as something to invent, to intervene in, to change and affect, to cause and to fail to cause–and not something to stand outside, to explain, resist, unveil, or critique. From this perspective, society ceases to be a problem and all of a sudden seems to be a resource, a toolkit, a field, a sandbox, a play (or a playhouse), maybe even a weapon. It involves not just a salubrious engagement with the 'real world' but the opportunity to retool social science for new environments, to engage in an active, creative, conviviality in places ranging from museums and cafes and art galleries to basements, hospitals, restaurants, to the internet, the campaign trail, the countryside, the war zone, the hot zone, or the border. It seems to exhume scholars from within the disciplines and their bloody-minded – but strangely persistent – norms, and expose them to the actual and vital eventful movement of that which they study. To invent the social is to create actually existing alternatives and real choices, to lay open means and methods to view and to invite others to tinker with them, extend them, break them, or repair them.

Now picture a hacker.

No, not that one.

The problem with the figure of the hacker is often that it is hard to see past the simple stereotype of the hacker into the figure itself. It should be an ambivalent figure: white hat, black hat, Unix geek, Facebook employee, social engineer, GCHQ operative, hacktivist, criminal, feminist, troll, gamer, maker: hacking comes in an under-appreciated variety of flavours today, ranging from morally repulsive to ideologically blinkered to creatively progressive. Some hack rootkits that own a server; some hack free software that runs the server, some hack pointless apps that spy on other people, some organise public protests that galvanise a movement, some make money, and some write things intended to criticise the very things the others are making, because even writing can be conceived of as a hack (Coleman and Kelty 2017; Murillo and Kelty 2017). At the heart of hacking is a certain commitment to *critique through making*. It is critique in a sense far more expansive than the kind that ostensibly belongs to 'critical social scientists' – it is more in line with what Foucault described as a refusal: 'we do not want to be governed *like that*' (Foucault 2007). So per-haps even more importantly, hacking is a particular kind of making – not the invention *de novo* (or creative destruction) of the engineer or economist, but a seeing-from-within, a making-as-exploiting, a kind of making that requires dwelling within precisely those ruins of past attempts to invent in order to find the weakness, the opportunity or the precise place to *build a critique*. Hacking is not confined to a class or a type of person, but is its own 'style of reasoning' (fittingly, see Ian Hacking 1992). It necessarily implies a collective, if not a social contract (though if the social is a shibboleth, *pace* Muniesa, hackers *love* cracking passwords).

So picture instead a collective of hackers. Perhaps something like the latter-day multicultural Star Trek crew of the television series *Mr. Robot* where the diverse collective society is led by a smart, savvy, female hacker, and includes a black felon, a young Muslim woman, a (now token) bearded white guy, and, tying them all together like a hoodie-wearing Spock, is a mentally ill drug addict. Which is to say, picture not the anti-social adolescent hacker of media stereotypes but a more gregarious group of friends and lovers and neighbours, engaged in problem-seeking and problem-solving in the face of a complicated world duct-taped together by big and small corporate experiments, previous hacks and kludges, broken technologies and a conflictual mix of expectations about the future and how to achieve it.

For one of the things that animates the hacker is precisely the fact that the existing systems (which are mostly technical, but also crucially composed of people, with their foibles and expectations), are complex accretions of past attempts at invention. Old systems, poorly maintained, full of vulnerabilities and human habits, are not failed inventions to the hacker, but opportunities to exploit, places to hang out and dwell (sometimes out of sight), and perhaps ironically, the very means to an expanded sociality, a way of being with others that, for whatever reason, has been denied them elsewhere. It is a way of seeing from the belly of beasts whose invention has been hard won and long in the making. Sometimes seeing from this perspective results in sabotage – the hacktivists of Anonymous, the trickster spirit that animates a 'fuck-shit-up' disruption (not a Silicon Valley innovator's-dilemma-disruption) (Coleman 2014). Sometimes seeing from this perspective animates a specific inversion – a way of making technology do something it was not designed to do. And sometimes seeing from this perspective simply makes clear a vulnerable spot in what has been invented – whether that be an operating system or a social system – that can be exploited for gain (e.g. ransom and ransom-ware), or re-made to be openly available (free software), or disclosed to embarrass and improve (outing, leaking and doxing), or squirreled away to await the highest bidder (zero day exploits for sale on black markets).

There is conviviality and competition in every hack, but it remains an ambivalent figure because it still contains elements of the anti-social, of a certain cynicism about progress and liberation, a certain toxic concentration of anomie, criminality and in some cases, a co-optation ill-fitting the name (e.g. Facebook – an engineer of the social *par excellence* – is at 1 Hacker Way and calls itself 'the hacking company'). There is failure, ineffectualness, pointless pursuit by the authorities, in-fighting, spying, accusation and informing. There is also, quite obviously, a problem of sociality in hacking: that it is mostly done by men and that it relies on exclusion through technical virtuosity, that it engages in reprehensible ethical and aesthetic actions. But not all forms of hacking have the same problems, social or otherwise.

What's more, hacking is ambivalent because hacks are themselves social problems. What can be good for some people (taking down the Sony network for political retribution) can be bad for others (a two-month outage in a beloved gaming platform) (Milburn 2015). A hack is mobile and self-contained, and by definition cannot be controlled by or confined to some entity or another.

I come thus not to praise the hacker nor to bury him, but to point out just what it is that the figure reveals today, and why *Inventing the Social* seems to me to be an emblematic expression of it. For there is something of the hackish impulse at work in the essays in this volume – perhaps most obviously, Andres Jaque's experiment with the basement of the Barcelona Pavilion. It is a literal inversion, in that it opens up the view from inside and below, and by doing so both displays and reinvents the social space and relations of the Pavilion. A different artist or a different activist might have done something different with the inversion – perhaps focusing on an environmental problem or a labour violation in order to shame the institution. For hacks can also be purely aesthetic or purely criminal: it is not the politics that makes the figure of the hacker useful, but the way it inhabits and observes existing structures, looking for concrete, technical ways to change them from the inside.

Hacks can also fail productively – not unlike the story that Wilkie and Michael tell of the Energy Babble: a device that provokes reassessment of the social order of environmental activism not by doing something instrumental ('solving a problem') but by, in part, flummoxing people. There is a bit of 'the lulz' in the Energy Babble: it is trolling environmentalists, artists, and the government agencies all at the same time.

Hacks emphasise the material – though that is the wrong word, since both software and social relations are sometimes said (mistakenly) to be immaterial. Hacks deal with things, but software, just like air and helium in Calvillo's piece, is not immaterial, just difficult to work with. Its characteristics require investigation and experimentation, much like those of helium, and the result of doing so is never only about helium (or software), but also about the social, spatial, and conceptual relations within which it has been installed. Hacking the air, for Calvillo, would not be just a metaphor: it would be a very specific orientation towards the air and its relations, and would be quite different to *engineering* the air, or controlling the air. That we leave to builders of Zeppelins, or worse.

Or again, in the work of Nold, to take the social as client is to see it from the inside, both its technical constitution, and the existing, hard-won previous invention of the social constituted around noise levels and decibel maps. To hack the social, here, is to transform that previous invention into something that displays, reveals, discloses – leaks or breaches – in order to potentially shame or perhaps simply inform. The noise around Heathrow is not changed thereby – but the inner workings of measurement and regulation are made public, and this act of disclosure is itself a kind of hack, dependent on an invented social it works from within.

And yet. And yet, inventing the social should also come with a significant anxiety. The heart of this anxiety is that trying to hack – to construct, tweak, experiment with, tickle, tease or prod the social into being – is to join the rest of the world. It is to face the reality of competing on a global stage, not just with other experts in the social (think tanks, development agencies, education specialists) but with experts in the social for whom the social itself is a means to other ends: power and capital.

One need only consider the naturalisation of social media as a site of the social: Facebook or Twitter's engineers are smug in their certainty that they now access 'the social' in huge pools and swells of data that poor university professors can only gaze at longingly from their rickety shacks on the shore. Though they may well be experimentally inventing the social (as Marres and Gerlitz show), their power comes from falsely but convincingly asserting that they stand outside it, observe it, and understand it better than anyone else. In this respect they ascend from the position of hacker to some even more monstrous form of the engineer – Facebook may call itself the 'Hacking Company' but its pretensions are not to hack, but to destroy the world and re-make it in its own image. They are not interested in *critiquing* the social, they are interested precisely in owning and controlling it – from the myriad everyday A/B tests that observe whether a blue font or a red font generates more clicks, to the controversial experiments in manipulating the news-feed, to the secretive and unknowable experiments in machine learning and algorithmic AI that guide users in everything from job ads to racial profiling of minorities to book-buying to driverless cars to, apparently, voting.

Or, for example, there is also the questionable fixing and staining of 'the social' engaged in by the elites of the bio-medical establishment, for whom the social is an evident problem, and where the refusal to engage with social scientists is both a misunderstanding of the object of their own expertise and a performance of their power over others – not just the sick and suffering, but those adjacent experts proposing other diagnoses and different treatments. Doctors do not 'hack' the social: but some do find themselves inside the layered ruins of past attempts. The responses to Ebola in 2014, for instance, dealt precisely with the frustrating failures of multiple different regimes, each with its own partial view of what makes the social work (see, for example, Rosengarten, this volume; also Lakoff, Collier, and Kelty 2014).

To invent the social as hackers is to bring ourselves into direct competition (by other means) with those who are busy inventing the social at scale, everyday. To my mind, this is the same problem that hackers proper have: they dwell inside a system of systems, tinkering, exploiting and exploring, but they do so against a backdrop of entities with much more money and power – who have the might if not the right to invent the social. To hack is to demonstrate the existence of alternatives to that might, and to do so through means other than critique and writing. And it has a greater chance of having an effect. Insofar as *Inventing the Social* aims at this goal, its clearest figure is the hacker – not the engineer or the scientist, much less the scholar. It somehow seems that a demonstration, an experiment or an event – even a small-scale one – both holds more persuasive power, and seems to reveal more, than an isolated act of writing, or some old method strait-jacketed in norms of distance, objectivity, or neutrality. The disadvantage is that we (social scientists) remain comparatively outside, underfunded, inadequately resourced amateurs in this game. The advantage is that by inventing the social we can lay bare the workings of invention, we can demonstrate how sausage is made, and perhaps thereby make it otherwise. The disadvantage is that our sausage shop is a street-corner operation in competition with abattoirs of shocking efficiency and cold chains of global reach. This is the anxiety that should face the inventive sociologist, the hacker sociologist.

Because what should be clear from the fact that 'critique has run out of steam' is not so much that it has run out of steam *for academics*, but that those in the world who regularly 'invent the social' were never really listening very hard to such critiques in the first place. It is quite possible that academic social science is just now emerging from a kind of legitimacy cocoon, within which critique seemed to be its main product, packaged in the butterfly garb of scientism or intellectual capital, and delivered to the world stage for everyone to gaze upon. But even if such legitimacy ever existed, that form of critique is in fact nearly exhausted (or perhaps more optimistically, awaiting a renewal from somewhere other than critique itself). What remains is for us to join the rest of the world, to invent the social, to build, to experiment, to make, to compete with the largest, the most powerful and the most extensive inventors of the contemporary social. But hacking demonstrates that there is more than one way to invent the social, that we are not all strictly in competition to invent the same social in just the same way, that it matters not simply *that* we experiment with the social, but *how* we do so. It is now necessary to say, perversely, that we invent the social *critically*, that our way of doing the social will demonstrate to others the nature of the problems we face more clearly, more precisely, or in ways that will lead to a better world, in ways that will be more theoretically correct, in ways that will compel us to think otherwise, because we make otherwise. If we want to invent the social *otherwise*, how should we think about the social (again)?

If the promise of inventing the social, or inventive methods, is offered in order to remake social science today, the figure of the hacker cannot be ignored. It is symptomatic of the social today, of the invented social we have inherited and are faced with exploring once more. But even more importantly, the promise of the hack is that it opens up competition to individuals and collectives with no power. Even though they compete with the largest, the richest, the most extensive – it is a figure that gives hope, even if it courts destruction as well.

REFERENCES

Coleman, E. G., and C. M. Kelty, 'Preface', in E. G. Coleman and C. M. Kelty, eds, *Limn Number Eight: Hacks, Leaks, and Breaches* 1.8 (2017) <https://limn.it/issues/hacks-leaks-and-breaches/> [accessed 30 April 2018].

Coleman, G., *Hacker, Hoaxer, Whistleblower, Spy: The Many Faces of Anonymous* (London; New York: Verso Books, 2014).

Donzelot, J., *L'Invention du social*. Essais. (Paris: Seuil, 2015).

Foucault, M., The Politics of Truth, in S. Lotringer and L. Hochroth, eds, *Semiotext(e) / Foreign Agents Series* (Cambridge, MA: MIT Press, 2007).

Hacking, I., *The Taming of Chance* (Cambridge: Cambridge University Press, 1990).

——'"Style"' for Historians and Philosophers', in A. Chakravartty, ed., *Studies in History and Philosophy of Science Part A* 23.1 (1992), pp. 1–20.

Lakoff, A., S. J. Collier, and C. Kelty, 'Introduction: Ebola's Ecologies', *Limn* 5 (2014) < http://limn.it/introduction-ebolas-ecologies/> [accessed 27 April 2018].

Milburn, C., *Mondo Nano: Fun and Games in the World of Digital Matter* (Durham, NC: Duke University Press, 2015).

Mitchell, T., *Colonising Egypt* (Berkeley, CA: University of California Press, 1991).

Murillo, L., R. Felipe and C. M. Kelty, 'Hackers and Hacking', in G. Koch, ed., *Digitisation: Theories and Concepts for Empirical Cultural Research* (New York; London: Routledge, 2017) pp. 95–116.

Rabinow, P., *French Modern: Norms and Forms of the Social Environment* (Cambridge, MA: MIT Press, 1989).

Rose, N., and P. Miller, *Governing the Present: Administering Economic, Social and Personal Life* (London; New York: Polity Press, 2008).

Tresch, J. *The Romantic Machine: Utopian Science and Technology After Napoleon* (Chicago: University of Chicago Press, 2012).

1 3

HOW CAN WE...? CONNECTING INVENTIVE SOCIAL RESEARCH WITH SOCIAL AND GOVERNMENT INNOVATION

Lucy Kimbell

IN THEIR INTRODUCTION THE EDITORS ARGUE THAT INVENTIVE APPROACHES to social research combine 'the doing, representing and intervening into social life' (Marres et al., this volume, p. 00). They emphasise how social life – and research – exists in the making and foreground why inventive approaches should be experimental. The carrying out and assessment of such experimentation in doing, representing and intervening into social life is always in question. They argue for the value of (researchers) pursuing long-term associations and changes to social life. But they point to the limitations of prioritising easily traceable, short-term associations between social research and social action which might result, for example, in *Das Kapital* not being seen as able to demonstrate research impact or policy relevance.

This afterword explores these ideas in relation to two contemporary domains of social life in which such creative experimentation is evident. It suggests how inventive social research as discussed in this volume might intersect with developments in the fields of social innovation and government innovation. Social innovation is one of the new socials identified by Marres and Gerlitz in their chapter, a term given to an area of practice and scholarship that aims to address social needs through creating strategies, infrastructures, ventures, products or services that involve new configurations of resources (Mulgan et al. 2006; Nicholls and Murdock 2011). A closely related area of government innovation is an emerging institutional practice within national, regional and local government administrations, where it often takes the form of 'policy labs' (e.g. OECD 2016; Puttick et al. 2014; Williams 2015). In such settings, diverse actors including governments, community organisations, funders and businesses conduct experiments into contemporary social life, sometimes in collaboration with academic researchers. In both areas, the devices and practices of 'social design' are increasingly visible as a resource to drive creativity and connect public servants and others with citizens and other publics, often with unclear results (Chen et al. 2016.; Julier and Kimbell 2016).

My aim here is to mix insights from this book with the creative practices that are tied up with how public policies, solutions and services are being constituted, researched, designed, developed and evaluated as they co-emerge in relation to social issues and policy agendas. In what follows I review some of the concerns of participants in this world of social and government innovation. I then identify opportunities for inventive social research to reconfigure these events, narratives and practices. Finally I suggest some issues that result from using an inventive approach in relation to social innovation and to government experimentation. As someone with stakes in these matters as a citizen, user, researcher, educator and consultant, my discussion is unapologetically interventionist and activist.[1] I take what I understand to be the possibilities of inventive social research, and explore how these can reconfigure devices, practices and narratives associated with 'innovation' to change how things are done in public policy contexts. My hope is that the academic discussion in this book, which recognises the potential for engagement between social research and creative practice and experimentation in social life, can intersect productively with the practices of social and government innovation through which public issues are formed and addressed. However, this might present some challenges because of the emphasis in these worlds on demonstrating short-term achievements and easily traceable passages between insight and evidence and action and outcome.

The word 'innovation' has gained wide currency in a context in which neo-liberalism increasingly pushes public servants, politicians and citizens to come up with novel solutions to social problems. Social and government *innovation* are perhaps better characterised as *invention* (Barry 2001), a term which fore-grounds the processual and performative nature of how novel solutions are constituted and re-made. Invention might be seen as a phase or stage within an innovation process, one that emphasises the reconfiguring of constituent elements into novel arrangements that cannot be predetermined (Garud et al. 2013). But more than a temporal phase, the concept of invention also points to the logics through which new combinations of resources are assembled and through which new publics and issues are brought into being.

Recent developments suggest the growing visibility of activities seen as, or hoped to result in, innovation in relation to public administrations, with close alignment to related experimentation happening in business. Arguments for 'mission-oriented' innovation in today's governments (e.g. Mazzucato 2013) intersect with 'agile' software development (e.g. Government Digital Service 2016), 'lean' start up (e.g. Ries 2011), 'smart' government (e.g. Noveck 2015) and new partnerships between government, business and social enterprise (Eggers and Macmillan 2013). Such developments have co-emerged alongside related activities within think-tanks and community and voluntary groups, as well as being informed by academic research.[2] They are also shaped by neo-liberal drivers within some governments to promote austerity, drive commercialisa-tion of public service provision and co-produce solutions with social actors, sometimes shifting the responsibility for addressing society's issues away from governments to others (Julier 2017). As a result, to differing extents, it is pos-sible to find big data analysis, digital platforms, social media engagement and analysis, randomised control trials, participatory design, and social and behav-ioural research used alongside one another to generate and explore solutions to policy issues (in the case of government innovation) or to address problems that may result from policy decisions and actions, or their lack (in the case of social innovation). Common to both social and government innovation are preoccupations with, and narratives about, experimentation, politics, participa-tion and systems change.

CHALLENGES IN SOCIAL AND GOVERNMENT INNOVATION

Much social and government innovation as it is currently organised is tied up with 'challenges'. Sometimes a challenge is simply expressed in the form of a summary of an issue and a question starting 'how can we...?'[3] Such challenges are articulations of issues that managers of public services, policy makers, funders, businesses and entrepreneurs, as well as universities and third sector groups, organise themselves in relation to, possibly with the involvement of academics and with academic research. Familiar topics include addressing environmental change, tackling obesity or improving prospects for people facing unemployment. The construction and articulation of such challenges takes a variety of forms depending on one's location in relation to an issue, with varying degrees of agency, accountability and legitimacy. For example funders, consultancies, universities, think-tanks, community groups and service providers may construct or be invited to respond to a challenge via mechanisms such as invitations to tender, calls for proposals, competitions, sandpits, jams, and design briefs, with associated platforms, resources, networks, funding and means of assessing to what extent a challenge can or has been addressed. Funders, policy teams, researchers and managers seek to mobilise diverse resources in addressing an issue, including researchers, professionals, citizens, activists or 'users' – often with uncertain motivations, accountabilities or rewards and different levels of urgency. They may also draw upon different institutional research capacities, organisational routines, datasets and modes of participation. Indeed, such is the extent of the challenge that there is now a centre studying and giving guidance on organising one.[4] Accordingly, in what follows I identify some of the current challenges within social innovation and government innovation, informed by my research and practice in the UK. As presented below, these challenges are also approaches or techniques used to address public issues. But they are themselves organisational issues with which public leaders and managers are preoccupied, in a context in which they are required to produce their 'innovations'.

THE CHALLENGE OF UNDERSTANDING
AND SETTING ISSUES

Often described as 'wicked' (Rittel and Webber 1972) or 'complex' (e.g. Snowden and Boone 2007), today's problems articulated in the context of social innovation or policy innovation are dynamic, multi-actor and multi-sited. Informed by perspectives in systems theory, futures and strategic management, there has been recognition for several decades that 'transdisciplinary approaches' (Bernstein 2015) are needed to address such issues. Issues such as, for example, the low educational attainment of white working class boys in the UK cross the boundaries of disciplines, organisational capabilities, sites of practice and scales of government, requiring actors to work together to understand the social world they want to change. These issues are seen as dynamic and in flux, and as having interdependencies, contingencies and feedback loops that make them hard to identify, describe or analyse. Issues co-emerge with publics; non-government stakeholders can play active roles in enrolling others into an issue (Marres 2005; Hillgren et al. 2016). But despite these moves, in many cases policy or social problems have endured, despite the application over years of different kinds of expertise, analysis, investments in organisational change, changes in leadership, technology, and other resources, as well as fluctuations in collective visions about which problems matter. Different assumptions play out here about what counts as evidence that there is an issue, what kind of issue it is and for whom. Big data and behavioural research are increasingly evident as resources and drivers of organisational attention in the policy ecosystem (Dunleavy 2016). Such evidence is often tied to the capacities of corporations to assemble, organise and analyse large data sets providing particular kinds of social data. But alongside big data there are also micro-social perspectives from ethnography, as well as participatory approaches to exploring issues through workshops, events and online platforms. The growing availability of and interconnections between different forms of data are reconfiguring social and government innovation landscapes.

THE CHALLENGE OF GENERATING
AND EXPLORING SOLUTIONS

In a context in which issues are seen as dynamic, multi-sited and multi-actor, advocates of social and government innovation often argue for an experimental approach (e.g. Breckon 2015). Different kinds of experimentality emerge in response to different social or policy issues involving different kinds of organisational apparatus. Some approaches – for example, healthcare improvement (e.g. Robert and Macdonald 2016) – recognise the value of allowing local actors who have a stake in an issue to be involved in generating and co-producing solutions – which handily coincides with a smaller role for government in a neo-liberal world (Julier 2017). Digital platforms are often implicated in the work of governing. Some responses to social or public policy issues, such as the OpenIDEO digital platform,[5] publish open challenges set by a policy team, foundation or corporate sponsor, and structure and enable processes that aim to engage people not previously connected to an issue to explore it and generate and iterate possible solutions. Alongside this kind of experimentation, other traditions have become more visible inside government and public policy. In particular, randomised control trials adapted from clinical sciences are promoted by some funders, researchers and civil servants as ways to test ideas and provide evidence for policy decisions about 'what works', often tied to behavioural theory (see Puttick 2012; Halpern 2015).[6] As in science technology studies (STS), for civil servants and social entrepreneurs a persistent preoccupation is scale, not as an analytical construct but as an operational achievement: how can solutions developed and tested *here*, be rolled out and made effective *there*?

THE CHALLENGE OF UNDERSTANDING CHANGE

Current practice in social and government innovation to some extent recognises that multiple actors are involved in constituting an issue and then shaping potential responses to doing something about it in order to achieve intended 'outcomes', reocognising that unintended consequences will also result. To understand a problem or to generate a solution, a civil servant or manager in a voluntary sector organisation may be asked to articulate a 'theory of change'. Such theories often foreground micro-social worlds and 'choices' made by individuals, rather than social practices (e.g. Shove et al. 2012) or are informed by, draw on, and deploy forms of technological determinism (e.g. Wilkie and Michael 2008). Some domains, such as healthcare improvement, allow an understanding of change that recognises multiple kinds of social worlds and researchers' and managers' participation within them, alongside the beneficiaries of interventions or users of services. But in other cases, innovation toolkits[7] and calls for proposals published by commissioners of services spread the idea that such theories of change can be adequately described in a page or two. Some funders, for example, require applicants to describe their theory of change underpinning a project (e.g. Nesta 2016). Elsewhere, methods drawing on participatory design in social or policy innovation workshops ask participants to materialise models of potential solutions and act out through role play how solutions might change a situation (Kimbell 2015). In describing how a desired change in a social world might unfold as a result of a proposed intervention, participants are asked to foreground 'barriers' to change and how these need to be addressed in implementing a solution. The temporal and spatial ordering of how change is constituted, experienced, understood, assessed and evaluated is downplayed. Discussions of who has agency to make change and the conditions and possibilities around this are often left unexamined.

THE CHALLENGE OF PARTICIPATION

From different perspectives, social innovation and government innovation are both premised on current and future relations between actors involved in an issue. Such practices foreground human actors – such as 'users', 'citizens' or possibly 'beneficiaries' – who are often already identified as involved in an issue and having particular 'needs' or 'capacities'. In social innovation and government innovation practice, emerging activities include generating insights about what is happening in a social world from the perspective of such actors; identifying and mobilising emerging practices; identifying non-obvious actors in an issue; and engaging actors in generating and possibly co-producing solutions. In the case of caring for older people, for example, human actors might include people directly experiencing the social or policy challenge (e.g. older people and their families, friends or neighbours), professionals (e.g. social workers, health visitors, nurses), service providers (e.g. carers working for municipalities or commercial firms), businesses (e.g. entrepreneurs or local shops or utilities), researchers (e.g. social or healthcare researchers, but also data analysts), and voluntary or community groups (e.g. those working with older people or carers). A perspective from STS would also emphasise the non-human actors that co-constitute adult social care, such as assistive technologies, particular kinds of housing arrangement and layout, concepts such as 'ageing' and 'caring', and financial models for care services. For people self-identifying as social or government innovators, the desire to acknowledge and engage a wide array of actors may be driven partly by openness to emergence and democratic ideals. Nonetheless, existing and future levels of agency and power relations may be under-examined. For innovators inside government, participation has a complicated relationship to formal democratic structures and processes, party politics and the media. For example, inviting responses via an online consultation or through participation in a policy workshop can privilege some contributions over others (e.g. Fortier 2010).

OPPORTUNITIES FOR INVENTIVE APPROACHES

These brief summaries of some of the challenges facing those involved in social and government innovation have highlighted concerns that resonate with inventive social research. While some readers may object to my emphasis on relatively short-term, easily-traceable intervention, I want to explore what inventive social research has to 'offer' service managers, delivery partners, policy makers, funders or communities entangled with these challenges. How might inventive social research express and connect social phenomena in the settings I describe, resulting in changes to how things are done, as well as in new insights? How does it challenge dominant notions of innovation in government and society? The things that inventive social research might offer or provoke, however, are not necessarily what these actors want, value, or have the capacity to engage with – a topic to which I will return later.

CHALLENGING THE CHALLENGE

As indicated in this book, a core characteristic of inventive social research is how it problematises an issue. Instead of taking up a challenge as initially articulated or framed, inventive social research starts with a query into a domain. It does not take as given the constituents of an issue. Through such research, a social or policy innovation challenge is likely to be reconfigured. This may allow identification of specific aspects that need to be addressed, or acknowledgement of the involvement of different actors from those originally thought to be part of the issue, or a shift in location, scale or timeframe. For example, in his chapter on making interventions to the Barcelona Pavilion, Andrés Jaque, by temporarily recomposing the constituents of the Pavilion, reveals the material practices, objects and materials associated with its maintenance and management. For social or policy innovators, inventive social science draws attention to the possibility that the challenge motivating their work is composed differently than they originally understood, which can be revealed through creative intervention. The actors or publics involved in constituting the challenge might not be the ones initially assumed to be part of it, and their capacities might also be other than originally understood (Stilgoe and Guston 2017).

SENSITISING PARTICIPANTS TO THE 'SOCIALS' BEING ENACTED

Inventive social research does not take the 'social' as a given but performs an emerging understanding of particular socials through experimental co-articulation – offering an 'experiential togetherness', as Savransky observes in his chapter. By intentionally modifying settings or prompting actors to express themselves or to perform differently, social phemomena become visible in new ways. Inventive research reveals the agencies and different kinds of social which may co-exist and interact with one another. Being able to identify, bring into view, or analyse these within a project can enable those working in social innovation or government innovation to develop and continually revise their understandings of the policy domain and how potential solutions are reconfigured. This can help them think through the ways in which the problem might change as experimentation proceeds – and draw attention to how a project's activities are implicated in articulating particular socials.

GENERATING INFRASTRUCTURES/PRACTICES THAT CONSTITUTE AN ISSUE OR PUBLIC

The versions of inventive social research that combine design and STS resemble some contemporary activities within social and government innovation. Expertise which bridges research and practice is now being developed as capabilities inside government teams and social innovation networks. For example, civil servants in the UK government are using creative approaches that combine the doing, representing and intervening in policy development (e.g. Kimbell 2015). By combining different kinds of research, materialising models of potential policies and organising participatory workshops, multiple understandings of the policy issue and potential interventions are brought into view, changing the issue and the institution of government, not just representing the issue. For social or policy innovators, adopting an inventive approach would allow them to better understand how policy agendas, devices, work programmes and publics are configured relationally. It would allow such practitioners to recognise and reflect on their roles in doing infrastructuring work by providing resources, designing work programmes and producing devices such as models, frameworks, guidelines and criteria (e.g. LeDantec and Disalvo 2014; Hilgren et al. 2016).

ENABLING ATTENTIVENESS TO SCALING

Scaling and the distribution of agency are long-standing concerns within STS and are evident in inventive approaches to social research. For example, Nold's macro and micro prototypes connect the issue of noise annoyance at Heathrow and publics within new configurations. Wilkie and Michael's chapter shows how the situated performances of the networked Energy Babble disrupted research funders' assumptions about 'community' and policy framings about the usage of information from smart meters. Inventive research in social innovation or government innovation contexts can highlight how scale is performed, rather than pre-existing, assumed or given. It has the potential to generate new possibilities enabling intended outcomes to be identified, assessed and revised, while being open to recognising how novel configurations and consequences unfold in practice.

OPENING UP THE WORK OF RESEARCHING

Inventive social research draws on traditions that highlight the distribution of agency across human and non-human actors, and the translations involved in producing knowledge and achieving technological change. Marres and Gerlitz's account of a collaborative analysis of a dataset from Twitter showed how categories such as 'frequency' or 'volume' got in the way of detecting the sociality of Twitter, which led to the research team refocusing their attention on developing other means to access dynamic interactions between Twitter accounts. In their chapter, Guggenheim et al. combine objects, situations and pressure to demonstrate the (creative) work that goes on in researching an issue. Bringing these orientations into social and government innovation draws attention to the material practices, events and actors involved in doing and representing research and intervening into an issue. Instead of analysing and reproducing 'what works' – a contemporary preoccupation within social or government innovation – this approach can highlight both what is required for a solution *to* 'work' and the practical accomplishments of doing research in social and government settings.

In short there is potential for inventive approaches to engage directly with social innovation and government settings. By 'directly' I mean by academic researchers working experimentally in collaboration with people (who may have research training) in local or central government, community and voluntary groups, think-tanks, service providers, entrepreneurs, activists or others in the policy ecosystem who are engaged in understanding a problem domain and intervening into it. Some of the challenges such individuals or teams face in doing the work of social or government innovation present opportunities to enact novel kinds of doing, representing and intervening in social worlds. While on the one hand this may be driven by, and result in, the prioritisation of short-term, easily traceable associations, on the other there is also potential for inventive research to also intervene in the institutional practices, devices and narratives that drive this short-termism.

IMPLICATIONS

Inventive social research can problematise accounts of policy issues and potential solutions developed in relation to them. It can propose modes of doing research by opening up theories of change, identifying how scale operates, acknowledging human and non-human constituents and agency, and examining the governance and styles of participation enacted in a project. In so doing, new possibilities will emerge. By engaging experimentally in reconfiguring projects that aim to address social or public policy issues, researchers may help articulate and detect new socials, develop new devices, infrastructures and methods, and produce understandings of their genealogies, possibilities and limits. They may also be able to situate themselves more closely in relation to some of the challenges that service providers, policy makers and activists are involved in by co-producing 'change' as well as 'knowledge' (Facer and Enright 2016).

With the possibility of closer engagement between inventive social research and social and government innovation come a number of matters that need further consideration. The first is the different temporalities that come into play in the worlds of academic research, which may not be aligned with those of social innovation and policy experimentation. Academia has its own temporal intensities that emerge, for example, when applying for funding, doing research, presenting at workshops or conferences, and writing papers or books, as well as moving between jobs or institutions. Some of these take place over days or weeks, some may take place over several years. Within social innovation and government innovation, timescales are equally varied and intense. Invitations to tender may have deadlines of weeks or months, research undertaken to shape policy making may take months, while efforts to research, develop and redesign a service might take months or years. In contrast, a minister might want a policy recommendation to be produced in a matter of days; a campaign to change regulations or the law might take years. Aligning the perspectives and resources of researchers in relation to organisational routines and resources inside public administrations and the organisational ecosystems around them is not a trivial matter, but, as Guggenheim et al. argue, the application of pressure may be productive.

A second and related issue is the accountabilities held by different actors involved in an inventive collaboration. Academics might hold themselves accountable to colleagues, current or future students, their institutions, funders, professional bodies or partners from civil society, business or the public sector. Managers, volunteers, activists or civil servants have other accountabilities, for example to colleagues, professional bodies, service users or residents, funders and donors, organisational partners, codes of practice, or to public bodies such as parliament. Bringing into view and articulating distinct accountabilities at different levels of institutionalisation and formality, recognising that these accountabilities may continue to change, requires attention and reflexivity.

A third issue is the jostling for power and negotiations between different kinds of expertise required to do inventive social research, which also emerges in other kinds of applied academic research. In their chapter, Guggenheim et al. propose that experts 'accompany' a lay person along an experimental path. Doing inventive social research in the context of social or government innovation requires awareness of different kinds and sites of expertise and the infrastructures, practices and devices that enable this. In different ways, the contributors to this book reveal some of the skills and knowledge required to undertake inventive socio-material and aesthetic experiments. As the connections between social and government innovators and creative practices continue to intensify, new patterns of expertise will emerge within inventive research. More intersections between the kinds of academic research discussed in this volume and the practices I have described will lead to the development of new tools, bureaucratic relationships and systems of valorisation and governance.

Each of these issues shapes the material practices, devices, infrastructures and processes of doing inventive research in the contexts of social and government innovation. By being attentive to temporalities, accountabilities and expertise as constitutive of inventive research, such experimental collaborations will play out differently.

To conclude, this sketch has suggested how inventive social research might engage with current preoccupations and practices in social innovation and government innovation. Shared concerns include experimentation, systems, participation, and the reordering and reconfiguring of a social world, and the politics of so doing. By drawing attention to the processual reconfiguring of resources and relations through a change process, inventive researchers and their collaborators in social innovation and government settings may add nuance, critical appreciation of, and insight to the claims made for and about innovation. My hope is that my description of the challenges I see in social and government innovation, and my brief outline of how this could unfold, will spark new engagements. At the very least, this account may prompt interest among researchers in some of these settings in more inventive doing, representing and intervening.

NOTES

1   I have been involved in different ways within these developments for over a decade: as an educator teaching design thinking to MBA students and social entrepreneurs; as former head of social design at The Young Foundation; as a researcher studying the emergence of social design for the Arts and Humanities Research Council (AHRC); as a researcher embedded for a year in Policy Lab, a team in the Cabinet Office of the UK government via an AHRC fellowship; as a consultant helping government bodies develop design capabilities; as a user of public services; and as an activist where I live.

2 There is a long tradition in the UK of think-tanks and other policy ecosystems that carry out research and undertake experiments in relation to social issues that are sometimes translated into public policy. An early example was the Institute of Community Studies, set up by Michael Young in 1952. Through his writing, work on the Labour Party manifesto in 1945, involvement in the creation of institutions such as the Open University, Young has long been recognised as an early social innovator whose expertise bridged social research, public policy and organisational action (Young Foundation 2017).

3 An exercise in which participants note down and then share challenges in the form 'how can we…?' is common in the work of Policy Lab, a team in the UK government's Cabinet Office. See https://www.slideshare.net/Openpolicymaking/policy-lab-slide-share-introduction-final [accessed 11 June 2016].

4 The UK's innovation agency Nesta set up a Challenge Prize Centre in 2012 to study and promote 'challenge-based' innovation. See http://www.nesta.org.uk/challenge-prize-centre [accessed 11 June 2016].

5 International design consultancy IDEO's platform partners with foundations, corporate sponsors and government bodies to set challenges for its users to respond to. See https://openideo.com [accessed 11 June 2016].

6 A leading example here is the UK-based International Behavioural Insights Team, originally set up in the UK government's Cabinet Office, which it now co-owns with the UK innovation charity Nesta and the senior management team. See the account of its chief executive David Halpern (2015). Such approaches are not without criticism.

7 See for example the Development Impact and You Toolkit, aimed at people working in development contexts, produced by UK innovation agency Nesta and funded by the Rockefeller Foundation. Available at http://diytoolkit.org [accessed 11 June 2016].

REFERENCES

Bernstein, J. H., 'Transdisciplinarity: A review of its Origins, Development, and Current Issues', *Journal of Research Practice*, 11.1 (2015) <http://jrp.icaap.org/index.php/jrp/article/view/510/412> [accessed 2 July 2017].

Breckon, J., *Better Public Services Through Experimental Government* (London: Alliance for Useful Evidence, 2015).

Chen, D. S., et al., 'Social Design: An Introduction', *International Journal of Design,* 10.1 (2016,), 1–5.

Dunleavy, P. '"Big data" and policy learning', in G. Stoker and M. Evans, eds, *Methods that Matter: Social Science and Evidence-Based Policymaking* (Bristol: The Policy Press, 2016).

Eggers, W., and P. Macmillan, *The Solution Revolution: How Business, Government, and Social Enterprises Are Teaming Up to Solve Society's Toughest Problems* (Boston: Harvard Business School Publishing, 2013).

Facer, K., and B. Enright, *Creating Living Knowledge. The Connected Communities Programme, Community University Relationships and the Participatory Turn in the Production of Knowledge* (Bristol: University of Bristol/AHRC Connected Communities, 2016).

Fortier, A-M., 'Proximity by Design? Affective Citizenship and the Management of Unease', *Citizenship Studies*, 14.1 (2010), 17–30.

Garud, R., P. Tuertscher, and A. Van de Ven, 'Perspectives on Innovation Processes', *The Academy of Management Annals*, 7.1 (2013), 775–819.

Government Digital Service, 'Agile Delivery' (2016), <https://www.gov.uk/service-manual/agile-delivery> [accessed 4 December 2016].

Halpern, D., *Inside the Nudge Unit: How Small Changes Can Make a Big Difference* (London: Penguin, 2016).

Hillgren, P. A., A. Seravalli, and M. Erikson, 'Counter-Hegemonic Practices: Dynamic Interplay Between Agonism, Commoning and Strategic Design', *Strategic Design Research Journal*, 9.2 (2016), 89–99.

Julier, G., *Economies of Design* (London: Sage, 2017).

Julier, G., and L. Kimbell, *Co-producing Social Futures Through Design Research* (Brighton: University of Brighton, 2016).

Kimbell, L., *Applying Design Approaches to Policy Making: Discovering Policy Lab* (Brighton: University of Brighton, 2015).

Le Dantec, C. A., and C. DiSalvo, 'Infrastructuring and the Formation of Publics', *Social Studies of Science*, 43.2 (2013), 241–64.

Mazzucato, M., *The Entrepreneurial State: Debunking Public vs. Private Sector Myths* (London: Anthem Press, 2013).

Mulgan, G., et al., *Social Innovation: What It Is, Why It Matters and How It Can Be Accelerated* (Oxford: Skoll Centre for Social Entrepreneurship, 2006).

Nesta/The Social Innovation Partnership, 'Guidance for Developing a Theory of Change for Your Programme' (2016), <https://www.nesta.org.uk/sites/default/files/theory_of_change_guidance_for_applicants.pdf> [accessed 2 November 2016].

Nicholls, A., and A. Murdock, eds, *Social Innovation: Blurring Boundaries to Reconfigure Markets* (Basingstoke: Palgrave MacMillan, 2011).

Noveck, B., *Smart Citizens, Smarter State: The Technologies of Expertise and the Future of Governing* (Cambridge: Harvard University Press, 2015).

OECD, 'Observatory of Public Sector Innovation' (2016) <https://www.oecd.org/governance/innovative-government/> [accessed 2 September 2016].

Puttick, R., *Why We Need to Create a NICE for Social Policy* (London: Nesta, 2012).

Puttick, R., P. Baeck, and P. Colligan, *I-Teams: The Teams and Funds Making Innovation Happen in Governments Around the World* (London: Nesta/Bloomberg Philanthropies, 2014).

Ries, E. *The Lean Start Up: How Relentless Change Creates Radically Successful Businesses* (New York: Crown Business, 2011).

Rittel, H. W. J., and M. M. Webber, 'Dilemmas in a General Theory of Planning', *Policy Sciences*, 4 (1973), 155–69.

Robert, G., and A. Macdonald, 'Co-design, Organisational Creativity and Quality Improvement in the Healthcare Sector: '"Designerly" or "Design-Like"?', in D. Sangiorgi and A. Prendiville, eds, *Designing for Service: Key Issues and Directions* (London: Bloomsbury, 2017), pp. 117–29.

Shove, E., M. Pantzar and M. Watson, *The Dynamics of Social Practice:*

Everyday Life and How it Changes (London: Sage, 2012).

Snowden, D., and M. Boone, 'A Leader's Framework for Decision Making', *Harvard Business Review*, November (2007).

Stilgoe, J., and D. Guston, 'Responsible Research and Innovation', in U. Felt et al., eds, *Handbook of Science and Technology Studies*, 4th edn (Cambridge, MA: MIT Press, 2017), pp. 853–80.

Williamson, B. 'The Digital Methods and Imagination of Innovation Labs' (2015), <https://codeactsineducation.wordpress.com/2015/07/16/methods-imagination-innovation-labs/> [accessed 21 September 2015].

Young Foundation, 'History' (2017) <https://youngfoundation.org/about-us/history/> [accessed 11 June 2017].

APPENDIX

14

INVENTIVE TENSIONS: A CONVERSATION

Lucy Kimbell, Michael Guggenheim, Noortje Marres, Alex Wilkie

THE SCENE: THE FOURTH FLOOR OF 1 GRANARY SQUARE IN KINGS CROSS, London, and the home, since 2012, of Central Saint Martins, one of the constituent art and design colleges of the University of the Arts London. Lucy Kimbell, the host, takes the visitors – Michael Guggenheim, Noortje Marres and Alex Wilkie – on a tour of the building and then invites them into a small room where a conversation ensues, the transcript of which has been edited by all four contributors.

LK: Welcome to this art and design school. Our building is full of people designing, making, creating, generating, exploring, performing, building, knowing and doing. There are students, staff and visitors whose work practices are intimately connected with investigating, proposing and enacting social arrangements, although they might not talk about it that way. Thinking of them as one audience for your book, I want to start by asking, why this book and why does it matter now?

NM: What has been interesting in making this book is that each of the editors has a different take on this. Some of us, I think, are quite okay with the rather sensational claim that 'the social is back' after it seemed to have disappeared for some time. You had a period in social theory, and arguably in public discourse – roughly speaking, during the 1990s – where 'society seemed to have disappeared'.[1] Today, by contrast, the social seems once again to be playing a central role in culture, the economy, science, politics – think of social innovation, social enterprise, social media, social design, social data. One of the questions then is how we approach this return of the social. What I think we're doing in this book is showing how these returning socials are different from how 'the social' has traditionally been defined and understood. These new socials are often about introducing technology and creative methods into other kinds of professional sectors. However, in the book we say 'Let's not be immediately dismissive of these new, creative uses of the "social" as a label, let's see what they are about, and what can be of interest in going along, at least initially'. That also means we don't simply want to criticise or reject the fact that sociality is today more closely inter-articulated with the technical and the creative. So that's one opening.

AW: Another way to think through the return to the social is to ask who or what decides what the social is? Here, and crucially, what counts as the social is being done in a myriad of ways outside, and irrespective of, the social sciences and other centres of expertise charged with determining the social. In other words, the disciplines that are conventionally sanctioned and obliged to proclaim 'this is the social!' This gives rise to both theoretical and practical concerns around how the social is conceived, composed, made and accomplished once the presumption of an extant social as pre-given and singular has been abandoned. Our attention, then, as social scientists, and in my case as a designer too, turns to sociality as process and multiplicity including the inventiveness and becomings of socials – where the s is underscored, meaning there is not one definition of the social, but a plurality of societies. It follows, then, that this implicates questions of methods and techniques and modes of doing research, as the 'practical' above indicates. So, in a sense there exists a multiplicity of concrete and possible socials that we and others are starting to recognise and locate, and this includes an appreciation of the situated role we play – as analysts and makers – in the emergence and patterning of socialities. Arguably, this requires an interdisciplinary engagement or an engagement that speaks outside the social sciences as well as inside them. The field of design is interesting in this regard, since its practitioners are accustomed to shaping and redefining the composition and compossiblity of socialities.

MG: The word 'social', *sozial* in German, has always had this confusion; in everyday parlance, *sozial* means something like 'just', or 'equally distributed'. There's also the notion of something being 'unsocial', meaning it's unjust. And basically, as a sociologist speaking German, you continually have to fight for this distinction that for sociologists there is no such thing as a non-social policy or whatever. Using social in this way isn't a discourse coming from the right, similar to the Thatcherite claim 'there is no such thing as society'. It's actually mostly a leftist use of the term social. As a sociologist, I'm tired of dealing with these confusions – they're not very productive. For me, the volume is really about what it means to invent the social. This is where there seem to be a lot of changes, which are mostly changes in the practice of social scientists, and in the way that social scientists now cooperate with people from other disciplines and away from academia.

LK: Colleagues and students here are involved in researching, designing and participating in some of these new 'socials', through their work inside the studio, and outside in bars, offices, clubs, prisons, galleries and online. I suspect they'd be comfortable with your ideas of multiplicity and becomings and would feel they have something to say, or show, about being inventive. But they don't necessarily want to be the objects of study for social scientists, which is what you are hinting at. As well as engaging artists and designers, who else are you addressing with this book?

NM: To recognise that the ghost of 'the social' is out of the bottle, that it doesn't necessarily comply with understandings of the 'social' that sociology has taught us, gets us into all sorts of trouble. For one, it is a highly sobering experience. For many, data science is the new social science and they are willing to accept that computing, physics and other sciences will provide the ontology for the social (think of contagion models for digital communication, where messages are assumed to spread like viruses). Design and art are today favoured by many as methods for representing society to society. There seem to be important shifts in the air, in terms of what are recognised to be the most valuable and effective instruments for knowing society, representing it, intervening in and engaging with it. To be sure, these various disciplines are critical participants in the doing of what we may want to call sociality, but I also think there are a lot of misunderstandings about their capacity to grasp the specificity of the social. If we say, to give only two examples, that an organisation is just like a neural network, or that making a painting can be the same as doing a survey (but better), then we're likely to be misunderstanding something about sociality. This is why it is important both to broaden who can participate in the doing and articulating of the social, but also to remain very critical about how it's done. In that sense, I have a possibly quite megalomaniac idea about who or what we are addressing, because I think we are addressing interested parties from these various backgrounds, whether it's computing, design, art, data science, sociology, architecture; they each have a stake, many of us have stakes in the reinvention of sociality.

LK: Today, it's as if nearly anyone can do social research and everything can be viewed as social. Design agencies offer ethnographic insight to spark innovation projects; managers and civil servants map the journeys of users and citizens engaging with their services to learn how to change them; artists create ways for people to visualise and play with data. There's a whole emergent field that, unfortunately, calls itself 'social design' which some funders and commissioners hope will enable design researchers to have academic impact, make designers feel useful to society (and not just capitalism), and lead to new solutions to policy challenges (Armstrong et al. 2014). For me, your book is valuable because it poses questions about what makes up the social, who defines and articulates it, the contexts for doing research into and inventing the social, the practices through which the social is made, and it sets this against the literatures of sociology and their histories. But I am left wondering how many data scientists or designers will engage with it? I want the book to open up to the people who are not yet critically aware of the socials they are co-constituting in their work.

AW: Part of the context is how sociology itself responds to the idea of its coming crisis, a predicament raised by Mike Savage and Roger Burrows (2007) about the efficacy, relevance and utility of sociology in the face of large-scale empirical research conducted on behalf of public and private institutions and made possible by new computational technologies of data production and analysis. Their response, however, is a lurch back into seemingly conventional ways of doing sociological description by way of combinations of existing empirical research techniques – a somewhat disappointing riposte, echoed by John Law's (2004) 'method assemblage', which entails a re-mixing of the discipline's existing methodological repertoire, and which, perhaps, the mutability of ethnography, for instance, has been well disposed to in any case. This book, alongside others, is trying to provide an alternative by saying, 'Well, actually there are other ways to respond', and these responses involve both theoretical novelty and methodological adventure, as well as a change in what might count as description – knowing that our descriptions, techniques and constructions add to the composition of the world. For my part, then, and having been committed to teaching novel empirical research skills to designers in order to resource and diversify their practices, this book can be used as an additional aid in the pursuit of equipping designers to develop their own explanations of situated design settings without relying on pre-fabricated explanations or methodologies.

NM: A lot of the excitement around social media has to do with the fact that they render recordable and traceable all these colloquial, semi-natural forms of interaction. As such, contemporary practices of recording have something to do with the methods of social research: sociologists and ethnomethodologists have long emphasised the value of analysing interactions and conversations 'in-the-wild' for understanding social life. However, today's interest in the social entails loads of other definitions, for example the social (engagement) as a placeholder for marketing, or the social as a placeholder for 'let's not use any government resources but free labour'. Having said this, they are also about the kind of socials that makes sociology exciting.

MG: But this excitement is somehow forty years too late, no? There's a great article by Mike Lynch and David Bogen (1994) about the excitement of conversation analysts in the 1960s now that they had these new tape recorders with which they could precisely record what was talked about and achieve what they thought was a natural science of the social. I think this was the decisive step in terms of being able to record so-called 'natural' interaction, and ironically, it seems to me, the new forms of treating these new data are in many ways less sophisticated than the practices of conversation analysis, and sociologically less interesting.

NM: I think social research is becoming more participatory today, and that is one of the big changes. One of the examples I like a lot is hetexted.com which is mostly young women posting screenshots of their SMS exchanges with mostly boys, and doing collective interpretations of these texts, like 'Is he dumping me here or not?' It's a wonderful spectacle of attempted communication across the gender divide, and my sense is that such experiments in interpretation open up possibilities that those sociologists of the 60s and 70s who invented conversation analysis weren't necessarily attuned to. But also, this is about the invention of a particular device, or *dispositif*, that enables a participatory form of social analysis. Here, recordability is not separate from interpretability, which is a mistake that some versions of data science make. It's the invention of a practice where recordability, interpretability and interaction all come together, and it's a very particular social, technical, material and aesthetic practice. There are many such moments of invention occurring today, and I do think there are different opportunities for understanding opened up by hetexted.com in terms of the politics of knowledge and politics of invention, as compared to the mostly gentlemen social scientists in the period of Sacks, whose aim was still to provide the authoritative account of interactional order, of what's happening in a pause.

LK: Given these developments, and the methods crisis within the social sciences, what are you adding to recent work on inventiveness?

AW: If we formulate the view that it's not just social scientists but also others, such as designers, architects, computer scientists, and so on, doing inventive social research, one approach, such as Lury and Wakeford's (2012) *Inventive Methods*, as well as the work Mike Michael and myself (2015) have been involved in, is looking back and asking what's interesting or who has done interesting work around expanding or adding novelty to the repertoire of empirical techniques that may be adopted (or not, as is more likely the case) and developed. For this book, however, I think how we've asked contributors to work is to think through the view that inventiveness is distributed and not the privilege or responsibility of a single actor. So it's not just a question of how methods in themselves are inventive (if at all) but also how the methods themselves are being deployed in order to understand inventiveness, and that's something that's distributed. I think this book acts as a kind of lure to researchers to think about how they themselves might take up some of these commitments in relation to their problems, their questions, their areas of interest, how the social pushes back at them and their work. In other words, rather than being inventive simply by taking up novel methods or describing the inventiveness of others, we are arguing for some kind of double capture where invention requires and begets inventive techniques and description.

MG: For me, part of the interest of the book is what follows from this for our practice as social scientists. Just to stick to the conversation analysis example, we would say 'okay, what is left for conversation analysis'? What is left for social statistics in Savage and Burrows' case, mentioned by Alex earlier? What is left for ethnography when there's all these examples of proto-ethnography? Shall we simply insist that we do these things somehow better, or more thoroughly? And I think that's mostly the answer that we are giving, but it's probably neither a really interesting answer, nor one that will make a lot of sense in the long run. Here, what the book is trying to explore is better, more interesting answers to that problem of reinventing social scientific methods in the face of all these changes.

NM: Besides the question of what is distinctive about social enquiry, there is also the question of how we participate in it. In the traditions we're referring back to, like the ethnomethodology and conversation analysis of the 70s and 80s, you could say there was a kind of a death drive present in them. Broadly speaking, their argument was that if social methods are being deployed across social life by social actors, and if methodologically accounting for social life is already part of how society operates, then we don't need sociologists anymore. I think that kind of approach was very much animated by this legislative and sovereign conception of what it is to do social enquiry, so it had to be completely distinctive and completely different from what was already going on, otherwise it didn't have a right to exist. We're now in quite a different context where the question is not 'Are we going to kill that big beast or let it live?', or if it can survive, 'How to secure a legislative space where sociology is in charge?'. To shift away from this is a risky move but one worth attempting. The question to ask here is, 'How do we participate in these wider processes?'. I think there's actually plenty of work for us to do when I look at other practitioners getting a taste for the social, for example the ways in which artists and designers working with found materials or found footage show a way into documenting social (dis-) order and social change. I also think there is a lot that social researchers and sociologists can bring to those practices: how does this work, how do we elicit sociality, how do we render social problems detectable in everyday settings? So, the question is how can we participate and how can we make this kind of contribution without any of us getting tricked into reducing our engagement to an issue of authority of who can legislate the social. You can't just say 'we're not playing that game', because the social is at stake and these are political issues. But still, asking how we can participate effectively, for me, is a more productive question than asking what's the little piece on the allotment where we still have absolute sovereignty as sociologists.

AW: It's slightly ironic and revealing that we're sitting here in an art school where there is a pronounced preoccupation with the role of aesthetics grounded on adding things to the world and the concreteness of what gets made here – and, of course, how the school publicly stages this style of invention and innovation to visitors and members alike. This is very much foregrounded here, and yet amidst all this we're fixed on an altogether different register – the problems of relevance and effectiveness facing the social sciences, but very much formulated as part of internal debates and problems rather than the new demands being placed on social science, which all this new stuff surrounding us incites.

LK: On reading the book, I was left grasping for the answer to the question 'What does this mean for me?', in my domain of design. What does it mean for the civil servants I know grappling with how to do experiments to provide answers to policy questions, who may not be able to engage deeply with sociological accounts that problematise their work, such as Ben Williamson's (2015) writing on policy innovation labs? What does it mean for funders and commissioners of arts venues or projects? We are sitting here in a recently-built art school, where the former head of college who commissioned this building, the architecture firm, the university administrators, the staff and students, the local government planners, and various others involved, were constituting an imaginary of a higher education institution, which is now continuously being re-articulated in the everyday practices of all these people and things. I doubt they consulted a sociologist along the way to discuss the sociality of a future art school. It's *already* in the practices of art and design to generate new social worlds through the devices, methods and objects they create. That's ordinary. But it's increasingly evident that designers and artists need to be aware of and held to account for the implications of the particular versions of the social that are imagined, enacted and unfolded in what they do, perform and make. I think artists and designers, managers and civil servants are concerned to understand which socials their work co-constitutes. But often people just get on with making it, and leave the studying of it to others. Your book shows how designers and architects are able to do research that is inventive, rather than being objects of study for sociologists.

MG: I think there's an interesting parallel to, say, psychoanalysis, where something similar has happened. Psychoanalysis has been in a decline for a long time now, but (pseudo) psychoanalytic theory has been taken up by everyday discourse and is used for everything. And if you look at psychoanalytical discourse, there's a huge amount of frustration about the decline of the discipline and its expertise in the face of its actually quite incredible success. I think one of the main problems from the viewpoint of its inventors is that they now have zero control over what they invented. Ideas or theories do not come with warning labels that have to be adhered to by users.

NM: I think it's fair to say that the wider condition is mostly one of mutual irrelevance. We carve up the world according to disciplines, and the prize or the cherry on that cake is the fiction of relative autonomy. You don't have to do all this diplomacy. But this can also be taken to mean that to produce situations of mutual relevance is a challenge, a task, and a job. And I think it's very important for us to keep remembering that it's a task, and not a given. That's one of the annoying things about today's revival of the social; when you hear social innovation, social enterprise, social media, it sounds as if the social is already accomplished in those environments, but of course it isn't. My colleague, Emma Uprichard, came up with this slogan, 'Just because it's called social, that doesn't make it social'. Sociology and supposedly non-creative disciplines are more of the underdog in some ways. They don't have the resources or the legitimacy to make a stronger claim and say that the experts tasked with inventing computational social science, or social media, are in many ways pretty bad at sociality, grasping it and doing it.

AW: And, of course, there are other organisations where the social is precisely the thing that is being harnessed. Much of the fieldwork I conducted on designers working for a multinational semiconductor manufacturer (2010) invariably featured interdisciplinary working practices that included various mixtures of designers, cognitive and social psychologists, ergonomiscists, mechanical engineers, computer scientists, and even anthropologists-as-corporate-ethnographers, all of whom could claim a certain expertise on and about the social, although some more than others. Here, I didn't experience mutual irrelevance between them, which suggests that they remained absorbed within their own disciplinary concerns and discrete domains of experience, as defined by an organisation. On the contrary, they were working with one another on a daily basis – often unproblematically. Their concerns were not with the practicalities of interdisciplinary collaborations, nor were they epistemological in terms of the kind of knowledge they were producing. Instead, their interests lay in new situations and possibilities brought about by faster, smaller, more energy efficient microprocessors, and the implications of this for creating new products, new applications, new markets, and, as a corollary, how to go about or inform how such new ways of living are colonised. Disciplinary concerns were less of a problem, because the problems were elsewhere and more ontological, for example, 'Where is the new market?', not 'Oh, you're worried about this social or that social'. And that goes back to Lucy's question of why it should matter. It does matter because what we see is organisations that are increasingly interested in people who can go in and tell them what the social is, how it operates, how it functions, precisely as a way to harness whatever knowledge practice can support an organisation's interests. Another way of putting this is to ask how epistemological resources are brought to bear on questions of practical ontology – about what and how to bring into the world, and the kinds of changes such new phenomena and entities – such as microprocessor- based technology will bring about, not least to the imagination of such organisations, a point made by Andrew Barry, Georgina Born and Gisa Weszkalnys (2008: 35).

MG: A lot of designers are operating and actually *need* to operate with an almost naïve belief that what they're producing will have the intended effect. I think this is holding a lot of sociologists back: the fact there has been so much research about social science itself, showing that this belief is mistaken, and that it can have unintended effects. We are all taught how the era of 1950s and 60s planning euphoria crashed because of, among other things, a related euphoria about the powers of social science (see for example Scott 1998). You have to follow projects to really understand what is happening, and you cannot just think 'Let's put social science here and then the world will be better'. Because we know about this history, we have also lost our own belief that we can really contribute in these ways, because we already know that it won't turn out the way we intended it. And I think this is a really tricky thing. I think in a way we need this naivety, or at least a little bit of it, to do interventionist projects at all. But we should also know, being STS scholars, or more broadly, social scientists, that it is going to turn out differently, and that it could actually go completely against our intentions. It appears that designers, and architects in particular, are just much better at forgetting how things went wrong previously, and continue to believe that their own grand projects will succeed. For me the solution is to design actual experiments rather than have specific ideas of what I want to achieve, in terms of outcomes. I want to set up experiments that open up options, that allow us to see options, to make them accountable. When I say experiments, I do not mean 'being experimental' in a fuzzy sense, but setting up devices that force us and participants to do things we would not do without the experiment, and which create situations that would not exist without these experimental setups.

NM: An experiment on society is often seen, in sociology, as a quite scandalous way of acting on society, something that's not ethical, but when Michael makes these remarks now, he's talking about the experiment as a particular trick for generating accounts and accountability of social life. When John Law says engineering is sociology by other means because it's all about making associations, that ontological claim is actually not enough. Now that we have a world full of engineering scholars who say 'Yes, we're sociologists', we know that there's actually more ingredients, more concepts that come into play, in the doing of sociology, namely the accounting for, and/or articulating of, practices that involve technology. We need these deliberate, expressive articulations of practices if we are to properly appreciate how social connections and heterogeneous associations come about in those practices.

LK: I think sociology could make more claims for being necessary to creating new devices, practices and institutions, by studying a situation and the collective work of creating the accounts of what is or could be happening in that situation. Andrew Barry, many years ago, introduced me to a version of the quote from Marx along the lines that social scientists study the world, whereas the point is to change it.[2] Similarly, in design research there's a long-standing but uncomfortable distinction between studying a situation and changing it, by devising courses of action to change 'existing situations into preferred ones', as Herbert Simon put it (1996: 111). Your book challenges this dualism in a stronger way than I've seen elsewhere. It recognises not only the need for accounting-for practices, but also the participation of those accounts in the creation of new practices in experimental setups. But I'm struck how, as a reader, while I am invited into the experiments discussed in the book, I cannot easily participate in them. We're speaking of opening up possibilities, and yet it's a text. Some of us need other ways or multiple ways of engaging with concepts. As well as the book I want the pop-out installation or the do-it-yourself inventive toolkit. How can I access materialised or digital instances of its discussions, and make the insights usable for the experimental contexts I work in, and for others who may not come across or read this book? How can I perform it?

NM: We shouldn't blame a book for being a book. It is clear that the works accounted for, or narrated, in *Inventing the Social,* have several different incarnations: they exist in some cases as an exhibition, or as an experimental device, or an intervention, or an art installation. And we have to introduce different criteria of evaluation, or wear different glasses, for these different instantiations. One of the things that stands out about the book, for me, is that it brings together an interdisciplinary set of contributors; another characteristic is its intentional confusion of roles. We attempt to move away from the kinds of abusive relations that intellectuals in previous times initiated in terms of how they connected with design, for instance: 'Now you're going to make my text look nice', or where artists say to the intellectuals 'Now you're going to write nice captions for my performance'. Where those experiments go wrong is where they end up as failed role reversals, the pretence to be something you're not. But role confusion is a kind of success. Is Andrés Jaque doing architecture or sociology when he is producing his Mies van der Rohe project as a chapter? Is this person still just writing as a theorist, or is there actually a methodology being proposed?

LK: It's disciplinary androgyny. It's a book and more than a book. How do different kinds of aesthetics play out in the different contributions?

AW: I think that's maybe one of the unanswered topics of this book, or one that it opens up to and invites readers to take up. To take an example from today, from where we are standing now, earlier we were looking into the window of one of the Central Saint Martin's fashion studios, and in there was a young student, dressed in a very particular way, all black, but the length and the cut of the cloth was not that of a typical garment. This is the garment of some-body who knows intimately about what they are wearing, and he was making something that wouldn't convert into a book, that would be hard to translate into written accounts and books. Instantiated in that costume and the way it is worn is years of training to acquire a certain sensibility about a certain mode and fashioning of aesthetics. And I think that's something that we as authors might admit, that this is stuff we find very hard to include, or to get at, namely experiences that escape linguistic or textual modes or that themselves demand experiencing rather than explanation. Having said that, books also circulate in this setting, and contribute to the aesthetic practices of the art students – a point I will return us to later.

MG: I've never understood the blaming of books or academic texts for being closed objects. For me, it is not about blaming particular forms; I think that's actually nonsensical. There is a reason why we still have, and should have, 500-page social theory books. We need them, with two thousand footnotes. And to assume, just because something appears as a 500-page theory book, that it is closed, is wrong, because obviously it pre-exists in talks, and there are reviews, and people talk about it and so on and so forth. At the same time, it only works in the way it does because it's this closed thing. For me, specifically with regard to sociology, we have to open up any default assumption that stuff should appear as a text. And I guess the other way around, with, say, design, I think we should give up the idea that the default product needs to be a three-dimensional thing. It's a matter of thinking about for which instance, for which situation, for which intervention we want to produce which kinds of materials and forms, and there are indeed many avenues to be explored here, once we leave our default assumptions behind.

NM: Our intention was precisely to invite non-professional sociologists into the format of the sociological text. In this book, we have multiply-trained contributors, some who have PhDs in sociology, some who only started reading sociology a few years ago and come from very different trajectories. We invited these people because we know, or we are confident that their practice speaks to this question about how the social is being invented today. And that partly has to do with a certain idea of how we do knowledge politics, but also with knowing what your competence is. When Alex speaks of this aesthetic competence, I know that this book can only work if it has the trust and the commitment of people who have that competence. But I also know that there are many who have only passive knowledge of that competence. So yes, it's about the specific purpose, and also knowing which strengths are called for when, and who possesses them.

LK: Given that data science is big business, and computing an academic field and a growing policy agenda, I'm struck by how the book's examples don't engage strongly with this. Where are the missing big data masses? There's obviously some computational work, but it's closer to people's experiences with devices, although the analysis reveals their interconnections with other worlds. Does the emphasis on particular scales and contexts discussed in the book matter?

NM: There's nothing about including a business chapter in this book that I would find intrinsically problematic, but it would probably be about the conditions under which those kinds of connections can be made to work, and what are the conditions under which they wouldn't work. One thing we're doing is talking to academia and saying 'Architects and designers are authors in our space that we should address *as* authors – not just as research subjects that we can interview and then anonymise'. So one of the interventions is in academic debates, and how they reproduce distinctions between the accredited and the unaccredited sociologist or social scientist. But the other intervention is about being ambitious across disciplines and fields about what it is that we can problematise. Because often when we talk about impact that kind of scaling down happens in another way, where it is assumed that 'we're not really going to intervene in problem framing, because that's just going to be confusing, and unsettling, and it's going to make it harder for us to demonstrate that we're relevant'. I think what we're saying is that in the labs of big digital industries, and in policy spaces, the social is being deployed in highly selective ways. This is how within Western governments social policy is recomposed as something else. This is how in digital industries what counts as a social community is being recomposed. And it is those kinds of framings that we also need to act upon in responding to the call to 'invent the social'.

MG: When we did our sandbox project, we set out to explore new methods of creating disaster scenarios (Guggenheim, Kraeftner, and Kroell 2013; Guggenheim, Kräftner, and Kröll 2016). We set up a sandbox in which participants created worlds with abstract figures and let disasters happen. The whole point was to create new and radically different, participative methods to counter existing forms of creating risk registers. We enrolled disaster researchers to play in our sandbox, and we also tried to interest government experts. But it quickly became very obvious that there simply isn't a straightforward way in which what *we* want to do can be in any way aligned with what these people are doing. We interviewed them, we played with some of them. But because the whole method fundamentally undermines the idea of what risk is, what a disaster is, and who should take decisions about these questions, it is difficult to convert government departments to adopt it. In the whole apparatus that is the government, the assumption is 'We do it and you don't'. Ideally, we would have been happy if they had said 'Oh yes, this is much better than what we are doing'. But it's not the scale of the project that prevented it. It's the fundamental incongruence between our interests and theirs.

NM: Being experimental also means that there has to be a space where confusion is possible. You need to allow for that possibility.

AW: There is also something about the fragility of these things which I quite like, the vulnerability, the temporality; but another way to understand this is through scale. How, for example, do devices or things necessarily scale up, if indeed they *do* they scale up? This is directly related to the question of policy and instrumentalisation. One example of this is discussed in the chapter I've written with Mike Michael, as well as our piece on speculative method (Wilkie et al. 2015), which is precisely about the failure of the rollout of sixty million smart monitors in the United Kingdom as a way to address climate change. Here, in fact, we find an ostensible solution that is being scaled up across an entire population, and yet reports are emerging indicating that people either can't use them, don't appreciate or comprehend the relation between consumption and calculation, or actually leave the lights on for longer – knowing they can do this with LED or low-energy bulbs. Arguably, it can't get bigger than that. And that precisely is addressing the question of what happens when policy finds itself in a mode of operating where there are reports that it's failing, and yet it continues on a particular logic and path. Another way to think about this, and another way to address qualms about the relevance of the practices included in this book to questions, arguably, of governmentality, is to situate the work being done in relation to what Latour (2007) describes as 'political-1' where new associations are coming into being and changing the composition of collective life. As a heuristic, I find this a useful way to appreciate the importance of and need for the work exemplified in this book, although, and as the UK smart monitor rollout illustrates, there are movements back and forth across the different political registers where smart monitors themselves are not fixed (to encode normative energy behaviour) but operate also to bring about new practical relations.

LK: Christian Nold's piece is in a similar vein, discussing the specifics of those material, digital, place-based community interactions that exceed the possibilities of the policy or programmatic question.

NM: I think there may also be some really basic confusion between intervention, and what, in a sort of vulgar language, is a provocation, as opposed to research, right? This book is mostly concerned with research *pre* any specific applications. That doesn't mean that research doesn't have any further output, and obviously I'm not a fan of that language at all, but I think it would be wrong to short-circuit it. The spaces of research are continuously expanding. There are the arts as a form of research, the museum as an urban laboratory, neighbourhoods as experimental settings. Bringing a research sensibility to social life is potentially relevant to these different environments where there is this moment of realisation 'Oh, what we're doing is really researching', or 'We're really doing a social experiment'. It's social research happening in spaces that don't have that accreditation. But the test has to be our capacity to problematise. I mean for me, in relation to this book, it's not so much about acting on problems, but how to pose the problems well. That's the business of this book.

AW: Earlier, as we were taking the lift to get to this room, someone got into the lift and then stepped out at the library floor. On the top of the pile of books the person was carrying sat a copy of Foucault's (1978) *The History of Sexuality*. Later, and whilst sitting in the room, I noticed someone walking by carrying Pelle Ehn's and his colleagues' *Making Futures* (2014). These books, these artefacts and their accompanying versions of the social, circulate. We're in this environment, having creativity reflected back to us, and yet, at the same time, the social sciences – for want of a better term – circulate and get mobilised in all manner of ways, by students in the first case, and by staff members as well as the design research practitioners who wrote the book, in the case of *Making Futures*. Clearly these books have an effect outside particular disciplinary settings and preoccupations. One key difference, perhaps, is that we are inviting others to contrive their own socials rather than use this book as a ready-made.

NOTES

1 The British sociologist Nikolas Rose published a paper 'The End of the Social' (1996), while Bruno Latour (1993) adopted Margaret Thatcher's slogan that there is 'no such thing as society'.
2 The actual quote refers to philosophers: 'The philosophers have only interpreted the world, in various ways; the point is to change it' (it is thesis 11 of Karl Marx's *Theses on Feuerbach* (1845)).

REFERENCES

Armstrong, L., et al., Social Design Futures: HEI Research and the AHRC (University of Brighton and Victoria and Albert Museum, 2014) <http://eprints.brighton.ac.uk/13364/1/Social-Design-Report.pdf> [accessed 28 April 2018].

Barry, A., G. Born, and G. Weszkalnys, 'Logics of interdisciplinarity', *Economy and Society*, 37.1 (2008), 20–49.

Ehn, P., E. M. Nilsson, and R. Topgaard, *Making Futures: Marginal Notes on Innovation, Design, and Democracy* (Cambridge MA: MIT Press, 2014).

Foucault, M., *The History of Sexuality* (New York: Pantheon Books, 1978).

Guggenheim, M., B. Kraeftner, and J. Kroell, "'I Don't Know Whether I Need a Further Level of Disaster": Shifting Media of Sociology in the Sandbox', *Distinktion: Scandinavian Journal of Social Theory*, 14.3 (2013), 284–304.

Guggenheim, M., B. Kräftner, and J. Kröll, 'Creating Idiotic Speculators: Disaster Cosmopolitics in the Sandbox', in A. Wilkie, M. Rosengarten, and M, Savransky, eds, *Speculative Research: The Lure of Possible Futures* (London: Routledge, 2016), pp. 146–63.

Law, J., *After Method: Mess in Social Science Research* (London; New York: Routledge, 2004).

Latour, B., 'Turning Around Politics: A Note on Gerard de Vries' Paper', *Social Studies of Science*, 37.5 (2007), pp. 811–20.

Lury, C., and N. Wakeford, eds, *Inventive Methods: The Happening of the Social* (London: Routledge, 2011).

Lynch, M., and D. Bogen, 'Harvey Sacks's Primitive Natural Science', *Theory, Culture & Society* 11.4 (1994), pp. 65–104.

Savage, M., and R. Burrows, 'The Coming Crisis of Empirical Sociology', *Sociology* 41.5 (2007), pp. 885–99.

Scott, J., *Seeing Like a State: How Certain Schemes to Improve the Human Condition Have Failed* (New Haven: Yale University Press, 1998).

Simon, H., *The Sciences of the Artificial*, 3rd edn (Cambridge, MA: MIT Press, 1996).

Wilkie, A., 'User Assemblages in Design: An Ethnographic Study' (PhD Thesis, Goldsmiths, University of London, 2010).

Wilkie, A., M. Michael, and M. Plummer-Fernandez, 'Speculative method and Twitter: Bots, Energy and Three Conceptual Characters', *The Sociological Review*, 63.1 (2015), pp. 79–101.

Williamson, B., 'The Laboratory Life of Innovation Labs' (20 April 2015) <https://codeactsineducation.wordpress.com/2015/04/20/the-laboratory-life-of-innovation-labs/> [accessed 5 May 2016].

MATTERING PRESS TITLES

An Anthropology of Common Ground
Awkward Encounters in Heritage Work

NATHALIA SOFIE BRICHET

Ghost-Managed Medicine
Big Pharma's Invisible Hands

SERGIO SISMONDO

Inventing the Social

EDITED BY NOORTJE MARRES, MICHAEL GUGGENHEIM, ALEX WILKIE

Energy Babble

ANDY BOUCHER, BILL GAVER, TOBIE KERRIDGE, MIKE MICHAEL,
LILIANA OVALLE, MATTHEW PLUMMER-FERNANDEZ AND ALEX WILKIE

The Ethnographic Case

EDITED BY EMILY YATES-DOERR AND CHRISTINE LABUSKI

On Curiosity
The Art of Market Seduction

FRANCK COCHOY

Practising Comparison
Logics, Relations, Collaborations

EDITED BY JOE DEVILLE, MICHAEL GUGGENHEIM AND ZUZANA HRDLIČKOVÁ

Modes of Knowing
Resources from the Baroque

EDITED BY JOHN LAW AND EVELYN RUPPERT

Imagining Classrooms
Stories of Children, Teaching and Ethnography

VICKI MACKNIGHT

www.ingramcontent.com/pod-product-compliance
Lightning Source LLC
Chambersburg PA
CBHW040141270326
41928CB00023B/3291